Praise for
Life after Lo

"Loss is a universal experience and too often, because they don't know what to say, well-meaning doctors, friends, and family say, 'Don't worry, you'll get over it.' We never get *over* a major loss but we can find a way through it to enjoy a full and fulfilling life. In *Life after Loss*, Bob Deits provides compassionate and practical advice for grieving and rebuilding a meaningful life after loss. As a palliative care physician, I care for people dealing with serious illness and those facing the end of life and their loved ones—where grief and loss are a constant presence. I will recommend this wise and important book as essential reading to all my patients and their families."

> —Steven Z. Pantilat, MD, Kates-Burnard and Hellman Distinguished Professor of Palliative Care, Director, Palliative Care Program, UCSF, and author of *Life After the Diagnosis: Expert Advice on Living Well with Serious Illness for Patients and Caregivers*

"Old grief is as important a work as new grief, and it resurfaces with brand new lessons. . . .Sooner or later, a difficult journey will come knocking (again), igniting the grief process. No one should be without this brilliant healing toolbox of a book."

> —Maryann Makekau, founder of Hope Matters and coauthor of *When Your Grandma Forgets*

Life
after Loss

Life
after Loss

A Practical Guide to Renewing Your Life
after Experiencing Major Loss

Sixth Edition

BOB DEITS, MTh

Da Capo
LIFE
LONG

Designed and set in 12 point Adobe Garamond by Cynthia Young

Cataloging-in-Publication data for this book is available from the Library of Congress.
ISBN: 978-0-7382-1961-5 (paperback)
ISBN: 978-0-7382-1962-2 (e-book)

Published by Da Capo Press, an imprint of Perseus Books, LLC,
a subsidiary of Hachette Book Group, Inc.
www.dacapopress.com

Note: The information in this book is true and complete to the best of our knowledge. This book is intended only as an informative guide for those wishing to know more about health issues. In no way is this book intended to replace, countermand, or conflict with the advice given to you by your own physician. The ultimate decision concerning care should be made between you and your doctor. We strongly recommend you follow his or her advice. Information in this book is general and is offered with no guarantees on the part of the authors or Da Capo Press. The authors and publisher disclaim all liability in connection with the use of this book. The names and identifying details of people associated with events described in this book have been changed. Any similarity to actual persons is coincidental.

Da Capo Press books are available at special discounts for bulk purchases in the U.S. by corporations, institutions, and other organizations. For more information, please contact the Special Markets Department at Perseus Books, 2300 Chestnut Street, Suite 200, Philadelphia, PA, 19103, or call (800) 810-4145, ext. 5000, or e-mail special.markets@perseusbooks.com.
LSC-C
10 9 8 7 6 5 4 3 2

This one is dedicated to June Deits, the only girlfriend, wife, and life partner I ever had. For 69 years she was the center of my life beginning at age 14. Her insights and influence come through the pages of this edition as they did in the previous five editions. It has the unmistakable imprint of her faith, love, courage, and compassion throughout its pages.

Contents

Introduction

The first edition of *Life after Loss* was published in 1988. During the ensuing years I have frequently received letters, e-mails, and telephone calls from people who credit the book for providing the strength to get through life's most difficult experience. Some have said, "It saved my life." I have met people at seminars and conferences who are carrying an older edition that shows the signs of heavy use. Professionals in the field have also praised it. Dr. Earl Grollman described it as "One of the classics in the field of crisis intervention." Dr. Howard Clinebell Jr. called it "The best book ever written in the field of grief and loss." More than 100,000 people have found help through the first five editions, not counting those reached through seven foreign-language translations.

My experiences as a counselor informed each of the previous editions. This edition, however, is different. My wife, June, died after a lengthy battle with Alzheimer's disease. She was my girlfriend at the age of fourteen—the only girlfriend I ever had—and my wife at eighteen. Her death came a month prior to our sixty-fourth anniversary. She and I were the definition of soul mates.

Dr. Alan Wolfelt says in his book *When Your Soulmate Dies*, "Whether they are also lovers or not, soulmates almost always describe themselves as best friends. They genuinely like each other. They communicate. They talk regularly and share things big and small. They confide in one another. They are loyal to one another. They make joint decisions. They go through life's ups and downs together as if on a bicycle built for two."[1]

> The death of a loved one is not the only source of grief.

This firsthand experience with loss and grief changed my perspective, and I wrote this edition not only as a grief counselor, but as one who has walked the same path as you are walking now.

Of course, the death of a loved one is not the only source of grief. When someone dies, it is the death of a body. Divorce is the death of a relationship and can be just as painful. It actually wasn't a death that first pulled me into a new understanding of grief and the work of grief recovery. It was relocating to Arizona from California. That loss entailed losing familiar places and faces, including leaving our first grandchild who was born a few months prior to our move. When June had to choose between losing a breast or a much higher chance of losing her life to cancer, that choice was not as easy or automatic as it might seem.

> *Learning how to grieve effectively is the most important skill anyone can learn.*

Whatever the source of our loss is, I am more convinced than ever that learning how to grieve effectively is the most important skill anyone can learn.

The challenge of grief recovery after any loss is to establish a "new normal" for life. It isn't easy, but it is possible. In the pages that follow you will find insights to help you avoid making an extremely difficult task worse than it already is. You will also find specific things to do to guide you through the process of recovery. The true stories of others who made it will inspire you.

The category of losses my wife, June, called quiet losses has affected many. These are major losses that seem more difficult to talk about with others. In the previous edition June told of being a survivor of both childhood sexual abuse and breast cancer and broke the silence about her new challenge of facing memory loss and early signs of Alzheimer's disease. In this edition, I am writing in memory of her and to honor her insights and gifts of healing to so many people.

> *The challenge of grief recovery after any loss is to establish a "new normal" for life.*

The subject of God and the role of religion in grief recovery is an important one. The temptation of "make a wish" religion persists and continues to be a barrier to healing. You will find practical help in choosing a healthy spiritual outlook so that your religious experience can be the resource it is meant to be.

The chapter titled "Losses in Later Life" will speak to an ever-growing number of people known as baby boomers who have become senior citizens. People are living longer, many into their nineties, even one hundred and beyond. Life as a senior citizen is another of those events for which we are not adequately prepared. You will find many helpful insights to guide you and enable you to better understand those who are already there and what lies ahead for you.

At the other end of the age curve, you will find good advice in helping children and adolescents cope with loss and grief. How the adults in their life respond at the time of a death or divorce goes a long way in determining what impact the loss has years later when they are adults.

If you have not yet experienced a major loss, you know someone who has. "What can I do to help?" is a question we ask because we often feel so helpless. This book is a great caregiver's manual. It will enable you to under-

An overriding purpose of this book is the survival of the survivors.

stand what is going on inside others after a major loss. It offers guidance on what to do or say—and what not to do or say.

It has been demonstrated by researchers that we face increased risks of cancer, heart disease, diabetes, and other chronic illnesses after a major loss. Dr. Glen Davidson and his team at Southern Illinois University identified the factors of the increased risk. After testing a hundred possible ways to avoid increased risk, they discovered five things to do that make a difference. You will find these incorporated into the "doing" part of the book.

An overriding purpose of this book is the survival of the survivors.

The act of grieving can actually be an avenue for personal growth. It will be demonstrated through the true-life stories of people who faced the worst and came out on top.

If you understand the principles of grief recovery spelled out in this book and put them into practice, you will have learned, in the words of Dr. Howard Clinebell Jr., "how to turn a miserable minus into a positive plus."

1

Loss and the Mourning After
A Universal Human Experience

> *For everything there is a season, and a time for every matter under heaven: a time to be born and a time to die; a time to weep and a time to laugh; a time to mourn and a time to dance.*
>
> —Ecclesiastes 3:1–2, 4

One of the things every human being shares with every other human being is that our life is mortal. We all die sometime. Until we die, there is only one other experience that is universal.

We all experience at least one major loss during our lifetime, and usually more than one. A major loss is any loss experience that destroys a significant piece of what makes our life normal. It might be the death of a loved one, a catastrophic injury to oneself, the trauma of divorce, or relocation to another city. These major losses happen to everyone without regard to economic status, ethnic origin, religious belief, or gender. If there is any good news, it is that we are never the only one to have major losses and feel as we do.

The emotional pain is beyond words. Therefore, no response is more appropriate than grief.

However, major loss and the grief that follows remain among the most misunderstood of all human experiences. When a friend loses a loved one to death, we don't know what to say. The same is true if that person goes through a divorce, is diagnosed with terminal cancer, or has a business that fails.

It's worse when the loss happens to you. You don't have words to express what you are feeling. The pain can exceed the worst toothache you ever had. Friends and family members may pull back, leaving you feeling abandoned. Equally frustrating and painful are the really stupid things said by people who don't have a clue as to how you are feeling—and who really don't want to know. It may seem as if you have fallen into a pit from which there is no escape. The world around you will act as if you should be back on your feet and functioning as though nothing has happened in a matter of days—a couple of weeks at the most. You can't do it—and you shouldn't.

You need to hear this: *Experiencing a terrible loss and the grief that goes with it is the most concrete proof there is that you are a real, live, normal human being.*

The first goal of this book is to help you avoid making the worst experience of your life worse than it already is. It's bad enough all by itself.

You will make it worse if you:

- Have unreasonable expectations of yourself.
- Keep your feelings and thoughts inside instead of talking about them with people who do understand. That often is in a grief support group with others who are walking a similar path as you.
- Believe that your religious faith can lessen the impact of your loss or give you a shortcut through grief.
- Get trapped in the "why?" questions and assume that you are the only one who has ever had such sadness.
- Believe you will always feel as you do in the first weeks and months. You won't.

You can also make the task more difficult by not taking your loss as seriously as you should.

You expect to grieve when a friend or loved one dies. But it is equally important to mourn the death of a relationship, a divorce, the loss of familiar surroundings when relocating to another city, the loss of a job, or any other loss that makes a major impact on the quality of your life. All the risk factors that follow a death also apply to these and other major losses.

You will not always feel as you do in the early weeks and months after a major loss.

If you even suspect that you may have been the victim of sexual abuse as a child, you are among a large group of people who have experienced this horrible trauma, which included June. Statistics indicate that more women than men have faced this experience that June called a "loss of innocence." However, the pain is just as great and the grief process just as difficult, regardless of gender.

Losing a body part to surgery is often more painful emotionally than physically. Women who have a mastectomy in order to survive breast cancer frequently struggle as much with the loss of one or both of their breasts as they do with having the disease. The same is true for men who have prostate surgery and have their sexual function damaged. These kinds of procedures can leave emotional scars that are far deeper than those on the body. June named them quiet losses. I address them in more detail in Chapter 13.

The death of a pet can be a terribly difficult experience for many people.

Throughout this book, you will find guidance on how to avoid making your journey through grief worse than it has to be. You will, in fact, learn how to take charge of your own grief and come out stronger than before your loss.

The Universal Experience

Loss is a fact of being alive in our world, and no one is immune from the experience. Rabbi Harold Kushner was absolutely correct—bad things do happen to good people.

Major loss affects good people, not-so-good people, and everyone in between. It does not check out the color of your skin, your ethnic origin, how much your grandchildren love you, or whether you are a faithful giver to your church, synagogue, or mosque.

You can get through every major loss without being destroyed by it.

One of the more challenging facts of loss is that there is no quota system. Having one major loss does not prevent you from having other losses. You need this book because *Life after Loss* will help you cope with present and future losses. Consider these facts of life:

- We live in a mortal, frail, imperfect world in which the word *fair* doesn't always apply.
- Every marriage ends one of two ways: death or divorce.
- Life is always a terminal condition. There really is a time to be born and a time to die.
- Every career comes to an end.
- Every relationship is temporary.
- The aging process is inevitable and so is the increase in frequency of the losses that come with it.

Now for Some Good News

You can get through every major loss without being destroyed by it. You can enjoy life to the fullest, knowing all the while that it will end. Everybody is capable of becoming good at doing grief work.

Healthy grief is not a passive experience. It isn't something that happens to you. The loss is what happens to you—grief is the normal, appropriate response to loss. Grieving is something you do to heal the wounds in your life after a major loss. There is much more for you to do in response to any loss than just wait and suffer. You can actually take charge of your own grief process. You are the one person who can turn the pain of any loss into a creative hurt—an experience from which you learn and grow.

The exercises you will find in subsequent chapters will teach you how to do everything from getting a good night's sleep to learning how to cry.

Real Stories of Real People's Victories

Ginnie's husband, Jack, died of cancer. She immediately joined the grief support group and put herself fully into the work of grief recovery. She remained in the group for ten years and occasionally led it in my absence. It was Ginnie who said the main task of grief recovery is to "create a new normal." It's a good image. Someone or something that was essential to making your life normal is gone and you can't get it or that person back. You have the difficult, but not impossible, job of letting go of the old normal and creating a new normal for your life.

Matthew was diagnosed with cancer on the day of his fourteenth wedding anniversary. His wife, Barbara, was at his side through chemotherapy. He seemed fine for a while, except for an unrelated back problem that resulted in surgery. The pain persisted even after the surgery. More tests revealed more cancer. Again, treatment seemed to be effective, but he grew steadily weaker. He had trouble breathing and tired quickly. This time, the tests revealed not cancer but pulmonary fibrosis—a side effect of the chemotherapy.

Four years after his cancer was diagnosed, Matthew died of pulmonary fibrosis.

Barbara was heartbroken and angry. She questioned why doctors could save him from cancer but killed him with the treatment. She was angry with God, who she felt had deserted them.

When Barbara came to our grief support group, she didn't have anything to say that was positive. Efforts to reach out to her were often met with sarcastic rejection. However, she kept coming, and over the course of time, a new person began to emerge.

Barbara would tell you that the key was the day she was able to forgive herself for not being able to save Matthew.

Today, she is a positive, outgoing person who is the life of any party she attends. For several years after Matthew's death, she drove a large motor home across country by herself. She maintains a cabin by a lake in Wisconsin during the summers and spends the winters in Arizona.

The life Barbara has is not the one she would have chosen for herself. Given a choice, she would give up everything to have Matthew back again. But she has a full, rewarding life that is good in its own way. She is also a stronger person for having overcome the tragedy life gave her.

Jan's story is different, but the pain was just as great. Jan was an accomplished roller skate dancer. She was as graceful on skates as she was dedicated to her sport.

That all changed just before Christmas one year. Jan was on her way to go caroling with her church group. A man ran a red light and broadsided her car. She was not wearing a seat belt. The impact threw her across the seat, and her head hit the passenger side door.

It was several weeks before she woke up out of her coma. When she did, it was clear that she had sustained serious and permanent damage to the motor section of her brain.

She had to learn to read and write—and to walk—again. Her sense of balance was damaged so much that she could never skate again. The amnesia she experienced was permanent. Among the memories lost was that of skating, which she said made the loss of that skill easier to accept.

Jan began walking every day. She again joined a choir. She went to the skating rink with her former partner and photographed the other skaters, then gave them the pictures.

Jan is another one who found a good and meaningful life after a terrible loss.

Jan and Barbara each went through a time of grief that was normal and healthy. The feelings they experienced were appropriate to the magnitude of their losses.

The grief recovery both of them achieved is not like getting over a case of the flu. It's like getting knocked flat on your back and working to get back up on your feet and recover equilibrium in your life.

It's this kind of grief recovery that you can have as well.

Not All Stories Have Happy Endings

Betty's husband fought cancer for five years before it took his life. Even as he became more and more jaundiced and gaunt, Betty remained certain that he was going to recover. Near the end, he was confined to a hospital in a coma. When I visited them, Betty assured me he would wake up soon. When he died, she was in shock and disbelief. She was also angry at God, the church, and me, as though we had somehow failed Matthew. She refused to take part in our grief support group. Over the next few years she became increasingly withdrawn and her own health began to fail. She kept Matthew's naval officer's uniform hanging in his closet with the cap on a shelf and his shoes freshly polished on the floor. She took the uniform to the cleaners on a regular basis. It looked as if it were ready for him to return any day. Betty was committed to the denial of his death. The result was years of broken physical and emotional health and, ultimately, her own premature death.

It Takes Time

Because it is an appropriate response to loss, grief is not a bad word! Neither is it a sign of weakness, nor does it represent a lack of religious faith. Grief isn't something to avoid at all costs and try to "get over" as quickly as possible. It isn't better to feel happy than to feel grief. It is certainly more fun to be happy—but it isn't better. If something good is happening, it is appropriate to be happy. If you have experienced loss, it is equally appropriate to be sad.

One of the greatest experiences of my life was standing in the delivery room of a hospital and watching our daughter give birth to her daughter on my birthday. It was an incredible gift of love and trust that our daughter invited not only her mother but also me to be present. That it happened on my birthday made it a rare experience indeed. If I was not overjoyed beyond words in that setting, I would be crazy by definition. At age sixteen, that same granddaughter was diagnosed with acute lymphoblastic leukemia. She underwent thirteen months of intensive chemotherapy. She was often vomiting for hours at a time, suffered extreme pain, and for a time was unable to raise her head or feed herself. I was overwhelmed with sadness and fear for her. If I wasn't, you would agree I would have been crazy by definition again.

The key word is *appropriate*.

If you have had a major loss, you already know that well-meaning friends will reward you if you can keep from crying in public. You will be told how strong you are and how "well" you are doing. In the first months after June's death, I heard that kind of message many times. The assumption seemed to be that because I have written books about grief, it must be easier for me. Wrong.

I'm glad I already knew that failing to cry is an inappropriate behavior that can put you at great risk of physical and emotional illness. Anyone who wants you to hold your grief in check is seeking his or her own comfort—not yours. To heal properly, you must express your sadness freely for as long as it takes to release it.

Many polls have asked the public, "How long should it take to mourn the death of a loved one?" The most common answer is, "Between forty-eight hours and two weeks." That misguided response has remained constant from at least the mid-1970s to the present. In truth, we have barely started grieving in that length of time. Research by Dr. Glen Davidson, a pioneer in analyzing the bereavement process, revealed it takes most people at least two years to begin returning to a normal life after a major loss.

In my experience it has seemed as if three years is the usual length of time before people have established a new normal for their life. Kay expressed it well in a grief support group when she said, "For the first year or two I went through boxes of tissues every day I cried so much. Sadness would pour over me in waves like those caused by a tsunami, powerful and crashing. Now that I am a little over three years out from his death, sadness still comes but it is like ocean waves coming up on a beach as the tide moves in and out."

There is even danger in establishing two or three years as a reasonable goal. I have known people who took as long as five years to finish mourning and came out healthy and strong. Yogi Berra, the colorful former major league baseball player and manager, once said that a baseball game isn't over until it's over. That's the way it is with the grief process. It's finished when it's finished.

I frequently hear a bereaved person say, "I'm so relieved to know that others still don't have everything worked out. I thought I was the only one who wasn't handling my loss as I should." A very dignified-looking gray-haired woman in our grief support group noted that an important part of aiding your own grief recovery is to not "should on yourself."

Very little is reasonable about grief. There is nothing sensible, reasonable, or fair about losing someone we love.

Nothing is easy about having a marriage end in divorce. Actually, there is nothing rational about any major loss. Whatever the loss, the experience is devastating. The last thing any of us needs at such a time is feeling guilty because we aren't responding in the "right" way.

If you are having problems with a loss after two, three, or four years, it only means you aren't finished with your grief. It doesn't mean you are weak. It doesn't make you less of a person. It just means you still have work to do. You don't have to feel embarrassed or shy about seeking help in doing it. My dad used to say there are those who enjoy hitting their thumb with a hammer because it feels so good when they quit. Don't inflict additional and unnecessary pain on yourself when you are grieving.

> *Grief is the last act of love we have to give those who have died.*

If you are surprised by the length of a normal grieving process, you aren't alone. It isn't negative or morbid. A grief reaction means the loss was significant and life-changing for you. The sadness and emptiness you feel are appropriate. It helps to remember this: *Grief is the last act of love we have to give those who have died.*

Grief is the final way we can say, "I care about you; you matter to me very much and your loss leaves a huge hole in my life." When June died, I took my own words to heart. Reminding myself that the overwhelming grief I was experiencing was the final act of love I could give her gave purpose to my sorrow and meaning to the pain.

Dr. Earl Grollman, an internationally known counselor on death and bereavement, has said that the loss of a loved one is the most stressful of all life's changes: "You may look into the mirror and not even recognize the way you now look. Something in you is gone that can never be regained."

Your grief is a symbol of the quality of relationship you had with one who has died. Rather than trying to hide your grief, I encourage you to wear the signs of it as a badge of honor. Your tears, the heaviness in your heart, and the overwhelming sense of loneliness all say, "This person, this marriage, this part of my life has been so important to me that nothing will ever be the same again. My grief is the last act of love I have to give, and I will wear it with pride."

Other Kinds of Loss

Those who survive permanently crippling injuries face multiple challenges. Burn survivors often have to undergo many surgeries and endure a forced alienation if they are visibly disfigured. Charlene had an idyllic life. She was attractive, talented, and athletic. Her executive position was second in importance only to the man with whom she shared love and adventure. They had condos in Florida and Colorado and an island getaway in the Bahamas to which they flew as often as possible in their own plane. On one flight something went horribly wrong. They crashed while attempting a landing on the runway adjacent to their home. Both were badly burned. Charlene awoke from a coma of three months to discover that the love of her life was dead. She was burned and scarred on more than 60 percent of her body, including face, neck, hands, arms, and legs. The life she had treasured was gone forever. People looked away and children acted frightened by her appearance. After four years spent in rehabilitation and forty-nine surgeries, Charlene had a new life. She said, "I never wanted to die. I always looked forward to reviving my life again." She subsequently remarried and works as a communication specialist developing programs and resources to assist burn survivors and others with physical differences.

Not everything is bad in a marriage that ends in divorce. The worst of marriages has seen shared times that are good and meaningful. These, too, are worthy of your grief.

The fact of divorce can be a terrible loss in itself. Nancy said to me, "I think I grieved over the fact that I was now a divorcée. It was a label I never wanted."

There is nothing wrong with acknowledging the significance of our attachment to a familiar place by grieving the loss of that place when we move away. Even less significant losses in your life will hang around in the recesses of your memory and emotions, gathering energy until they have enough combined force to make themselves felt.

Grief and Accumulated Loss

Have you ever found yourself overreacting to a minor disappointment? Do you have times when you are irritable and short-tempered without knowing why? Such behavior often results when some relatively minor loss experience calls forth the gathered energy of several buried losses from the past—losses that were not adequately acknowledged at the time they occurred. Thinking back about these losses is not enjoyable, but it is necessary if they are to be healed. I once heard Elisabeth Kübler-Ross say that it is as if every loss, great and small, is filed in a loose-leaf notebook in our memory. When a new loss happens, the notebook is opened again and we are confronted by any losses from the past that have not been resolved.

The desert community in which I live often experiences a gathering of thunderhead clouds on summer afternoons. Sometimes the result is little more than higher humidity and soft breezes. On other occasions the breezes become a screaming dust storm, followed by intense rain. These monsoons happen when the atmosphere has stored up the right conditions and something serves as the trigger to turn it loose.

Our accumulation of loss experiences is like that. We store them up over time until something happens to trigger the outpouring of all our pent-up feelings. It should be no surprise that we sometimes cry our eyes out over a seemingly minor disappointment.

Norman Cousins said, "Death is not the enemy. Living in constant fear of it is." I would paraphrase that to say, "*Loss* is not the enemy. Living in constant fear of it is."

Because of books such as this one, the lid is off the subject of loss and grief. Earl Grollman once noted that "Grief is the last pornography." I don't think that is the case any longer. While it is true that people who have not had a major loss often don't understand your grief, it is no longer taboo to say you are grieving. As we begin accepting grief as an appropriate and normal response to loss, it becomes something we are free to experience without seeing ourselves as weak. Understanding that it isn't a forbidden subject, we can lay aside any sense of guilt and break the silence about our experience. We can take the opportunity to grieve at the time the loss occurs—and for as long as it takes to recover from it.

These are the first steps toward discovering a full and rewarding life after any loss.

2

First Responses to a Major Loss
When Your Worst Fears
Become Real

My mother died in her sleep at age fifty-four from a heart attack. I was at a conference when someone called to give me the bad news. I knew she had health issues, but none of it seemed life threatening. Like many people, when the death of a loved one comes suddenly, I was in such a state of shock that I don't remember much else about that day.

By contrast, June died slowly. I had watched her decline several times over the years, then rally back. Then came a time that was different. No one had to tell me she was dying. I could see it with my own eyes. On the day she died I helped our grown kids care for her until the moment she was gone and I closed her eyes with my fingers. But even though I knew it was coming, the moment I saw color drain from her face, I collapsed over her in tears. The next few hours could only be called surreal. I helped the mortician zip up the body bag around her, helped push the cart to the van and lift her body into it. I functioned calmly off and on interspersed with spasms of uncontrollable anguish.

Responding to Death

What happens when you are told a loved one is dead? If death was sudden, most people go into a state of shock and are apt to do just about anything. The first seven to ten days are often a blur about which little is remembered later. If death was prolonged, it takes on a surreal quality that makes it difficult to distinguish between reality and what seems like a nightmare from which you will awake.

It's nearly impossible to function well in either situation. Moreover, you can't anticipate how you will react to the death of someone dear to you. Even if you have had other losses before, each experience is different and you may react in quite different ways.

If you haven't "let it all out" after three or four months, you probably should seek counseling.

Whatever your reaction is to the bad news, it will be normal and okay. Some people faint; others are icy calm. Some fall apart in tears, while others become the world's greatest organizers. No particular reaction is better or worse than any other. It doesn't mean you cared less if you don't become hysterical. It doesn't mean you are weak if you do.

In the long run, tears are a good thing.

You know yourself better than anyone else knows you. If you aren't given to tears in general, you may not cry at a time of loss. If you don't feel like crying in the first few days, don't worry about it! If after some time you feel like crying but can't, seek professional help. A good rule of thumb is, if you haven't "let it all out" after three or four months, you probably should seek counseling. You will find an exercise on page 233 titled "A Programed Cry." It has helped many people break through the "I can't cry" barrier.

Caring for Yourself after the Death of a Loved One

Take special care of yourself in the wake of any major loss. Start with the following seven steps to help you through this difficult time:

1. Assess your state of health before your loss. If you have been under a doctor's care recently, or if you have a history of heart problems, stroke, high blood pressure, or any other serious health issue, get in touch with your doctor as soon as possible.

2. Be careful about what you eat and drink. Food may not interest you at all. Nevertheless, you need all the energy and emotional strength you can muster. Going long periods of time without eating, then consuming foods with little or no nutritional value, or drinking large quantities of beverages with caffeine or alcohol is not helpful. When June died, I found myself eating out several times a week and mostly eating "comfort" foods. It wasn't a good plan. I gained 5 pounds in the first month. I began weighing myself once a week and writing the results on the bathroom mirror with erasable pen. It helped me be more aware of what I was eating. See Chapter 20 for nutrition guidelines.

3. Talk about the deceased person. Talk with anyone and everyone who will listen to you. Reminisce about past good times and tell stories that are unique to the one who has died. Do not hesitate to talk about the events surrounding the death. You may find yourself telling the story of how the death occurred over and over. That's normal and good. A hospice worker was the most helpful person to me following June's death. She called regularly for a time to meet—and was persistent in the beginning if I was reticent to meet with her. I quickly learned that I could talk freely to her and that my tears were not a problem. I came to look forward to her calls and visits, which continued for a year.

4. Make time for solitude. Before the funeral or memorial service at some point, take time to be alone. Dedicate an hour to this important task, if you are able to. Say out loud to yourself: "___ is dead; he [or she] has died." Don't say *gone*, *passed away*, *passed on*, or *passed*. Use the word *dead*. You need to hear yourself say it. Don't be afraid of your emotions. Not even hysteria will hurt you.

5. Keep your normal routine intact as much as possible. Go to bed as close to your normal bedtime as possible, even if you don't feel like sleeping. Avoid tranquilizing yourself with medication, drugs, or alcohol. Many people experience disturbed sleep. A common sequence is to go to sleep, then wake up in the middle of the night and be unable to go back to sleep. Pay attention to what you do, eat, and drink before going to bed. It's okay to discuss sleep aid medications with your doctor.

6. Allow your family and community to help you. This may be your church, synagogue, mosque, friends at work, or members of a lodge, a club, or any other group in addition to your family. Many people won't know what to say, but that doesn't matter. Their presence is what counts. It's nice to let them know you appreciate their concern.

You may find that prayer and other religious practices do not come easily. That, too, is normal. In the first hours, you may even forget the name of your rabbi, priest, imam, or minister. Again, don't worry about it. Your faith will catch up with you along the way.

7. Allow yourself to have angry feelings. If you find yourself angry at medical personnel, the world in general, and at God in particular, it's okay to feel those emotions. It won't hurt the world, God, or you! Remember: Even if you know the answers, it is always okay to ask "why?" It has seemed to me that there are two basic reactions people have to a death. One is anger and the other is denial of their anger. Writing down your feelings is a good exercise. You aren't sharing the writing with anyone else, so be blunt and honest.

Preparing for the Funeral or Memorial Service

A funeral service means the body is in a casket and will be buried in ground or in a mausoleum.

A memorial service is held when the body is cremated and no casket is present. The cremains may be present in an urn or not at all.

A funeral typically takes place three to five days after a death. Even with modern embalming techniques, the body needs to be interred in less than a week. When cremation is chosen, there is no fixed time line for having a service. The decision be-tween casket burial and cremation is most often guided by cultural differ-ences in various parts of the country or religious doctrines. In the western part of the United States where I live, cre-mation is the dominant choice. In the Midwest, East, and Southeast, more in-ground burials take place. Religious doctrines may also determine the method in which the body is handled after death. Occasionally, surviving family members opt to have what is called a service of celebration, which is held in a home or outdoors at a park or beach.

> Don't say **gone, passed away, passed on,** *or* **passed**. *Use the word* **dead**. *You need to hear yourself say it.*

However you decide to deal with the deceased person's body, your time for the next few days or weeks will be consumed with decision making. If you are responsible for making arrangements, you have to:

- In some circumstances, decide whether there is to be an autopsy.
- Select a mortuary or cremation service. Contact a minister, priest, rabbi, imam, or other person to lead a service.
- Decide how disposition of the body will be handled. This will guide your decision regarding having a funeral or memorial service.
- Make decisions about the place, date, and time of the service. As an example, June died on February 18. She was cremated. Her memorial service was held on March 19 to allow time for family members living out of state to arrive and to fit into the minister's availability. A second brief service of placing her cremains in the memorial garden of a church we had served for a long time was held later with only a few family members and close friends present.

- Choose embalming or cremation. If cremation is chosen, decide whether the cremains are to be buried, placed in a niche, or scattered.
- Make seemingly endless yet necessary phone calls, each of which is just as hard to make as the one before it.
- Locate any insurance papers, birth certificates, and military records.
- Arrange to obtain copies of the death certificate. You will probably need several. The funeral home will usually handle this for you.

You will not want to do any of this, but it must be done. You might find all the activity to be a blessing in disguise. Friends or relatives who have no demands made upon them often find it is harder to cope in the first few days than do friends or family who have assumed responsibility for making the arrangements. For many people, making funeral arrangements and doing the other necessary tasks gives structure to an unstructured time and provides some clarity at a time when everything else seems so unreal.

One mother found comfort in dressing the body of her thirteen-year-old son for his funeral. She was at work when he accidentally shot himself with his father's handgun. She had felt helpless from the time the news reached her. Dressing him, she said, provided the first sense of being able to do something for her son. She did not want strangers to perform this intimate task, and it allowed her to touch him and "fix" him as she had done when he was a little boy.

I had my family with me at the very moment June died. Before her body was picked up for cremation, our daughter and a daughter-in-law removed the pajamas she had been wearing and dressed her as if she was going out for a special occasion. It also made June look more like she did in the past when she was going out. It was something they could do for her after death that made them and the rest of us feel less helpless.

It isn't fair to have to make decisions with long-term consequences (such as the cost of the funeral) when you are in a poor mental state.

Social Media

The advent of cell phones and websites, such as Facebook and Twitter, opened a whole new opportunity for notifying individuals and groups of people about a death or other major loss. Instead of leaving voice mails on others' telephones, you can often text them so the message is received even before you talk to each other. Care needs to be given to the mental and emotional state of those to whom you send a text message. I suggest not notifying all family members with a single e-mail or Facebook post. Be sensitive to each person. Before sending a group message, ask yourself whether anyone needs a personal contact, perhaps by voice from you.

When June died, I was able to use Facebook to notify people from seven churches of the place, date, and time of the memorial service. People we had not seen in as long as forty-seven years traveled hundreds of miles to come to her memorial. I received cards, letters, texts, e-mails and phone calls from more than two hundred others.

The circumstances of deaths and divorces will determine how much information you wish to disseminate. What you share with immediate family may contain information that may not be appropriate for general sharing.

Facebook is good place to post photographs of one who has died, showing the person at an earlier time and listing accomplishments. These posts can be placed throughout the first year after a death and, if you wish, on the anniversary of the death in subsequent years.

However, choosing a disposition of the body and doing something about a funeral won't wait until you feel better.

At this time, a trusted outsider can be a tremendous help. Don't hesitate to call on a friend to help you with these decisions or to act as a sounding board while you work out for yourself what to do. You could also call on a neighbor, counselor, or clergyperson. Ask this person to go with you to the mortuary, help select a casket, and assemble clothing for the funeral, if needed. If you must drive a car during the first few days, be very careful. You will be easily distracted and your reaction time may be considerably slower than normal.

> *If you must drive a car during the first few days, be very careful.*

The funeral director can also help with many details and offer good counsel. I have heard stories about unscrupulous morticians who take advantage of people in crisis, but in more than fifty years of being involved with funerals, I have never encountered such a person. The funeral directors I know are honest businesspeople who have a genuine concern for their customers. Don't be hesitant to ask about costs and services—and to compare with other mortuaries in your area. When possible, choose which mortuary or service will handle arrangements before they are needed. In the area where I live, the cost of cremation ranges from a few hundred dollars to more than two thousand dollars for basically the same service. The cost of funerals is typically thousands of dollars more.

Viewing the Body

You may have to decide whether to view the body of the deceased before or at the funeral, or whether to view the body at all. If you prefer, you can choose a private family viewing before anyone else arrives to allow time to get over the initial shock and be more in control in public. If the body is cremated, viewing typically has to be done no more than a day or two after death, unless you go through the expense of embalming and purchasing or renting a casket. The body of a dead person does not look like those you have seen in a casket when burial is in ground. You may want to discuss this with the mortuary if you are considering this option.

There is only one hard-and-fast rule about viewing the body: *Do whatever you feel like doing or not doing.* There is no right or wrong way to do it. Many people find that viewing the body prior to the service helps them comprehend the reality of the death. Seeing the body of your loved one in a casket makes it difficult to run and hide from the loss. It also can

> It isn't wrong to touch the body. Choosing not to view the body is okay, too.

bring a sense of comfort if you were not present when your loved one died, or if that person had suffered a lingering, debilitating illness and now appears at peace.

My mother-in-law was a victim of Parkinson's disease for many years. Her mind remained sharp, but the disease ravaged her body. In later years, she struggled with constant pain. When she died, her wish to be buried in a casket was honored. My wife and I both found comfort in how relaxed and at ease she appeared at last.

It isn't wrong to touch the body. When my wife's brother was killed, she was not able to accept the reality of his death and begin mourning until we went to the funeral home and she touched him. If you have never touched a dead body, it helps relieve the initial shock if you know that the body will feel very cold to you and the skin has a somewhat leathery texture.

Choosing not to view the body is okay, too. You may want to remember the person as you last saw him or her. Because I only saw June in an ever-weakening condition for the last four years of her life, I had a very difficult time trying to remember her when she was healthy and think of all the great things we did together. I found several boxes of pre–digital age photos in the closest that June had assembled over the years. Going through those brought back memories I needed to recall. I posted twenty photos on the hutch over my computer where I would see them every day. I also created some albums to keep the memories fresh.

It may be that the circumstances surrounding the death itself make it impossible or undesirable for you to view the body. If the body is to be cremated, there is often not a time of viewing once it has been picked up. Also, consider your own health: if you have heart problems or high blood pressure, it may be preferable for you to deal with the loss more slowly.

Whatever you decide is perfectly okay as long as it is not a way of denying the death or spending money that you really can't afford. If you can't decide what to do and are in good physical health, I suggest you view the body in private, then decide what you want to do at the funeral if it is to be a casket burial. If cremation is chosen, I suggest not viewing the body after it is picked up and having a memorial service whenever the time is convenient for the greatest number of people. It has become quite common for a short video presentation about the person's life to be shown at the memorial service. Using PowerPoint or another presentation software program, up to sixty photos can be shown in seven minutes.

The Day of the Funeral or Memorial Service

The day of the funeral or memorial service is unlike any other. If you are a family member, you are the center of attention, especially if you are the central family figure. You may think the whole world is watching you suffer. Hopefully, you are surrounded by people who love and care for you. There were nearly 250 people at June's memorial service at the church, including 34 family members. I greeted almost all of the people as they arrived. I was surrounded by individuals or couples for a long time after the service. I found it much more positive than challenging. If tears came, they came, and no one was injured in any way by them, including me. However, this, too, has to be an individual decision. It is just as appropriate to have family members gathered in another location and enter when it is time to begin the service.

One of the most healing things that happens at the time of a loved one's death is that the extended family gathers for a reunion. Telling stories, recalling the past, and giving one another support can provide you with a special measure of strength.

Many religious communities provide food at a reception following the service or bring food to someone's home for the family on the day of the service. It relieves the pressure on you and your family to take care of feeding people after the funeral. If anybody offers to provide food, accept.

Avoid Drugs and Tranquilizers

Don't take tranquilizers, drugs, or alcohol before the funeral. The service is designed to help you as much as it is to honor the deceased. To get the most help from the funeral, you need to:

- Be as aware as possible of what is happening.
- Be in touch with your feelings.
- Express your grief.

The service may be the first time the death becomes real for you. As painful as this moment is, experiencing the reality of your loss at the service where there are others to comfort you can be quite important to you a few weeks or months down the road because the only way out of grief is through it (see Chapter 6).

Also remember that at this time neither you nor anyone in your family needs to be strong for each other or for friends and community. This is not the time to play *Marvelous Christian*, *Noble Jew*, or *Super Trouper*. It is not your job to show how well you can care for everyone else.

If anybody offers to provide food, accept.

I learned that lesson early in the ministry. A woman in our church who was considered saintly and deserved the title lost her husband to a heart attack. At the service she was taking care of everyone else. She stood at the back of the church as the service ended, greeting people, comforting them and assuring them her faith was holding her strong. We were all impressed. Eighteen months later we were doing her funeral service.

First Response to Divorce

The death of a family member is not the only loss that triggers grief and mourning. What do you do when the loss is one of divorce? That announcement is no less shocking than that of a death.

Suppose you have been reasonably happy in your marriage. It has not been all peaches and cream, but then, whose marriage is? One day, out of the blue, your spouse announces that he or she wants a divorce.

Or suppose you have been unhappy in your marriage for several years. Perhaps you have "hung in there" because of the children, or maybe you hoped that one day the relationship would be different. Now it has become intolerable to go on with the charade. You have gathered your courage. Tonight you will tell your spouse that you want a divorce.

Whether you are the one who initiates the divorce or the one who is shocked by your spouse's decision, divorce represents a major loss. Regardless of the side you find yourself on, a number of questions surface when a divorce is imminent. You may wonder:

- Can I cope with my feelings of failure?
- Am I doing the right thing?
- How can this be happening to me?
- What will our friends think?
- How can I face my family?
- Can't I just wake up and this will be over?

In a divorce, it is not a person who has died but a relationship, along with memories from your wedding day and a big part of your self-esteem. Despite the number of divorces that happen in our society, I have yet to perform a wedding in which the bride and groom expected anything less than a lifetime of marriage that will have far more happiness than sadness.

Acknowledging that your marriage has failed is very much like hearing that your spouse is dead. Some divorced persons have told me they think it is worse!

Sally spoke for many when she said, "If my husband were dead, I would at least have a body to bury and something I could do. This way, he is still walking around and I have only my pride to bury. If I were a widow, I would get sympathy from our friends. As a divorcée, I get blamed for it!"

In a divorce, it is not a person who has died but a relationship, along with memories from your wedding day and a big part of your self-esteem.

Caring for Yourself after Divorce

The first seven days after the announcement of a divorce is a time when you would do well to take special care of yourself.

1. Assess your own state of health prior to your divorce or separation. Yes, this is the same as the first step after a death. If you are under a doctor's care, or have a history of heart problems or high blood pressure, contact your doctor right away.

2. Be careful of what you eat and drink. Yes, this suggestion is the same, too. You may want to respond to your anger and emotional upheaval by going on a food or alcohol binge. The desire is understandable, but the results are not helpful.

3. Find someone with whom you can talk freely. What you need more than anything right now is an understanding ear. Find a person who will listen without making judgments or offering too much advice, someone who genuinely cares about you. It is important to talk about how the decision to divorce happened. Did you make the decision? Or did your spouse drop the bomb on you? What are your feelings? Talking about it is crucial!

4. Don't keep your divorce secret. Let family, friends, clergy, fellow employees, and business associates know your situation as soon as possible. The fear of other people's rejection is almost always worse than reality. The sooner you can be open about what is happening, the better. You have nothing to be ashamed of. If family members, friends, or clergy don't understand, it's their problem!

5. Don't give immediate feelings long-lasting importance. If you are like most divorcing people, your emotions will run the gamut between anger and panic. If you were the one to make the decision to file for divorce, you may go through a period of sheer euphoria. If you had no idea that a breakup was coming, you may feel betrayed and crushed.

Try to remember that you won't always feel as you do now. If you are high, you will probably experience a sudden drop along the way. If you feel torn apart, you will recover.

6. Seek legal advice and emotional or spiritual help. Get both before you make decisions that can't be changed. I can't begin to tell you the amount of unnecessary grief I have seen people bring upon themselves because they acted on their own volatile emotions instead of seeking legal counsel.

Likewise, everyone I have known who has come out of a divorce truly on top of life has benefited from good psychological and spiritual counseling. When children are involved, this step is an absolute must.

Responding to Other Losses

What do you do when they say the word *fired*? Or the words *cancer*, *amputation*, *moving*, *early retirement*, *bankruptcy*, *dementia*, *failure*, or any word that identifies a loss of security, love, or familiar places and faces?

Without a doubt, some losses will affect you more than others, but all losses do affect you. Whenever you experience loss of any kind, doing the following will help put you on the right track through your grief.

1. Identify precisely what you have lost. For instance, in a bankruptcy the loss of money or income often is not as traumatic as the loss of self-confidence. Make a list of the loss or losses. (One major loss may imply a number of associated losses. This is discussed in more detail in Chapter 7, starting on page 96.) Identify the feelings you have about each by using the list of feeling words in Appendix A. Which loss calls forth the strongest feelings? That's the one with which to begin your list.

2. Take a personal assessment. What is your physical, emotional, intellectual, and spiritual condition *right now*?

These dimensions of your being are not isolated from each other. Your attitude affects your emotions, your emotions affect you physically, and your physical condition affects both your emotions and attitude. Your spiritual outlook affects everything else.

In which areas do you need help? Identify the best source of help for you in that area. You might need counseling or just a vacation. Follow up on seeking whatever help you need.

3. Talk about your loss and your grief. Tell anyone who will listen to you about your loss. Tell as many people as you can. Don't hesitate to call your reaction by its correct name: grief.

Set a goal to tell at least one or two people about your loss every day for the first week. Keep a journal of whom you talked to about your loss and the date you talked with them.

4. Find a supportive community. You need people who will give you emotional support for the duration of your grief, whether that means a few days or several years.

If you belong to a church or synagogue, you have a ready-made source of support. Your religious community either has an existing support group or needs one. You can be sure there are other people waiting for someone like you to call a group together.

If you are not part of a religious community, you can find a church or synagogue that has such a group, or look for people in your neighborhood, service club, or workplace. If you can't locate an existing support group, you may have to create one. Or, if you feel comfortable doing so, you may find a supportive community online.

It's not as difficult as you may think. Loss and grief are universal human experiences. Many others around you need the support as much as you do. Reaching out can be difficult when you are struggling with grief. But you will be rewarded with a strong network of support that makes the path through grief easier.

The Deafening Sound of Silence

For some days following the death of a loved one, you will be surrounded by caring family members and friends. But all too soon the day comes when family members must return to their own lives, and friends seem too weary of coping with your grief.

All too soon the day comes when family members must return to their own lives.

If you are divorcing, friends and family will rally to your side and be ready to listen to your complaints and comfort your tears—for a few days. Then, they will go back to their own lives and expect you to get on with yours.

Two weeks after her husband's death, Marjorie said, "One day you are the center of attention and it seems everybody cares about you and shares your loss. You wake up the next day and everybody is gone. You are more alone than you have ever been in your entire life. It is so quiet that the silence is deafening." The initial shock of Marjorie's loss had worn off at about the same time her support system went home.

Those of us in churches, synagogues, and mosques have failed people by pouring out compassion and care for about a week when someone dies—and then disappearing like fog before the rising sun. Being with people through the funeral is good. But it is *after* the funeral that the real work of grief recovery begins—and lasts for a long time. Three years or more is not unreasonable or abnormal.

Preparing for the Weeks Ahead

After any major loss, you may have a difficult time reaching out for help.

People will tell you to call them whenever you need them. At the moment you need them the most, the thought of calling others may never cross your mind! You will feel lonely and confused. You will wish somebody would come along to do something without your having to ask.

It is after the funeral that the real work of grief recovery begins— and lasts for a long time.

Most of the time, no one will come. It doesn't mean no one cares. It simply reflects the truth that the only people who really understand loss and grief are those who have experienced it themselves. It is time for you to begin taking charge.

Write the following information on a notepad and put it next to your telephone. If you have a smartphone or tablet, you may want to enter it on one of these. By writing down this information and keeping it by your telephone, or with you in your telephone, you don't have to remember names or telephone numbers in an emergency or when you are distraught. It is also a way of beginning to take charge of your life again.

1. The name and telephone number of your minister, priest, rabbi, or imam. If you haven't had regular contact with a clergyperson, use the one who officiated at the funeral. If that isn't feasible, think of the emotionally strongest and most understanding person you know. Put that person's name on the pad.

In the case of divorce, do the same. Ask yourself who has been divorced and seemed to grow through the experience. Test the reliability of this source of help by calling that person before you really need him or her. Ask if you can call during the night in a crisis. Remember, a "no" answer doesn't mean you are rejected. It means that the other person is either overstressed, is not able to cope with your grief, or has some other valid reason for being unable to respond to your request.

At one of my churches the congregation was very large during winter months. There was no way I could always be available to everybody. I was fortunate to have three associates and a group of specially trained laypersons to help carry the load. Still, occasionally I had to say no when I was asked for my time.

If your first choice can't help you, call the next person on your list. Once you have connected with someone who is available, be sure you:

- Never call at an inconvenient hour unless it is a crisis time for you.
- Never hesitate to call when you do have a need. If you don't reach the person, leave a voice mail or text message.

2. The name and telephone numbers of your doctor, including the after-hours number and address and telephone number of the nearest hospital.

3. The names and telephone numbers of family members with whom you can talk the most freely. These should be the relatives you would want notified in the case of any emergency.

Back to Work

If you are employed, go back to work as soon as you can. Let the appropriate people know that for the next few weeks or months, you may not function as efficiently as you did before. Assure these people—your supervisor, business associates, or other contacts—that your performance will return to normal, and believe yourself that it will! As a minister, I was uncomfortable with the probability of "coming unglued" while leading worship. I took three Sundays off before giving it a try. I learned to be careful about any reference to June. Like most people, choking up could "come off the wall and bite me." It took several months before I felt at ease again.

At times you may find that a day is going along reasonably smoothly, when suddenly something calls you back to the intensity of your loss and grief. At that point you will need to go home or take a break until you can regain your composure.

It is not uncommon to think you see your deceased loved one in a crowd or hear him or her in another room. An ad on radio or television can recall a poignant memory. So can a song or the conversation of fellow employees. If it was your spouse who died, having to be the only single person in a group of couples can be overwhelmingly challenging. Normal events like these can trigger a barrage of tears. Those with whom you work need to know that it doesn't mean you are falling apart. On the contrary, your tears are a sign of your recovery process.

Changes at Home

Going home to an empty house can be terrifying. So can being at home waiting for your loved one to pull into the driveway at the usual time and suddenly remembering that this beloved person isn't coming home now or ever. Parents who have lost a young child to death may have an especially hard time at the hour of their child's nap or bath, or when other children are coming home from school.

> "Don't let the house be completely quiet unless you are ready to deal with your feelings."

Many people report that it helps to have the radio or TV playing when they get home. They use these diversions to distract themselves from former routines. "Don't let the house be completely quiet unless you are ready to deal with your feelings" is the frequent advice given in our grief support group by those who have been there.

You may find it difficult to leave the house. Facing the world again as a widowed or divorced person is a strange sensation. One widow had not driven a car for ten years before her husband's death. When he died, she had to learn again. Not only was it frightening to face traffic, but each time she got behind the wheel she was reminded that she was there only because her husband was dead. For several months her grief intensified each time she drove. Many widowed persons struggle with eating alone in a restaurant after years of always dining with their spouse. Like most people whose spouse has died, I have never grown comfortable marking "widowed" on a form that lists only "single, married, divorced, or widowed" as the only choices. I continue to wear my wedding ring and will as long as I live.

Changes with Divorce

The divorcing person has most of the same things to face as the widowed person, plus others. Widowed people get sympathy in the early going at least, but few friends or relatives will seem to care how much your divorce hurts.

One or both of the spouses will relocate, so with the loss of partner also comes the loss of one's home. Housework and laundry can be real problems for someone who wasn't used to doing every one of these tasks before. People seem to expect that every male who gets divorced is overjoyed at gaining his "freedom" and can hardly wait to start playing around. Actually, most of the men I talk with are scared of reentering the dating scene. Their grief at losing their marriage, home, and family is often intense.

> *The divorcing person has most of the same things to face as the widowed person, plus others.*

Those with young children have the awesome task of becoming single parents and trying to meet the needs of their youngsters without much help. Typically a divorce is costly enough that the family home must be sold, both persons must work, and childcare must be arranged. The standard of living can decline dramatically.

Like everyone else who experiences grief, you will have to face many challenges for which you are not ready. Sometimes you will think you are the only one ever to have felt what you are feeling. You may think you are losing your mind. You may wish that you could run away or die. You will feel as lonely as you have felt in your entire life.

Hear this message: You are normal! What is happening is to be expected. It is a necessary step through grief. It must be faced. It will pass. You will conquer this thing.

3

Sudden Loss or Prolonged Loss
There Is No Easy Way

All major losses happen in one of two ways: suddenly or gradually. In the long run, the grief process is about the same. However, for the first several months, even a year, your reaction to the loss will be different depending on whether it happened in the blink of an eye or was prolonged over a lengthy time.

Dale and his wife were in Arizona for the winter from Minnesota. A granddaughter was visiting and traveled with them as they drove back to Minnesota for a wedding. They were driving on a rural highway when an eighteen-wheel truck ran a stop sign and broadsided their vehicle, sending it tumbling into a field across the road. Dale's wife died on the way to the hospital. His granddaughter was seriously injured. Although he was knocked unconscious, his injuries were minor. In one instant his entire life was turned upside down. A year later images of the truck hitting them and their vehicle rolling over and over haunted him.

> *There is no easy way to lose someone dear to you or something meaningful to you.*

Howard and Betty had been married for twenty-two years. It was the second marriage for both due to the death of their previous spouses, each of whom died suddenly from a heart attack. Betty was in a rehab facility after a knee replacement when she had a heart attack and died.

Howard said this time he at least had some idea of what to expect after her death, but his grief was just as intense.

My wife, June, died very slowly over a period of twelve years from Alzheimer's disease. At first her decline was barely noticeable. As the years went on it progressed slowly but relentlessly, taking away one piece of her life at a time. First memory was impaired, then physical skills, such as riding a bicycle, and art skills. During the last four years of her life, she went from being able to walk only with help, to not at all. At this point I could no longer keep her safe at home and moved her to a memory care facility. As the disease progressed, she became unable to dress, undress, feed herself, go to the bathroom, or perform any function of caring for herself. By trial and error I learned to perform all of the functions she needed and over time it became second nature. I tried to keep her dressed as attractively as possible, but pants could have no buttons or zippers and blouses had to be stretchy. She had a brace on one leg, so only special shoes could be worn. Finally, her body shut down and would receive no more food or liquids. I had a cot brought into her room and stayed there the last few nights of her life. Our three children, two spouses, and a granddaughter spent time with her every day. When she died, I was overcome with a sense of grief and sadness that I had never experienced before. But it was not a shock. I knew it was coming.

When a death is prolonged, those who are closest to the person often experience what is known as anticipatory grief. I did. It means as you watch your loved one decline, you anticipate the feelings of sadness and grief that will come with the person's death. There is a certain "getting prepared" for the loss you know is coming. The downside is the surviving primary caregiver is so fatigued by that time that body and emotions are exhausted. The stress is such that statistics have shown 65 percent of caregivers die before the one with Alzheimer's.

Sudden deaths include death from a heart attack, stroke, an accident, or murder. Prolonged losses include death after months or years of struggling with cancer, pulmonary disease, Parkinson's disease, ALS, diabetes, Alzheimer's, or Lewy body dementia. Suicide is in a class by itself. Suicide is an instantaneous event, but there may have been threats or previous attempts over months or years before it actually happened.

Sometimes a divorce has been "brewing" for years. When the marriage ends, neither partner is surprised. Other times, one partner's announcement that the marriage is over catches everyone off-guard, including the other partner. It is not unusual for one person to contemplate a divorce for a long time while the other person in the marriage is blissfully unaware of the impending crisis.

Jim was blindsided by Pat's sudden announcement that she was leaving him and wanted a divorce. He was happy in their marriage and devoted to their children. He provided a comfortable home, was involved in the kids' sports and other activities, and thought of himself as a near ideal family man. It turned out that Pat had an entirely different view of their lives and marriage. She was frustrated by Jim's occasional "black moods." She felt lonely and unfulfilled. Eventually, Pat had turned to another man for affection who was considerably older than her. She and Jim were well into the divorce proceedings before Jim learned of her involvement with the other man. He was as shocked at the end of his marriage as he would have been if a terrible accident had happened and Pat or one of the kids was killed. Pat wasn't shocked. She had contemplated the separation for several years, but didn't have anywhere to go until the other man came into her life. In the years afterward, both of them faced quite similar issues of grief and loss. In the beginning, however, it was quite different.

All major losses are painful beyond words and require a lengthy time for healing. The appropriate response in every case is grief. There is no easy way to lose someone dear to you or something meaningful to you. However, soon after the loss, it may seem as if *any* other way to experience your loss would be less painful than the way you have experienced your loss. If your loved one's death was sudden, you may wish there had been time to get used to the idea. If the loss was prolonged, your emotional and physical strengths have been drained to the point of exhaustion. You feel as if you have no resources left with which to deal with the pain and grief. You are sure a quick death would have been less painful for you.

The issue of sudden death or prolonged death comes up all the time in grief groups. Sometimes people who lose loved ones suddenly think it would not have been as painful if they had time to get used to the idea of the other person dying.

But some people who deal with the prolonged loss of their loved one are so tired, stressed, and worn out, they have little resources left for coping with death when it comes. One man never did show any signs of grief recovery because even though he had been with his wife in a nursing home many hours every day, she died when he went home to rest one day (he was in his upper eighties). He never could forgive himself.

The Special Dynamics of Sudden Loss

A sudden loss is a momentary incident that changes your life forever.

One night Tom and three friends went to a basketball game, then decided to go to a sports bar. When they were ready to leave, they realized it was not safe for any of them to drive a car. They decided to take a cab home and sat down on a bus bench to wait. A young woman walked by behind them, turned around, and walked by again. The third time she pulled a gun from her purse and shot Tom in the chest. The others ran but one of them was shot in the leg. Patrons from the bar ran out, knocked the woman to the ground, and held her until the police arrived. Tom died in the hospital. No words passed between them. They had never met. To this day no one knows why the woman shot him.

His friends and family were shocked. The manner of Tom's death was like a blow to the midsection.

Years later the impact of that tragedy continued to haunt those who were close to Tom.

The special dynamics that people like Tom's family and friends experience are typical of sudden losses.

1. Lack of preparation. There was no chance for anyone to say "goodbye," "I'm sorry," or "I love you." His parents and friends had no forewarning of what would happen and were not prepared for it. Tom was healthy, talented, and successful. His parents' hopes and dreams for their thirty-two-year-old son did not include the possibility of an untimely death. At his memorial service Tom's mother said, "Heaven has just gotten a lot happier with Tom there."

When losses happen suddenly, there is a horrible sense that "I did not have time to be ready for this." Practical issues often complicate emotional ones. For example, perhaps one person in a marriage always handled the finances, and that person dies suddenly. The survivor has to cope with the new challenge of taking care of money matters at a time when he or she is least prepared to do so. The other frequent challenges are women learning to put gas in the car and men learning to cook.

Every bereaved person is angry.

Common wisdom says we can never adequately prepare for any major loss. That's true under any circumstance, but the reality is all the sharper when the loss occurs suddenly.

If you experience a sudden loss, you may believe that if only you would have had the chance to prepare for it, your loss would be easier to face. No one would argue with you—except people like me whose losses occurred over years.

2. Difficulty accepting reality. The unreal nature of a death, divorce, or job loss can be magnified if that loss happens suddenly. Questions are urgent and intense and usually focus on trying to make some sense of what has happened.

You may wake up in the morning, hoping to find you have been dreaming, only to realize yet again that what happened was no dream. Your loss is real, and it is permanent.

3. Anger. Virtually every bereaved person is angry. Those whose loved one died suddenly are more aware of their anger, and it is often more intense than it is for those whose losses are prolonged. If responsibility for the loss can be identified, the anger will also be more focused. Tom's parents are angry with the young woman who shot him. The fact that she is in jail for at least forty-two years and will not see her own son grow up does not alleviate their hostility.

Frequently I hear people express anger at doctors and other medical people for not saving their loved ones. The tacit assumption is that if the medical professionals had done their job, the person would not have died. When sudden loss occurs, it's as if we revert to that point in childhood where *somebody* must be to blame. By contrast, those who cope with a prolonged loss have time to work through the blaming phase. They come to understand that people die, even with the very best and most talented medical help.

If yours was a sudden loss, it's important for you to know that the anger you feel is normal. It's also important that you find a creative way to release your anger by granting forgiveness or by making peace with the flawed and frail nature of this mortal life. A trusted friend, your minister or rabbi, or a counselor may be able to help you get to that point.

4. Guilt. The two most frequently used words by those who experience a sudden loss are *if only*. "*If only* I had done something different." "*If only* I had been more aware of his symptoms." "*If only* I had called 911 sooner." "*If only* we had talked more, this divorce would not be happening."

Jean was driving the family car when she and her husband were involved in an accident. Her husband died instantly. Jean's list of "if only"s was almost endless.

The issue is *guilt*. Guilt is the flip side of blaming someone else for the loss. With guilt, we blame ourselves. The most common experience of guilt with a prolonged loss comes if the survivor was not present at the time of death.

5. Secondary anxieties. If a death happens suddenly, survivors are left to wonder, "Did he or she suffer?" "Was he or she frightened?" Often I hear people in grief support groups agonize over what might have been going through their loved one's mind just before the incident that caused the death. Secondary anxieties can be pervasive and long-lasting.

My parents died six months apart. Each of them was alone at the time of death. For many years, I wondered what each was thinking and feeling.

I have been present with family members when dozens of persons stopped breathing and died. Their family members have typically remained free of the kind of anxiety that is felt when no one is present and the person dies alone.

My granddaughter Carrie was driving on a freeway late at night when she spotted an object in the lane ahead. As she swerved to avoid it, she was shocked to see it was a person, down on the freeway. She stopped and ran back to find a badly injured young woman. Others stopped and began to wave off oncoming cars as Carrie knelt beside the victim and comforted her. The young woman tried to speak but could only mumble incoherently. Seeing fright in the woman's eyes, Carrie wrapped her arms around her and held her. The young woman died in Carrie's arms. In the months that followed, the parents of the young woman called Carrie frequently to ask about their daughter: Had she been in pain? Did she seem frightened? They invited Carrie to their home for dinner and expressed a deep gratitude to her. The fact that their daughter had not died alone on the street was a great comfort to both of them.

Other questions survivors ask frequently are, "Can we view the body?" "Are there photographs?" and "Did the deceased person say anything to anyone before death?" These and questions like them are ways survivors try to understand what happened and to make contact with the event retroactively.

If your loss happened suddenly, be assured that your reactions, however bizarre they may seem to you, are probably no more extreme than those of anyone else who has had a similar experience.

You will be okay! Over the long road of grief recovery, your experience is neither easier nor more difficult than if your loss had been prolonged. You will find much in common with others who have had similar losses. You can recover your balance, create a new normal, and move on with your life.

Traumatic and Catastrophic Losses

Every loss has a traumatic impact on every person's life to some degree. However, now and then a multiplicity of sudden deaths happen that impacts family and friends with such trauma that it goes off the scale in terms of suffering and shock. I call the worst of these catastrophic losses.

Fortunately, these kinds of deaths happen very infrequently.

A catastrophic death typically happens in a violent way without warning and includes more than one person. The aftermath of grief is prolonged beyond the two to three years that typical grief recovery requires. The usual methods of comforting and helping people after the loss of a loved one can seem to be ineffective after a catastrophic loss. The level of suffering is so great it's like a tidal wave of suffering flooding over efforts to bring comfort and healing.

During the night before a Thanksgiving, a thirty-nine-year-old veteran pilot left a small airport in Mesa, Arizona, in a private plane with his three children, ages nine, eight, and six, and two friends to fly to his home in Safford for the holiday. Something went terribly wrong and he flew into the steep face of the Superstition Mountains at 200 miles per hour, instantly killing everyone on the plane.

I attended the memorial service, which was packed with hundreds of mourners.

The mother's level of grief and the shock and horror on the face of everyone gathered was something I have only seen after such catastrophic events. Five years later it was still having an impact on those closest to the victims.

A similar catastrophic loss happened to a young man and his wife who were married in our church. In time they had four children, two girls and two boys. His work took them to Texas, where they headed out for a vacation one summer. A tire on their SUV blew and the vehicle rolled. When it stopped only the father and his eight-year-old daughter had survived. The mother, the other daughter, age eighteen, plus both sons, fourteen and eleven, died at the scene.

Several hundred people attended the memorial service at which there were four caskets across the front, all closed because there had been too much physical trauma to those inside. The church was filled with an invisible cloud of sorrow and the sounds of sobbing.

I had close contact with the father and parents of the mother, who were grandparents of the children over the next year. The father just wanted to die himself. He did not want expressions of sympathy and let everyone know that he resented efforts to try to make him feel better. The couple who were parents and grandparents of the deceased kept asking for some way to find their way through the loss and feel any sense of hope again.

On the anniversary of the accident, the father held another memorial service at the site of the graves. He addressed the crowd that gathered with him. Here is an excerpt from what he said:

> When people ask how I am, I tell them "I'm okay." Today I will tell you how I really am. *Hate* is a very strong word. I hate everything. I hate the sun hitting my skin; I hate the wind in my hair; I hate the food that I eat and the air that I breathe. I hate every day when I wake up and realize that I'm alive and most of my family isn't. I hate what my little daughter's future will be. I live in a nightmare I wish wasn't true, but it is.

Those are the unfiltered, raw emotions of a man who was hurting beyond words.

The amazing part is that as I listened to him, I felt growing sense that he and his daughter were going to survive. It will take many years—but both are young enough and strong enough to have a chance to make it through. His determination and willingness to face the full force of their catastrophe is the promise of it. It's the same thing required of all of us in times of major loss. It's just much greater in its magnitude.

When traumatic and catastrophic losses occur the incidence of PTSD (post-traumatic stress disorder) for those who mourn are significantly higher than for the general public, even when measured five years after the event.

Because of this, it is always good to have counselors available who are specially trained in helping people cope with PTSD.

When Loss Is Prolonged

Not all losses happen abruptly. Many times, losses happen over a period of months or years.

The word that seems to describe the experience of survivors best is *fatigue*. Although you may feel deep shock when the illness or situation is first disclosed, that feeling is eventually buried under the incredible burden of coping with prolonged loss. Emotions soar and fall with every hopeful or discouraging development. When all is said and done, prolonged loss involves just as much grieving and feelings of emptiness as sudden loss. There is the same terrible finality to contend with. But some aspects of the adjustment are different in the first months.

> *Prolonged loss involves just as much grieving and feelings of emptiness as sudden loss.*

I was called to a hospital to visit a woman who was gravely ill. Arliss had struggled with pulmonary disease for several years. She was now at a place where it seemed as if any quality of life was impossible. Her survival was in jeopardy. Her lungs continued to fail for reasons that weren't showing up on tests.

Her husband, Marty, sat by her side, holding her hand, stroking her hair, and offering words of love and encouragement. He appeared as calm as he did strong—until you looked into his eyes. When Arliss was sleeping under the effects of medication, I said, "Marty, you look tired." He responded, "I've never been more mentally, emotionally, and physically exhausted in my life."

Guilt and Prolonged Loss

People who care for a dying person for a prolonged period sometimes struggle with guilt. Typically their guilt is not nearly as intense as it is when the death happened suddenly. The most common expressions of guilt I hear after a prolonged illness have to do with the survivor's not being able to prevent the decline and death of the loved one or not being present when death finally comes.

I was with June six to nine hours a day from the time she had to be in a memory care facility. I would go help get her ready early in the morning, feed her breakfast, and make sure all was okay before I left for work at the church. I was back by three thirty in the afternoon, fed her dinner or took her out to dinner, got her ready for bed, and stayed with her until she was asleep. The last three days of her life I was there constantly, sleeping on a cot beside her. She was in my arms when she died. Nevertheless, I struggled with a sense of guilt that I had not done enough, or missed something she needed. It was not a rational perception, but it is normal.

By day's end, he heard the awful truth: Arliss was dying. She went home a day or two later and was placed under the care of hospice.

The level of grief Marty faced when Arliss died was every bit as deep as that of people who experience a sudden loss.

The Role of Hospice

The emergence of hospice has been a wonderful development for the physical comfort and emotional care of those who are dying and of their loved ones. Hospice is a medically directed, team-managed service program that focuses care on the patient and family. Professional and volunteer hospice workers provide not only good medical and social services, but they also bring the added benefits of dignity for the one who is dying and compassion for his or her family.

Hospice care is palliative rather than curative, with an emphasis on pain and symptom control, so that a person may live the last days of life as fully as possible, with dignity and comfort. Palliative care frees the patient, the family, and medical personnel to talk openly about the end of life.

If they are alert enough, dying people are able to help survivors make decisions. Funeral arrangements can be made, plans for a surviving spouse's support can be put in place, and family and friends can visit. Perhaps the most significant part is that all of this can be done with the person living at home or in a hospice-served facility where family and friends are around them.

When death occurs, the hospice workers are either present or arrive within minutes. They are able to take over contacting the funeral home and arranging for transportation of the body.

They offer emotional and spiritual support to the survivors until other family members, friends, or spiritual leaders arrive. My sister was diagnosed with a rare cancer. She was able to hold it back for a while, but eventually it was clear that the cancer was going to win the fight. As the end drew near, she entered a hospice-run facility. Her room was furnished much like a normal apartment might be, except for the medical equipment. She was able to check out her room, garden outside her window, and join the community gathering area outside her door. Two days later, she was in a coma. The hospice staff and volunteers were comforting and gracious to all of us in her family. If she needed pain medication, it was provided within a minute or two. As her coma deepened, someone explained the signs we could expect to

Hospice personnel are typically prepared to stay involved with the family for as long as a year.

see that would indicate death was nearer. She died peacefully in her sleep with her husband and children by her side.

Hospice personnel are typically prepared to stay involved with the family for as long as a year. Their comfort level with the subject of death and grief provides strength and stability for the survivors, especially when other family members and friends begin to depart. They can greatly soften the "thud" that comes with being alone with grief for the first time.

Chances are there is a hospice group near you. Check your telephone book, talk to your doctor, call your hospital, or ask a librarian at your local library for reference help. Hospice organizations have my highest endorsement (and admiration).

Prolonged Loss in Divorce

I don't know of any hospice-type group for dying marriages, but it would be a valuable resource. It isn't easy to find a pastor or other counselor who is willing to counsel for divorce. The focus often seems to be on doing something to save the marriage, not on finding ways to allow it to end peacefully.

Jean and Joe were married for seventeen years. They had three children. Throughout most of those years, one or the other, or both, were unhappy. They didn't fight. They weren't mean to each other. There were few harsh words. They just didn't fit well together in terms of what it took for each to feel fulfilled. For the last seven years of their marriage, Jean grew increasingly despondent. She tried to stay in it for the children, her parents, and as some kind of act of contrition. It didn't work. Finally, she told Joe she was leaving and filed for a divorce.

Fortunately, Jean and Joe were counseled by a sensitive professional who understood that the dynamics between them were incompatible. Families who supported each of them without blaming anyone helped both Jean and Joe through the process.

Jean and Joe held hands as they filed their divorcing papers. They went through the process without lawyers or court appearances. They agreed on joint custody of the children and an equitable sharing of assets and liabilities.

They both continued to attend school and church functions that involved the children. Birthdays and holidays were celebrated with both parents present.

In time, first Jean and then Joe remarried. The two couples met regularly over the years to discuss matters relating to the children, one of whom is now married and a parent herself. The others are young adults with successful careers. Jean's second husband was a groomsman at Joe's second marriage. In times of crisis, the two couples rally together—as when one of their daughters was battling leukemia.

> *Families who supported each of them without blaming anyone helped both Jean and Joe through the process.*

Jean and Joe have demonstrated that it is possible to go through the dissolution of a marriage, with emotional pain as severe as any death, and still maintain dignity and respect for each other and cause as little distress to children as possible. Another divorced woman commented to Jean that her relationship with Joe was "weird." Jean's reply was, "No, what we have is normal. It's the other way that is weird." Joe and Jean have fully recovered from their loss and have moved on to very happy lives.

Common Factors of Sudden and Prolonged Loss

Once initial adjustments are made, the grief process takes the same path, whether a loss was sudden or prolonged. Grief is finally grief, whatever its cause. The length of time required, the work to be done, the "mileposts" that mark your progress, and what it takes to have life be full again are about the same.

> *Grief is finally grief, whatever its cause.*

The shock of sudden loss wears off with time and effective grief work. The fatigue of prolonged loss typically doesn't last long. Loneliness is every survivor's long-term adversary.

No matter how difficult the circumstances may seem to you right now, believe this: There is no "easier" way your loss could have happened. However your loss occurred, acknowledge it as "the way it is" and take charge of your grief. Keep going. Talk to people.

4

Recovering Your Balance
Creating a New Normal Experience

Recovering from a major loss is not like getting over the flu. Grief is not an illness. It doesn't help to take two aspirin, go to bed, and wait for the grief to go away. Neither is there enough alcohol in the world to make the pain disappear. When you experience a major loss, it is as though the rug of life has been jerked out from under you. Someone or something that made your life normal, gave it meaning and joy, is gone forever. You don't know which way to turn or what to do. Getting back on your feet is a difficult but important first move toward recovery. It can take much longer than you expect to feel normal again. It will not be the former normal. That one is gone. The first task of grief recovery is to begin the challenging task of creating a new normal. It will be different. In the beginning it won't feel good. But with time and effort, it will take you beyond your loss and make your life feel worth living again.

The Urge to Escape

More people than I like to remember have tried to medicate their way through grief. It never works, but I have to admit it's tempting. It isn't difficult to find a doctor who is willing to prescribe tranquilizers for the first few days or weeks. The problem is that being tranquilized can create a fog around your emotions and block the beginning of grief recovery. The abuse of prescription painkillers is like a plague in many places in the world.

The side effects can include hallucinations, nausea, and impaired judgment. They, too, inhibit the first steps that are necessary to grief recovery. Taking medication is sometimes necessary, but it should always be the last resort. If depression persists for weeks or if anxiety attacks are frequent and severe, it is time to seek professional intervention. The issue is one of *intent*. Medications that are taken to keep from facing the reality of the loss do more harm than good. To take control of your grief, you must face your loss directly, with all your senses and your mind working. You can't do that while you are blissfully tranquilized—any more than you can safely drive a car while under the influence of alcohol.

However, it is also true that antidepressants can give you needed strength to make the decisions that will enable you to create your new normal and take you to recovery. Hundreds of people whom I have counseled have used antidepressants in the course of their grief recovery with no apparent negative effects. Getting back on your feet after a major loss is one of the most difficult tasks you will ever face. There is no more shame in using "a crutch" to accomplish this task than using one while a broken leg heals.

The Challenge of Getting Up Again

After the death of a loved one, the shock of divorce, the disillusionment of bankruptcy, or a catastrophic injury, people often say something like "It knocked me flat." It is not an overstatement; rather, an accurate description of experiencing a major loss. You are affected emotionally, physically, and spiritually. You will feel disoriented, uncertain, and weak in the knees. Your sense of equilibrium will be impaired. You may feel so tired that even *thinking* requires tremendous effort. Your religious faith may seem as shattered as your life appears to be. Many people have reported how difficult it was to go back to church. Memory losses and forgetfulness are almost universal.

Other family relationships are often affected in dramatic ways.

One of the most frequent and emotional topics in our grief support group centers around disillusionment and hurt feelings with family members. We are inclined to think everyone will rally together at a time of loss, but that turns out to be more fantasy than fact. Sometimes, relationships can be damaged for years. Sometimes they are permanently destroyed. In either case, the sadness of the loss is multiplied many times over. I have seen people's healing blocked by anger and conflict until some kind of resolution is found with estranged family members. The source of the conflict doesn't seem to matter. It is often related to money in some way, but can also be centered on children (young or grown), some artifact, or simply a lack of emotional support and understanding. If your marriage was a second marriage and your deceased spouse had children by his or her first marriage, you may find a noticeable difference in how they relate to you after the death of their parent.

Taking medication is sometimes necessary, but it should always be the last resort.

- The death of a child produces incredible stress between the parents. Statistics have shown that the divorce rate among parents who lose children is very high.
- Parents and siblings of a deceased child often struggle with their feelings about one another and the siblings' place in their parents' emotions.

No One Response Fits All People

Janet's husband, Don, left for work at the same time that he always did. It would have been like any other day if she hadn't received a telephone call an hour later from a sheriff's deputy. Don was only 2 miles from home when an eighteen-wheel truck turned in front of him. Don died instantly.

Janet was filled with disbelief and horror. She was sure it was a mistake and Don would call to say he was okay. But Don didn't call. Weeks after the funeral, Janet would find herself going to the door and looking for him. Then the anger set in. She filed a lawsuit against the trucking company. I'm convinced that it was the energy of her anger that sustained her over the next two years. It gave her a reason to get up in the morning and a purpose for living. In time, the lawsuit was settled and her life began to take on some sense of a new normal.

Mary was driving a group of neighborhood children to the ice-cream store. Somewhere along the way, her own toddler choked to death in the backseat. Mary was unaware of any problem until she arrived at their destination.

On the day of the funeral, the family called me to say Mary was hyperventilating. As soon as she could breathe again, she would begin screaming hysterically until her breath was once more gone. Family members had tried everything to get her calmed down, without success. I went to the house and ordered everyone out of the room, except for Mary.

When we were alone, I told her that I was there to be with her, that I understood the immensity of her loss and her sense of guilt. I said, "Mary, you can respond any way you want to this terrible thing. It's okay with me if you hyperventilate, scream, throw up, wet your pants— anything that will help you get through the funeral this afternoon. I won't let you be harmed, and there are plenty of people who love you who will clean up any messes."

She looked me squarely in the eyes for a long time—I think to see whether I really meant what I said. I did not take my eyes off her and tried not to blink any more than I had to. She threw her arms around my neck, sobbing not in hysteria but in an anguish that was totally appropriate to the loss of her baby. Later, after the funeral, she could not remember being out of control, only that she felt better after my arrival.

Dan was an engineer who designed computer hardware and programs. His work was brilliant in part because of his skills and in part because he never let his emotions guide his response to any challenge.

When his son was murdered, Dan conducted interviews and press conferences without a tear in his eyes. We never sat down in chairs so I could "counsel" him. We walked, sometimes for miles at a time, while he talked about his son's death—never about his own feelings. His response seemed to break all the rules of good grief recovery process, but it worked for him. This was the way he functioned normally, and he did not vary from it under the stress of grief. He went on to make a full recovery and has led a full life in the ensuing years.

It isn't better to remain calm like Dan, angry like Janet, or hysterical like Mary. There was nothing wrong with the way any of them reacted to their loss. They all responded in ways that helped protect their shattered life and emotions. Each of them was beginning to recover long before being aware of it.

You will react to a major loss in your life in ways you can't predict ahead of time. It will seem as if the foundations of your very existence have crumbled. Before you can pick up the pieces and get back on your feet, you will need to regain your sense of balance.

Creating a new normal for your life is an enormous task that takes a long time.

Think back to some loss in your life.

- Remember how your life seemed to crumble.
- Write down some of the feelings you had at that time. See Appendix A for a list of words that describe feelings.
- With whom did you talk about those feelings?

If you are like most of us, you kept most of your thoughts and feelings to yourself.

Trust Yourself

Loss and grief are subjects we should be talking about frequently—before losses occur. The fact is that we have not been talking about these experiences very much, even after the losses. Because of this conspiracy of silence that is mostly unintentional, the task of grief recovery is made more difficult. We think there is something wrong with a perfectly normal reaction, such as intense crying, bitter anger, difficulty sleeping, or overwhelming fatigue.

A frequent statement I hear from people in grief support groups is, "You mean other people do that? I thought I was the only one and that I was going crazy!" Actually, a very small percentage of people experience mental illness after a major loss, but almost everyone does "crazy" things. When a loved one (even a pet) has died, you may struggle with issues of security and depression. Even if you were a fabulous caregiver, you will be haunted by the times you know you failed. You will do and think things that seem strange to you and, perhaps, to others. This is one of those times in life when "weird" means normal.

Forgetfulness

You may find that you have forgotten how to do tasks that had been routine. Sue was a secretary who regularly typed eighty words per minute with flawless accuracy. A month after her divorce, she complained she could not type her own name without making a mistake. I had my own introduction to this phenomenon when we moved to a different state after thirty-three years of being in the same area. In the next six months, I locked my keys in the car four times. I went through forgetfulness again after June died. I was very grateful and fortunate that cars now had push-button gadgets on car keys that opened and locked doors. It was impossible to leave them in the car when locking it! However, I "lost" my cell phone an average of four times a day for months.

Whenever I meet with a group of bereaved persons, we inevitably spend some time laughing at ourselves for our forgetfulness. What's happening is the emotional equivalent to overloading an electrical circuit. Our mind and emotions can absorb just so much stress and then they "short out." That isn't a bad thing. I see it as a protective mechanism, an automatic reflex that functions like a fuse or circuit breaker. It's a necessary step for most of us that enables our emotional resources to gain strength for the difficult task of grief recovery.

Keys and Signs

"Veterans" who have been dealing with grief for a while tell newly bereaved people to anticipate and guard against forgetfulness. They suggest if your car doesn't have electronic remote entry, to keep a set of car keys in a magnetic box placed discreetly out of sight. It's always a good idea to have a trusted neighbor keep a spare set of house keys. Make signs to put on the inside of the door you use most to leave the house. They should say such things as "Have your purse?" "Cell phone with you?" More than one person in a grief support group has said to add a sign that reads, "Do your shoes match?"

This advice applies to any major loss, not just to the death of a loved one. Forgetfulness hits almost everyone regardless of the source of grief.

You will continue to recover your emotional balance as time goes on and you gain more skills in coping with your loss. The more you understand what is happening to you and that it is normal, the less forgetfulness and other common occurrences will frighten you. Take hope and comfort in knowing others behave in the same ways.

The following exercise has been well tested by thousands of people. It can help you begin to recover your emotional balance and get back on your feet.

Write each of the following statements on a separate piece of paper in your own handwriting. (If that doesn't work for you, print them out from your computer or smartphone.) Make three copies.

- I will not always feel as I do now.
- I am doing okay. Grief will not destroy me.

- I will make it through this experience just as others have before me.

Post one copy of each on the door of your refrigerator. Put another
in your bathroom, either on the mirror you use most frequently or on

You aren't falling apart;
you are coming together.

the lid of your toilet. (You will use these
household items regularly, regardless of
your grief.) Keep the third copy with
you. If you use a smartphone, consider
adding these statements to a note on
your phone, or setting a digital reminder to pop up when you might
need it.

Every time you see these statements, read them aloud. Keep reading
them until you know them by heart and the words come automatically
in times of special sadness. Being forgetful is only another aspect of
your grief experience, just like sadness, fatigue, and anger. It is a sign
of your movement along the pathway to recovery. You aren't falling
apart; you are coming together.

In spite of your feelings to the contrary, you won't always feel as you
do early on in the process. You will recover your balance, get back on
your feet, and have a good life.

Tears

On your journey to recovery, you will shed more tears than you thought
your body could hold. Four months after her husband's death, one
widow said, "Now I understand why they say the human body is mostly
water. I've cried enough tears to fill a swimming pool!"

I am a big believer in tears. There was always a sign in my office that
read, "People and tears are welcome here." There was always at least one

Big boys don't cry,
but real men do.

full box of tissues in plain sight and more nearby.
When someone came to talk about a pending divorce, the death of a loved one, or a child who
has run away, I wanted that person to feel free to
cry as much as needed. When our grief support

group met, there were always boxes of tissues around the circle in highly visible locations. The tears of a newcomer or "veteran" are met with a casually passed box of tissues. The clear message is, "Your tears are okay here." In the weeks and months after June's death, every time I broke into uncontrolled sobbing I told myself it was a good thing that was making me better—and reached for my tissues.

I am among the men who have grown up believing that "big boys don't cry." I don't know who ever taught us that bit of foolishness, but we never should have listened. Women are smarter and healthier, not weaker, because they typically have an easier time crying. The two best things men have going for them these days is (1) being in the delivery room when their children are born; and (2) watching massive football players weep openly on television. Being present to the birth process softens them up, and it doesn't take a rocket scientist to conclude that if the really big boys can cry, so can I. A good motto for men is: "Big boys don't cry, but real men do."

Tears can be embarrassing if they flow in public. They most certainly turn your eyes red, cause your mascara to run, and make your face look puffy. But those are the only negative aspects of crying. Crying is actually one of the healthiest things anyone can do. Studies have shown that tears of sadness have a different chemical makeup than tears of joy. Tears of sadness stimulate the production of endorphins that have a calming effect. It is no myth that you will feel better after a good cry. Some studies indicate they are also washing stress hormones and toxins out of the body—which means not crying is holding these poisons inside.

Add this to your list of notes to be posted around the house: *Tears are a sign that I am on the way to recovery.*

Jack came to see me a few months after his wife died of a heart attack while they were on a skiing trip. He had been absent from church since her death. In the past, the two of them rarely missed a Sunday. He told me he had reached the church door several times but just couldn't come in. He would begin to cry uncontrollably as the memories rushed over him of having Helen beside him and listening to her sing the hymns. Each time he tried to come he would get a step or two inside the door, then turn around and go home to cry alone. He didn't want anyone to see him "acting like a sissy."

As we talked, I discovered that he wasn't sleeping well and was eating infrequently. He also reported that he was having occasional chest pains and shortness of breath.

I suggested to Jack that his unwillingness to cry was hurting him and blocking his ability to get back on his feet after Helen's death. It may sound unkind, but I scolded him for his foolish pride that kept him away from church and for his lack of confidence in the rest of us to be able to understand his grief.

I told him our church Cry Room at the back of the sanctuary was not only for parents with babies but also for adults who did not want to cry in public. I urged him to join the grief support group where he could talk and cry with people who would understand perfectly. Jack accepted both suggestions.

He used the Cry Room for a few weeks and then rejoined the rest of the congregation. Without doing anything else, he began to sleep better and eat better. His chest pains disappeared, and in time his physical health was back to normal.

The Pattern of Recovery

Getting back on your feet and creating a new normal after a major loss will follow a fairly predictable pattern—which may seem like the pattern of a crazy quilt. It isn't as though you will ride an escalator from the basement of grief to the penthouse of recovery. Neither is it like climbing a set of stairs with a firm tread and a good, solid handrail.

If you are like most of us, you will have times when your recovery seems like a hopeless maze with no way out. Sometimes, moving forward will seem to you like slipping backward. About the time you have some part of your grief figured out, a new challenge is likely to appear.

The best image I can think of to describe the pattern of grief recovery is to picture yourself trying to walk the greased tracks of a roller coaster in the dark . . . in a wind-driven rainstorm . . . with lightning flashing all around. It's frightening. It's almost impossible to figure out which way is up and which is down. You think you will fall at any moment. You take three steps forward and slip back two. It feels terribly "messy" and uncomfortable. Sometimes, you will think you are going to die. Other times, you will wish you could die. But in the end, you make it.

Like Jack, you will be able to cope with your losses and grief better if you have some idea of what to expect of yourself on the journey to recovery. You need to know that

- Forgetfulness is common, and it doesn't last.
- Tears are a sign of healing.
- You are not alone in your feelings.
- Grief recovery takes time—it is measured in years, not weeks or months.
- You will move through various stages of recovery.
- If you know what to look for, there are visible signs of progress.

Any loss is upsetting. It isn't only death that can knock you off your feet. Divorce, relocation, financial loss, chronic illness, and children leaving home are among many other experiences that can devastate your life. The experience that taught me what grief is was not a death, but being transferred to a church in Arizona after living most of my life in Southern California. June went through all the struggles and emotions that I did. It took three solid years for our new residence to become home.

Recovery takes time, attention, and hard work.

These kinds of experiences are part of being a human being. They happen to everybody. They knock you off balance, leaving you feeling flattened and defeated. You must recover your balance, create a new normal, and get back on your feet before life can go on. This is the task of grief recovery.

This recovery takes time, attention, and hard work. If you don't take the time to pay attention to your grief and do the work it calls for, life after a major loss will never again be as full as it could be.

But in the end you will make it. You will stand tall. You will reach your destination. You will know that you have achieved a significant victory. Life will be whole again. You will have created a new normal and you will be content with it.

5

Perception
The Key to Healing

Iam convinced the key to healing after a major loss is a thing called perception.

Perception is what we "see" from inside our head. It is the way we interpret the events of our life. Perception incorporates such words as *insight*, *awareness*, and *discernment*. All these are elements of what we call attitude, which has to do with outlook, mind-set, and a way of thinking.

Our perception of the losses we experience is far more important to healing than the circumstances of those losses.

> *Our perception of the losses we experience is far more important to healing than the circumstances of those losses.*

A difference in perception determines why one person experiences a major loss and comes out of it a stronger person—whereas someone else has an equally painful loss and is destroyed by it. It's the age-old question of how full or empty the glass is. The added question is "What are the chances of having it filled again?"

Joe and Wilma were married for sixty years before her death due to a combination of cancer and congestive heart failure. Several years after her death Joe still said nothing had really changed. He felt as lost as ever. The best he could say was "I'm getting by." His sense of guilt for not being at the hospital when she died remained undiminished. The fact that he had been at her side week after week, going home only for necessary sleep did not bring comfort. Joe lived out his remaining years without ever getting through his grief or making any effort to create a new normal for his life.

Joyce also lost her spouse after more than fifty years of marriage. Her response to her loss was quite different than Joe's. A few months after his death, she was not sleeping well and food had no interest to her. She lost weight and was tired all the time. She often did not bother to get dressed all day. She chose to go to a psychiatrist and received a prescription for an antidepressant. When her symptoms of chronic depression did not abate, she agreed to be hospitalized until she was able to get on top of it. Once released, she joined our grief support group.

Two years later she was able to withdraw from all medication. She purchased a new town house and over the course of four months slowly moved her things into the new dwelling. Joyce said it gave her time to take leave of the home they had lived in for almost twenty years. She purchased new furniture for the bedroom that she said expressed her new life—lots of "flowers and frills," as she put it.

Joyce emerged as an upbeat person. Her new normal includes smiles and laughter as she talks about her travel plans. She became a volunteer at the hospital where her husband was treated and where he died.

The difference between Joe and Joyce is one of perception.

I have been leading grief support groups since 1978. In that time several hundred people have come to the groups and, eventually, moved on. Their losses were everything from deaths of loved ones by disease or accident, to suicide, murdered children, divorces, loss of jobs, relocation, the death of pets, loss of body parts, catastrophic injuries, and many other major events. Those who recovered and successfully created a new normal for their lives were not the ones whose losses were "easiest." It was those whose perceptions of their losses permitted them to work through their grief and move on.

An Exercise in Perception

Here is an exercise to help you get in touch with perceptions that you can choose—and which will enable you to choose healing after any loss.

Using your imagination: Suppose you do not know the date of your birth and do not own a mirror. How old would you be?

> *Suppose you do not know the date of your birth and do not own a mirror. How old would you be?*

If you think of yourself as "old," whatever that means, you will be old. Being "old" has little to do with age. It has to do with perceptions.

If you have a spirit of adventure within you and have the desire to do things spontaneously now and then, you are anything but old, regardless of how long you have lived. A friend of mine made his first skydive on his seventy-eighth birthday. Now in his upper eighties, he has done multiple zip line tours and bicycled down Mount Haleakala in Maui, Hawaii. He works out four days a week, does extensive yard work, and is an avid golfer. He does not perceive himself to be old. The important thing to note is that your perceptions define your expectations of life and yourself.

A major loss has come to your life. A loved one has died, the marriage you thought was made in heaven has ended in the hell of divorce, you have lost your job and everything you worked for, or you have been injured in a catastrophic way. Whatever the experience, it has wiped out the substance of your life.

If you are like the vast majority of us, when a major loss happens, the first thing you want to know is "Why? Why me? Why my loved one?" It's a normal perception. We don't expect tragedies to come to us. We see stories in the news daily, but they are other people's stories, not ours.

When tragedy becomes our story we look for a reason for it.

One of the defining experiences of our lives happened two months after June and I were married as teenagers. Her six-year-old brother, Ronnie, ran into the street in front of his parents' home. He was struck

_____

*When a major loss
happens, the first thing
you want to know is
"Why?"*

_____

by a car and died on the way to the hospital. In the midst of our family's grief everyone wanted to know why such a terrible thing could happen. Well-meaning people told us that everything happens for a reason. Some suggested Ronnie might have had a terrible life. Others said it was God's will and we should not question such events. A neighbor said Ronnie was in a better place and we would all get over his death in time. I found myself filled with the desire to hit the next person who had some simple explanation for a tragedy that seemed at the time to destroy our lives and the lives of June's parents.

Decades later, June and I vividly remembered where we were when we heard the news. We could picture the faces of those who had to tell us and what the weather was like as we drove to her parents' home. We could also recall the pain we felt that day.

The list of platitudes and explanations goes on and on when major losses occur. Books have been written trying to bring meaning and understanding to events for which meaning has to be created and which no reasonable mind can ever fully understand.

In the ensuing years since Ronnie's death, there were more losses for our family. Our grandparents and parents all died, as did my younger sister, older brother, and some members of our extended family. Two of our three grown children have gone through divorces. One of our closest friends died from ovarian cancer after an eight-year battle. I have officiated at the funerals or memorial services for numerous people who have been important in our lives. Most recently, my beloved June died from Alzheimer's disease. In addition to our personal losses, I have been immersed in the major losses of other people on a regular basis since 1978.

Out of all these experiences I finally found a perception that works every time in the face of a major loss. It is the one effective answer to the question "Why?"

I suggest you write this down and read it as many times as necessary until you have it memorized:

**THIS IS A MORTAL, FRAIL, IMPERFECT WORLD
IN WHICH THE WORD *FAIR* DOESN'T ALWAYS APPLY.**

This is why terrible tragedies take place. It's why your loved one died. It's why children make a brief mistake and are killed. It's why all kinds of bad things happen to the most wonderful people. It tells you why natural and human-caused disasters take place.

To anyone who asks the question "What did I do wrong to deserve this?" is the answer, "You were born. That is the only thing you did wrong."

It is a very uncomfortable perception to people who think bad things must be deserved or those who want to see divine, demonic, or karmic causes to human suffering. It's not yet a popular perception. It is reality.

Sometimes, the only meaning there is to a major loss must be created by you.

There was nothing fair about June's long struggle with dementia that only ended with her death, or her brother's death as a child, my sister in the prime of her life, or your loved one. There is nothing fair about those who suffer catastrophic injury. There certainly is nothing fair about the immeasurable suffering of people in third-world countries and the 45 million people in the world who were held in some form of slavery at the time this book was published.

It is a fact of life that we are real, live, mortal human beings who live in a mortal, frail, imperfect world in which the word *fair* doesn't always apply. There is no other option.

Once you accept this perception, you will no longer think you have been singled out for suffering. Your attitude will not be "Why me?" but "Why *not* me?" You will know with absolute certainty that you are not the only one to feel as you do or hurt with the depth of pain that you do. If misery loves company, coping with major loss and grief loves it even more.

Perhaps the greatest benefit of this perception is the freedom from searching for some meaning or purpose for every major loss. The word *accident* means just that. Human beings are capable of being very cruel to one another—even to children. Sometimes, the only meaning there is to a major loss must be created by you as you respond to your loss.

The best-known example of this is John Walsh, who was host of the popular American television program *America's Most Wanted*. John and his wife lived in Florida, pursuing their dreams of a successful business and life. All that ended in 1981 when their six-year-old son, Adam, was kidnapped and murdered. The Walsh family had to wait over twenty-five years for the case to be closed; the police announced in December 2008 that they were satisfied that Ottis Toole was the killer. John's response to their tragedy was to take on the cause of abducted children and to seek ways to apprehend fugitives who have committed horrendous crimes. Under his leadership, *America's Most Wanted* became not only a popular television program, but contributed to the arrest of more than one thousand fugitives. In addition, a television movie about Adam's abduction and murder led to the recovery of sixty-five abducted children. He was successful in getting a law passed titled "The Adam Walsh Child Protection and Safety Act." He is the author of many books.

Little Adam Walsh lost his life because in this mortal, frail, imperfect world in which the word *fair* doesn't always apply, there are evil, sick people. John Walsh and his wife took every parent's worst nightmare and gave it meaning through their perception of the tragedy and their response to a crushing grief.

Wounded soldiers also face the challenge of creating meaning for the damage to their body. J. R. Martinez was nineteen years old when the vehicle he was driving hit a land mine in Iraq and caught on fire. He was trapped inside. By the time he was pulled to safety, he was burned over more than 30 percent of his body. When he finally saw his face in a mirror some months later, he was horrified. He says, "I constantly asked, 'Why me?'" Then, a new perception took over. J. R. remembers thinking about how he could use the experience to help others. "Eventually, I became happy this happened to me," he said. He began visiting other burn survivors in the hospital. Less than five years after his injury, he began traveling across the United States, speaking to injured soldiers.[1]

I met J. R. at the World Burn Congress in 2008. He is one whose physical healing is due to skilled doctors, but whose emotional healing is the result of his own perception of his experience. You may remember him as the season 13 winner of *Dancing with the Stars* and as an actor in a daytime television program.

Control What You Can

Here's another important perception: We can't always control the events of our life, but we can always control our attitudes toward those events.

When my wife was dealing with breast cancer, she coined a phrase that speaks clearly to the issue of perception. She said, "I realize that I don't have a choice about whether or not I have cancer. But I can choose whether I will be a victim or a survivor. I choose to be a survivor." She didn't mean that cancer wasn't a problem or that it didn't have the possibility of taking her life. Her perception was not a denial of reality. It meant that she would not be passive in dealing with cancer. She took an active role in her treatment. Doctors had to explain the reasons for everything they planned to do or not do. She wanted to know what her odds of survival were with or without each treatment and what side effects were likely. One surgeon called her a walking question box. He said her kind of patients made his job more difficult compared to those who just went along with his decisions. She asked him which kind of patient had the best rate of survival. He responded, without hesitation, "Your kind."

We can't always control the events of our life, but we can always control our attitudes toward those events.

Grief recovery is like that. We can't choose not to have major losses. Remember, that choice gets taken away with birth. We can, however, always choose how we will respond to any major loss. Exercising those choices keeps us from feeling helpless as we try to cope with whatever has happened. It also is another way to avoid making a terrible experience even worse.

Time Out for Laughter

One of my favorite comic strips comes from *Calvin & Hobbes*. Calvin is sitting in a wagon, racing down a hill. He is saying, "We're so busy watching out for what's ahead of us that we don't take time to enjoy where we are."

That's a valuable insight about life and its inevitable losses. We will experience major losses in our lifetime, but that doesn't mean that life is not good. There is still ample reason for laughter.

If you were to walk by the meeting place of our grief support group, you would be as likely to hear the sounds of laughter as the sounds of crying. A single meeting frequently has plenty of both. It's a good reminder that even with the worst of losses, not all life is bad or destroyed.

One of the funniest people I have known was a ninety-three-year-old woman named Dorothy. She came to the grief support group because her husband was dying from Alzheimer's disease. She went to the nursing home every day, even though he no longer recognized her. He had been there for almost seven years when she joined the group. A few days after his death, her sister moved in with her because she was dying from cancer. Dorothy took care of her with help from hospice until the end. Dorothy's tears flowed freely as she expressed her sadness, but she also had a great sense of humor. She was a retired teacher. I arrived late for the group one day. Dorothy didn't say anything, but the following week she brought a tall stool and a dunce hat for me to wear in penitence.

Dorothy's best contribution to laughter was the "Dammit Doll." I still have the original one she made for me. As long as she was able, Dorothy made them for every new person who came to the grief support group. It became the symbol of what it means to be a survivor instead of a victim.

It's a funny-looking cloth doll with orange flowers printed on the cloth. It has button eyes, a painted frown, and ribbon around what passes for a neck. On top of its 14-inch-length is orange hair made of yarn.

A paper tag pinned to the middle has this verse:

> *When you think you want to climb the walls*
> *or stand right up and shout,*
> *Here's a little Dammit Doll you cannot do without.*
> *Just grab it firmly by the legs and find a place to slam it;*
> *Then as you whack the stuffing out,*
> *say DAMMIT! DAMMIT! DAMMIT!*

With the doll and her perception of her own losses, Dorothy enabled other bereaved people to enjoy a lighthearted moment in the midst of heavy-duty grief.

She also demonstrated that the people who heal the most effectively and completely are not those who try to get through it the quickest, or keep the busiest. It is those who choose to not only cope with major loss, but to conquer it.

Since grief is personal and is something that you do, the one who is finally in charge of it is you.

Take Charge of Your Own Grief

There is another perception that is crucial to healing. Almost everyone discovers it along the way to grief recovery. It is also a hard sell to anyone who has recently experienced a major loss.

It goes like this: Since grief is very personal and is something that you do (not something that happens to you), the one who is finally in charge of it is you.

Having the mind-set that says "I am in charge of my own grief" is almost shocking at first. When our worlds are turned upside down by tragedy and sorrow, we feel helpless. Life seems totally out of control. In truth, it is, until we decide that it's not the way it's going to be.

There is an insight from the motivation field that applies here:

IF IT IS TO BE, IT IS UP TO ME

These have been called the ten most powerful two-letter words in the English language. They apply directly to taking charge of your own grief. Please note: I said nothing about its being easy. There is nothing easy about any part of recovering from the death of a loved one or any other major loss.

I tell this fictional story in every lecture I give on loss and grief:

> A man was shopping in an exclusive men's store. He selected a pair of pajamas that cost $500 and took them to the clerk. "Look," he said, "before I pay $500 for pajamas, I have a question. The label says they are shrink resistant. What does that mean? Will they shrink or not?"
>
> The clerk, in a tone of voice heard only in exclusive men's stores, said, "Sir, it means they will shrink, but they really don't want to."

Taking charge of your own grief is something you can do—but there will be many times when you really don't want to.

Taking charge of your grief means doing some specific things, including:

- Making the conscious choice that you will live
- Giving yourself permission to have a life that does not include the one who has died, except in memory. If you are coping with divorce, it means letting go of your emotional ties to your ex-spouse. In other circumstances it could mean letting go of the body you used to have or the familiar surroundings of a former place you lived.
- Putting yourself in a grief support group
- Facing and accepting the myriad of feelings that flood over you
- Taking care of your physical needs
- Allowing others into your personal life

- Over the course of time becoming willing to invest your love and emotions in other people, while recognizing they, too, could be taken from you
- Finding simple ways to take time out from grieving. You will find some examples on page 241.

I am never sure which is the more amazing, the fact that doing these things works 100 percent of the time, or that 100 percent of people like you are capable of doing them.

Loss and Grief Are Not Our Enemies

Since experiencing loss is a fact of life and grief is the appropriate response to it, neither of them is our enemy. However, living in constant fear of them is.

Nobody wants to be brokenhearted. Nobody wants to mourn the death of a loved one, go through divorce, be catastrophically injured, or face the cold truths of aging. You know what? That's too bad! It's part of being alive.

It's easy to get philosophical about these things when life is going smoothly. I've heard it said that our losses give depth to life and make our joys all the more precious. That's a fine thought—until our first major loss comes along. Then, it is not so easy. When talking about multiple losses, my wife liked to say, "They told me to cheer up, things could get worse. So, I cheered up and, sure enough, they got worse." June had many "cheer up" years in her lifetime.

In addition to the experiences described in Chapter 13, June lost two of her closest women friends one month apart. Both died of cancer. She was there to support grieving spouses and other family members. Some months later, she began to have increasing back pain. In time, an MRI revealed degenerative disease in her spine. Disks were deteriorating, arthritic spurs appeared on her vertebrae, and her spine twisted with scoliosis.

When various therapies did not help, she underwent back fusion surgery. Two titanium rods, eight screws, and a cage were placed in her lower back. All went well and she cheerfully anticipated getting back to her normal, energetic life. However, the stress placed on her spine above the newly fused area was too much and it gave way. One vertebra twisted and slipped to the side, endangering her spinal cord and crushing a nerve. The result was extreme pain in her back, hip, and leg. Months of extensive physical therapy and steroid injections did not help. The only alternative was another fusion surgery. When it was completed, she had a total of seven layers of vertebrae held in place with two rods, twelve screws, and another cage. Her spine was straightened and anchored in place.

We both hoped she was finished with "cheer up" experiences, but we were not so fortunate. It turned out that Alzheimer's would have the last word and there would be no further life to cheer up.

Ray's experience was different, but the role of his perceptions was equally important. He was married to his high school girlfriend shortly after they graduated. Ten stormy years and a child later, they were divorced. Ray had a difficult time letting go of his marriage dreams. He berated himself for failing to hold his family together. It was some time before he could again perceive himself as worthy of another person's love and trust. He married again and fathered two more children. After seventeen years, this marriage, too, was ended. During the most troubled times, he experienced a business failure that put him on the brink of bankruptcy. Ray turned to his spiritual roots and found a renewed perception of himself and his purpose in life. He recovered financial stability, allowed his job to take him to another part of the state, and in time married again. He would tell you that he learned much from the challenges in his life.

It is never a question of whether or not we will face multiple losses in our lifetime—we will. Some we can anticipate, some we can't. The important thing is we can always find healing for any and all of our losses if we make the choice to do so.

They told me to cheer up, things could be worse. So, I cheered up and, sure enough, they got worse.

The story of David and Goliath is more than a biblical narrative. Songs have been written and movies made about this story of perception. It is a story of two armies facing each other in a turf battle. One of the armies said to the other, "Why should all of us get killed in a battle for this ground? Let's each of us pick one soldier to fight for our side. We will let them settle it for us." The other army was not as excited about this plan since the one proposing it had a giant warrior who towered over everyone else. One by one, their soldiers took a look at Goliath and said, "He's so big. He's so gigantic. There's no way I can kill him." David, who was actually smaller than others in his army, looked at the same Goliath. He picked up a couple of stones and his sling, and then said, "He's so big. He's so gigantic. There's no way I can miss!"

We can always find healing for any and all of our losses if we make the choice to do so.

Some of our losses are big. Others are gigantic. The pain these losses cause is huge. The question is, do you feel helpless? Or do you contemplate recovery and say, "I can't miss?" How you answer will depend upon your perceptions as you face the challenges before you just because you were born into this mortal, frail, imperfect world in which the word *fair* doesn't always apply.

6

Steps to Recovery
A Common Path to Wholeness

Recovering from a major loss is like being forced through a twisting maze that presents you with one dead end after another. To complete the journey successfully requires perseverance more than anything else. Put another way, life seems shattered in a million pieces, and your challenge is to make it whole again.

How any of us experiences grief varies as widely as our personality and life history. Picture yourself as one of twenty people in a grief support group. Each person is asked to place his or her thumb on an ink pad and then make a thumbprint on a piece of white newsprint fastened to the wall. When everyone has completed the task and sat down, all would agree that they are looking at twenty thumbprints. Nevertheless, no two thumbprints would be exactly the same. The same is true for grief: No two people experience it exactly the same way, but there is enough in common that we can help one another.

You can expect to take certain steps along the path to recovered wholeness that are similar to those of everyone else who is recovering from a major loss. Some of these steps will seem out of your control. Others will require enormous willpower. Some steps may take a few weeks to accomplish; others could take three years or more.

Understanding these steps will help you deal more effectively with grief. You will know you are making progress, even when it feels as if you are slipping backward. You will not have the added burden of thinking something is wrong with you when actually you are reacting in a perfectly normal way. You will be able to describe your experiences to family and friends and tell them how they can support you most helpfully.

The steps everyone has in common are:

1. Shock and numbness
2. Denial and withdrawal
3. Acknowledgment and pain
4. Adaptation and renewal

1. Shock and Numbness

In the first seven to ten days after a major loss you will probably feel stunned, shocked, and overwhelmed. You may feel emotionally "frozen"—or hysterical. Either way, you will have a difficult time later remembering much of what took place. A frequent comment is "It seems surreal."

Whatever your initial outward reaction, you will have a certain numbness inside. Your emotional system has shut down for the time being. I like to think of it as God or nature supplying us with temporary protection against the full impact of our losses. The experience of shock provides us with a brief, sheltered rest before we begin the long journey through the agony of grief as we move toward a renewed sense of joy.

This is a poor time to make decisions that will have a lasting impact on your life.

A few days after the death of a loved one, when the funeral is over and relatives have gone home, the shock begins to wear off. This is a good time to have someone with you. It is a poor time to make decisions that will have a lasting impact on your life. People who give away clothing and possessions, decide to move from their home, or quit a job within a few weeks of a loved one's death often regret those decisions.

In the case of divorce, the shock comes either with the announcement by one spouse to the other of the desire for a divorce, or the actual filing.

I answered the phone one day to hear the familiar voice of my dear friend Jim. He was calling from another state. His voice was hushed as he said, "Bob, Marge wants a divorce. She doesn't want to be married to me anymore. I keep saying this can't be happening to us, that I'll wake up any minute—I can't believe it!"

Now it was my turn to be shocked. June and I had known Jim and Marge for more than twelve years. We had shared many family experiences together. I thought I knew them as well as anyone in my own family. They were the last couple I would have expected to divorce.

I mumbled something to Jim about telling me what happened, but I don't remember what he said after that. My mind was racing back over the long hours June and I had spent with Jim and Marge over the years, talking about future plans— the mythical restaurant we had planned in the greatest detail, the trips we would take, and sharing our children's weddings. None of this would happen now. For June and me, the shock of losing our friends as a married couple was magnified by the loss of the dream we had for the future. I found I could not approach this divorce with any sense of professional detachment.

The shock attached to relocating comes when we first confront the strangeness of our new environment.

For Jim and Marge, the shock came in facing the reality of their lost dreams. Children loved by both had to live in separate homes. There was property to divide. Friends and family had to be told. It wasn't the way they had planned their lives.

Jim and Marge taught me that the shock and grief that comes with divorce is not less than that which comes with death. It takes the same week or so for the shock to wear off. And it takes much longer than that to complete the recovery.

The shock attached to relocating comes when we first confront the strangeness of our new environment. A young couple came to my office one day in tears. They had arrived in town a few days earlier with their baby. Everything had seemed okay. They had a place to live. Their belongings had arrived undamaged. His new job would start on Monday.

But on that particular morning the baby awakened with a fever. All of a sudden the shock hit: They didn't know where to begin looking for a doctor in this large city. They had come from a town with 1 percent of our population. Back home they knew the doctor, the druggist, and even the mayor on a first-name basis. This wasn't home, and they felt lost.

Other loss experiences have a similar effect. You may have been cool and collected as you prepared for surgery and then found yourself "coming unglued" as you were being prepared for the operating room. The realization that "it" is really going to happen can stun the strongest among us.

Shock follows every loss experience to some degree. The important things for you to know about shock are:

- It is a necessary first step to recovery.
- It doesn't last long.
- It is not a time for long-term decision making.
- It is good to have a trusted friend with you.
- When shock goes away, pain arrives.

2. Denial and Withdrawal

When the shock of your loss wears off, you will want to deny what has happened with all your strength.

No one can begin to describe the incredible depth of pain we feel when a loved one dies. If you have already had that experience, you understand. If you haven't lost someone to death, think about another very painful personal loss you have had. A pet's death can be very painful. People grieve over lost friendships, mourn the move from familiar places, and agonize over bitter disappointments in their lives.

As unavoidable and natural as loss is, we are seldom ready to admit that loss is a normal part of our own life. No one plans on a divorce at the time of marriage. When we think about relocating, we are usually more aware of new places to be seen than old ones to be lost. We seldom stop to think that our parents, spouse, or children are going to die someday—and that the loss of these important people can be within our lifetime. No one anticipates an injury that causes permanent disability.

It's natural to deny a loss when to acknowledge it leads to so much pain. After an initial reaction of "Oh, no!" The most significant fact of this step is that it is often happening *without our being aware of it*. Behavior and attitudes may change for a while. Health can suffer, too.

Physical and emotional effects you may experience after the initial shock of the loss wears off include:

- Feeling weak and drained of energy
- Inability to perform routine tasks
- Lack of appetite
- Lack of sleep or oversleeping
- Forgetting names, phone numbers, and other significant data
- A persistent dry mouth
- Physical aches and pains
- Lack of concern with personal hygiene or grooming
- Fantasies of the deceased or divorced person
- Expecting a dead or divorced person to come back
- Disillusionment with your new city or home
- Anger

These are all normal reactions to loss. You may experience one or several at a time. It's possible you will think you are done with one reaction, and weeks or even months later it will return.

If you know to expect these signs of denial and withdrawal after a loss, you can comfort yourself by saying, "This reaction is normal. This is another step on the path through grief. It won't last forever. I will be okay again." In the weeks following June's death, I could not seem to stay focused on any one task that needed doing. I would start to carry it out, jump to something else, then leave that for yet something else. The result was I did not complete any of the tasks I needed to do. I repeated the words I have told others to say for many years: "This reaction is normal. It's another step on the path through grief. It won't last. I will be okay again."

During this step, disappointment with family and friends may surface. Your closest friends and members of your immediate family may not respond to your grief in ways that are helpful. Even those who know you best will not understand your grief any better than you do. Well-meaning people who really care about you will want you to "be okay" much more quickly than you can be. Most won't know what to say. Some people will avoid you. Reactions like these aren't unusual, and you aren't alone if you experience any of them from friends or family members.

At the same time, you may be too fatigued to ask for help. Even making a telephone call can seem like an insurmountable task. I once woke up in the night feeling nauseous. I went to the bathroom and the moment I threw up, I found myself on the floor, unable to get up and in excruciating pain. It turned out I had herniated a disk in my low back. I crawled back into bed but could not escape the terrible pain. June was sleeping next to me, but I could not make the words come out of my mouth to tell her I needed help. The initial pain of grief can be like that. You will want others to reach out to you, but you will not be able to tell them what to do or say to help.

You will want to tell the story of your loss again and again.

In time you will want to tell the story of your loss again and again. You may find that the world around you will be through listening long before you are through with the need to talk. Some will "reward" you with kind words and more frequent visits if you pretend to be on top of things. It won't seem to matter to them that you really feel as though you are dying inside.

If you understand that conflicts such as these are normal, you can be more patient with others—and with yourself. This is especially helpful when anger surges within you during this step, either because of such conflicts with others or because you want to blame *someone* for your loss.

Linda came into our grief support group two months after her husband's death. She was filled with a furious anger, blaming everyone for his death, including herself. As a part of a grief support group exercise, she wrote a letter to herself that appears below.

The anger and blame in Linda's letter may be unreasonable, but little is reasonable about grief at this point in the recovery journey. Read the letter again and picture some hurtful loss of your own as you do. Change the names and circumstances to fit your experience. See whether Linda didn't express feelings and anguish that you have also felt. These kinds of angry reactions are signs of your denial of the loss. They are a symbol of your mind's effort to withdraw from the pain. It isn't wrong to have these reactions. It may even be necessary for your survival in the early months after a major loss.

Dear Linda,

Did you do all you possibly could to help Earl? Do you believe everything a doctor says? Don't you know that most doctors are in it for the money and not to help people? They took the easy way out with Earl. All they wanted was their thirty pieces of silver!

Linda, don't you think you should have noticed Earl's health more? Instead of going for a walk with him, you could have taken him to a heart specialist. You say you didn't know anything was wrong. Why not? If you had been a little more observant, my partner Death and I would not have paid you a visit.

Sincerely,

Grief

Denial and withdrawal is a difficult step in grief recovery because you are least able to reach out when you most need to do so. Others are also least able to help at the time you most need it. The more you know about the step of denial and withdrawal, the less isolated and helpless you will feel. Be assured this phase will pass.

3. Acknowledgment and Pain

The classic term that psychologists use for this step is *acceptance and pain*. I do not refer to this step as *acceptance* because of Ann. She joined our grief support group after her husband choked to death in his sleep. I was talking about accepting our losses one day when Ann broke in to say, "Bob, the word *acceptance* carries with it some sense of approval and there is no way I will ever approve of my husband's death. I'm ready to acknowledge that he is dead and he isn't coming back, but I refuse to accept or approve it!" Every person in every group I have talked with since agrees with Ann.

> Acknowledging a loss is the most important step of your recovery.

Acknowledging a loss is the most important step of your recovery. It is at this point that you will again take full charge of your life and full responsibility for your feelings. A noticeable sense of balance is coming back into your life when you can acknowledge that your loss is real—and permanent. It represents a giant step toward full recovery.

If you have had a loss through death or divorce, you will probably be ready to acknowledge your loss fully in about three to six months. However, if it takes you a year or more to get to this point, you won't be the first. Nor will it mean you aren't doing as well as someone else. Everyone reaches this stage of grief at his or her own pace.

When Rae joined our grief support group, it had been eighteen months since her husband's death. When asked why she had decided to join at this particular time, she replied, "I thought I was doing fine. I handled the funeral okay and went to work shortly afterward. I was lonely at times, especially in the evenings. But all in all I thought I was

doing pretty well. In the last month, it's as if I'm right back at the beginning. I didn't cry the first time around, but now I cry all the time."
Rae had not been ready to acknowledge her husband's death "the first
time around." Now she was. It was important for Rae to see that crying
now meant she was going forward, not backward. She wasn't "worse"
than she had been for eighteen months, she was *better*. She was ready
to move on. In the months that followed, she did just that.

If you have never endured a major loss in your life, you will not be
able to understand the depth of pain that acknowledging such a loss
can bring. It's another of those times when you can only understand
after walking the walk.

Grief is like that. It takes you into new territory. When I first
started meeting with a group of widowed persons, I had to say to
them, "You are the experts here. I am an amateur. My parents have
died, my brother-in-law died at age six, I have moved to a strange city,
and all my children have left home. These losses I can understand. But
I don't know what it feels like to have my spouse
die, and furthermore, I don't want to know! You
will have to tell me about that experience, and I
will try to understand." Thirty-eight years later
I became an expert too when June died. I
learned more in the weeks and months after her
death than in all the years of careful listening to
the grief experiences of others. The first time I sat down with a grief
group after June died, one of the men greeted me with "Now you are
one of us."

*You will not always
feel as you do at
this moment.*

There is nothing easy about saying "I am divorced" or "My child is
dead" or "This part of my life is over." It hurts! But it won't hurt forever.
Emotional pain is another sign of your progress toward a full life. It is
important at this point of your recovery to remind yourself—often—
that you will not always feel as you do at this moment.

You will be tempted to slip back into denial of what has happened.
You can do that periodically and you will feel better—for a little while.
But the only pathway to balance and a new normal for your life lies
through the pain of acknowledging your loss.

A support group or professional counseling can be invaluable in this step of your recovery. People around you will ask, "How are you?" They expect to hear that you are "fine," regardless of how you actually feel. If you *aren't* fine and you tell the truth, many people will ignore your words and behave as though you hadn't said a thing. Then you may feel worse than you did before trying to say how you are really feeling.

A counselor or a support group can give you the opportunity to talk freely, express your feelings, and gain much-needed insight. You can be sure that your counselor or others in the group will hear you and understand you. You need little else right now as much as that understanding! This acknowledgment step takes time. It is extremely important that you have a strong support system in place as you make your way through it.

Slowly but surely, the good days begin to outnumber the bad ones.

This is an up-and-down part of the journey through grief. You will not stay immersed in agony for a year and then suddenly wake up one morning to find yourself finished with it. You will make progress one day and encounter difficulties the next. You may have a few good minutes or hours, followed by all-night restlessness as you relive the details of your loss. An entire day or week can be going fine when, all of a sudden, sadness comes off the wall and bites you. Overall you will be heading in the right direction. As one of those who have been there I assure you that slowly but surely, the good days will begin to outnumber the bad ones.

4. Adaptation and Renewal

The first sign that the roughest part of your grief is over is when you notice a change in the questions you ask yourself. From the time of your loss, the most haunting and persistent question is "Why did this happen to me?" The day will come, often a year or more after the loss, when a new question will emerge: "Now that this thing has happened, what do I do next?" That question is typically followed by: "How can I grow through this tragic event to become a better person?"

When you stop asking "why?" and begin asking "how?" you are beginning to adapt to your new life without the person, place, or condition that has been lost. You will have begun creating the new normal for your life that you never thought was possible.

Elizabeth came to our grief support group at the urging of a friend. She was as angry about her husband's death as anyone I have ever met. For several months, she had nothing positive to say. She was angry at the doctors, the insurance company, family, and anybody else she could think of, including God. I'm sure it seemed to Elizabeth as if no one had ever grieved as deeply as she.

Slowly, however, her outlook became more positive. She became the source for some of the best laughter experienced in the group. She brought in clippings and quotes that were meaningful to everyone. On some occasions, she filled in as group leader in my absence. She became the person that newcomers in the group turned to most often.

Six years after she lost her husband, Elizabeth found a new love in her life in Larry. They were exploring and developing their loving relationship when he died in a tragic accident. Elizabeth was again plunged into grief. Once more, she went through all the steps of grief recovery.

Elizabeth worked at ways to make her life as enjoyable as possible. In time, she adapted to her second loss and emerged as a new, even more compassionate person than before.

"Why?" Questions

The worst thing about "why?" questions is that the person asking really doesn't want to know the only answer that makes sense. Questions that begin with "why" reflect a desperate yearning for meaning and purpose. People look for someone or something to blame for the loss. They are sure there is some reason for what happened. They think they might feel better and hurt less if only they could discover that reason.

Lois's son was playing golf when he was struck by lightning and killed instantly. Four young men were standing together when the fatal bolt struck. Her son just happened to be the tallest of the group. For months the one question that dominated Lois's mind was: "Why

Derek? He was happily married, had a great job with a great future. Why him?"

You may be asking:

- Why did I get this cancer?
- Why did my husband die when he was such a good man and others who don't care about their families live?
- Why did this catastrophic injury have to happen to me?
- Why did my loved one not survive when other military personnel did?
- Why did my wife want someone else when I've provided so well for her?
- Why did we have to move to this godforsaken place?

The answer to "why?" is, of course: *This is a mortal, frail, imperfect world in which the word* fair *doesn't always apply*. This is the only answer that matters, but is not one that brings much comfort in the immediate aftermath of a major loss.

"How?" Questions

Questions that begin with *how* indicate we are ready to face the reality of our losses. They also express our searching for ways to put life together again after the loss.

Pauline's mother died in May. A year later her son died in the same month. Two years later her husband also died in May. When she came to the grief support group more than a year after his death, she said, "I had to wait until I was finished asking 'why?' before I could come. I reached a point where I had to move on with my life or die. I have come here to find out how I can keep going."

These questions touch on issues such as:

- How can I fill the void in my life that my wife's death has left?
- How can I learn to cope with the injury that has changed my life completely?

- How do I learn from my divorce so I won't make the same mistakes again?
- How can we make friends in our new city so we will feel more at home?

It is certainly difficult for us to accept that some things, even deaths, happen for no purpose. It's easy to forget the word *accident* means just that—something that happens because this is not a perfect world with a perfect script written for life.

When your questions begin to change from "why?" to "how?" you are beginning to accept that accidents include your own tragic loss.

I want you to be able to say this with confidence:

The loss I experienced is a major event in my life. Perhaps it is the worst thing that will ever happen to me. But it is not the end of my life. I can still have a full and rewarding life. Grief has taught me much, and I will use it to be a better person than I was before my loss.

These words are not easy to say. It isn't easy to think these thoughts after a major loss. It is even more difficult to say the words aloud. You can't rush them. But working toward saying them with conviction is a reasonable goal.

When you can acknowledge these truths about your loss, you will find a renewed energy and enthusiasm for life. You will begin to adapt to a new life that does not revolve around your loss experience and grief. You will have a new sense of self-worth. If you are like most people, you will find a new calmness within yourself. Little things won't irritate you as much. You will take yourself less seriously, and you will laugh more. This is a good time to obey an urge to try a new hairstyle or wardrobe—or both! It may be a good time to redecorate a room or take a trip. It's time to establish new goals for yourself over the next two to five years. As time goes on you will realize that recovery is a lifelong process of adapting to all kinds of changes and losses. As with any ability, you will get better at this as you continue to use the skills you have learned from this loss. You won't forget your loss. It will always be a part of your life history. But in time you will be able to think about the person, the place, or the condition that was lost to you without pain.

The day will come when you will know deep inside that you have recovered your balance, completed your journey through grief, and are ready to get on with a good and full life. You will have created a new normal. On that day, you will be a stronger person than you have ever been before.

Healthy versus Distorted Grief

Grief is the nuclear energy of our emotions. Understood, respected, harnessed, and directed, it can be a creative force. However, when grief is out of control, distorted, and misunderstood, it can become a destructive force.

It is important, therefore, to recognize when your grief is healthy and when it is distorted. If you have a common cold, you know how to care for it. You don't need a doctor or a hospital. But if your cold becomes pneumonia, it would be foolish not to seek professional help. So it is with grief.

As you have read through the steps to recovery, I hope you found your fears diminishing. I hope you learned more about what to expect from yourself as you experience healthy grief. Reactions and feelings that may have frightened you are in most cases normal under these extreme circumstances, and they will pass. However, I also want you to know some signs of distorted grief.

Five Symptoms of Stress Overload

Here is a list of five symptoms that indicate you have had all the stress you can handle alone. The presence of any of these symptoms says it is time to call in professional help. Remember: There is no shame in seeking help. The only shame would be to need help and not get it.

1. Persistent thoughts of self-destruction. The key word is *persistent*. It is not unusual to have suicidal thoughts while experiencing grief, but they should pass quickly. They typically come out as a desire to be re-united with the one who has died. If you begin thinking of a specific method and occasion for taking your life, seek help. "I will live" is a necessary decision for healthy grief.

2. Failure to provide for basic needs. If you find yourself changing your patterns of activity and avoiding friends and family, it is time to seek help. Interaction with other people is essential to healthy grief.

Equally important is paying attention to your physical needs, including nutrition, fluids, exercise, rest, and personal hygiene. If you are failing to take care of these fundamental needs, it is time to seek help.

3. Persistence of one particular reaction to grief. Depression that immobilizes you for weeks is a sign professional help is needed; so is continued denial of the reality of your loss, or finding yourself still without feelings months later. Help is needed when any normal grief reactions persist too long.

4. Substance abuse. This means everything from using tranquilizers or sleeping pills for too long, to engaging in alcohol or drug abuse. It also includes eating too much, too little, or surviving on junk food.

There is no shame in seeking help. The only shame would be to need help and not get it.

5. Complicated grief may include feelings of anxiety, yearning for the one who died, and feeling that life has lost its meaning. Other relationships may suffer for months at a time and the ability to perform at work can create additional problems. The emergence of these signs indicate what has come to be called complicated grief. It does not respond well to antidepressants or the usual kinds of therapy that help with normal grief. A good rule of thumb: If you see the signs of complicated grief in yourself, seek the help of a professional counselor who is familiar with complicated grief.

If you are on the fence about seeking psychological help—get it! Your minister, priest, rabbi, or imam can refer you to someone who specializes in grief counseling. When you first contact a counselor, don't hesitate to ask if he or she has experience working with grief. You will know within one or two sessions whether the person will be helpful. If you sense that person does not have a good understanding of your grief process, try another counselor.

7

The Inward Search
Grief Is a Personal Experience

Any major loss is first and foremost a personal experience. Your loss is yours, regardless of how many other people are affected by it. Because of this, it will be difficult (it may seem impossible) to share your feelings with others. It will be equally difficult for anyone who has not experienced a similar loss to understand what's going on inside you.

To recover your balance and to get back on your feet will require you to search within yourself for strength and hope. No one else will be able to give you satisfactory answers to the questions that dominate your thoughts. Your journey through grief will have many aspects in common with others who have also had terrible losses. But you will not respond exactly like any other person. You are a unique person, and your grieving will reflect your uniqueness.

A perfectly normal reaction to a major loss is the conviction that "no one else has ever felt as I do." There is a sense in which that is true. Bereaved people tell me that having another person say, "I know how you feel," is much worse than the sound of fingernails across a chalkboard—especially if that person has not had a similar loss. Nobody knows exactly how you are feeling, including your family and closest friends. Those who offer you pat answers and simple formulas for "getting over it" need to be politely ignored.

If your spouse has died, you are concerned about other family members. If you have divorced, you may worry about the welfare of your children. After a business failure, you may care about other investors or employees. But your first concern is the sense of *personal loss*.

You will not ask, "Why has this happened to us?" You will ask, "Why has this happened to *me*?" Others can offer help and encouragement, but only you can take charge of your grief and your recovery. Only you can decide if making your way through grief will be an occasion for growth. You can't escape the sorrow, but you can choose to make it be a positive force in your life.

Think of a loss you experienced in the past. If that loss was severe enough, it was all you thought about from morning to night. As far as you were concerned, it didn't matter whether the sun was shining brightly. To you the days were dark and gloomy. It did no good for some well-meaning person to try to cheer you up with reminders of all the reasons you had to be thankful. Your loved one was gone, that place

> You can take charge of your grief and your recovery.

called *home* was far away, or your dream was shattered. You were in no mood for platitudes. In your heart it was pouring rain—and the sadness was about to leak out of your eyes. The orders you gave yourself to calm down were futile.

You had lost something or someone very important to you. That loss hurt beyond words.

The thing you wanted more than anything else was a glimmer of hope. You wanted to know whether there was a light at the end of the tunnel of misery. If there was such a light, you wanted to know it was not an oncoming freight train loaded with more heartache.

You did not look around you for answers because you were sure nobody else understood exactly what you were feeling. No one else could take away your pain. As much as you wanted someone else to come to your rescue, you knew that, ultimately, you had to work it out for yourself.

If you have experienced the things I've just described, you understand the true meaning of *personal grief*.

Once you understand it, you have to decide what you are going to do about it. Will you be a victim or a survivor? Victims are passive, feel helpless, and let circumstances dictate their feelings. Survivors are assertive, take charge, and understand that whereas they may not be able to control their circumstances, they can always control their attitudes toward those circumstances.

Betty's husband died after a lingering battle with cancer. His death hit her hard. They had worked together in their business, sang together in church choirs, and just enjoyed each other's company. When her husband died, Betty joined a grief support group where she talked openly about the anguish of watching her husband die slowly and how empty she felt with him gone. Her tears flowed freely at times, but there was always a glint in her eyes that said, "I am going to overcome this." She divided time between our community in Arizona and the midwestern city where she and her husband had lived for several years. My wife and I visited her in that place about two years later. She was active in her church and community. She had again become "life-oriented." During another winter in Arizona, Betty met a man who had lost his wife at about the same time she had lost her husband. They found they had common interests in music and many other things. Eventually, I had the privilege of officiating at their wedding. They lived in a retirement community and had a wonderful life together until his death some years later.

To successfully cope with your personal grief requires that you decide:

- You will live.
- It's okay and quite possible for you to have a full life after your loss or losses.
- You can take charge of your own grief.

- Although you can learn from the experience of others, strength and hope will come from within.
- You will reach the place where there are less tears and more laughter.
- Making decisions like these will help you get back on top of life again!

Reflecting on Personal Losses

Put the following questions on separate pieces of paper. Write your answers to them using as many pages as necessary to express your feelings. I suggest answering one question each day so you have time to think about it and consider more than your initial response. This is another place where you may want to utilize your computer, tablet, or smartphone.

- What do I need to do to survive the loss I have experienced?
- Can I be happy again knowing that my life will be different because of my losses?
- What can I do to begin creating a new normal for my life?

Read your responses aloud to yourself. See what they say about your inner thoughts and feelings. If you recorded your responses into your smartphone, play it back and listen.

The more resources you have, including healthy religious beliefs, family traditions, and supportive groups, the more fruitful your inward searching will be. The more you understand about what to expect of yourself, the better you will be able to recognize the signs of grief recovery and growth.

On another piece of paper, write the name of your most recent loss—a person's name or "my marriage," "my home," or whatever best describes the loss. Under the heading of your major loss, list the additional things you've lost as a result of it. For instance, if your spouse died, your list might look like this:

Major loss: My husband, Joe, died.
*Resulting losses: financial security; companionship; may lose
home; retirement dreams; close ties with Joe's family;
independence; sense of personal value*

My wife referred to these other losses as "the stacking nature of loss."
It's a good and useful way to view them; other losses stack up under the
original loss.

The same kinds of things are often lost if you are dealing with divorce instead of death.

Make your list as complete as possible. Take a look at your resulting
losses. Do any of them suggest even *more* disappointments? If so, add
these to your list.

Notice that whatever loss you experienced caused you to have a *series* of "stacked-up" losses. *Each one hurts.*
Each one hits at the core of how you measure
your happiness and the value of your life.

Bill was thirty-two when his wife committed suicide. He said to me, "I didn't just lose a
wife. My sense of self-worth and all my plans
for the future for our children and me went
into the ground with her! What do I do now?"

> Notice that whatever
> loss you experienced
> caused you to have a
> **series** of "stacked-up"
> losses.

Nancy, whose husband divorced her after
twenty-eight years of marriage, said, "When he walked out the door, my
security went with him. I've got to find some way to earn a living."

Jack lost everything in a business venture. He said, "I had to learn to
see my personal value as separate from my dreams of success before I
could give up the idea of killing myself."

Minor Losses

Not all of your losses will be as serious as the death of a loved one, a
divorce, or other major loss. Nevertheless, even so-called minor losses
can have a far-reaching impact on your life.

After driving safely for thousands of miles and many years, June and I had two automobile accidents in less than forty-eight hours. There was no way to avoid either of them. The first was a drunk driver who lost control, jumped a curb, and hit us as we were pulling into a parking lot. The second was a head-on collision with a truck that crossed the center of a forest road on a blind curve. June's head hit the windshield. After the impact, I looked at her and saw blood streaming from her face and coloring her white pants a bright red.

Within minutes, people who were total strangers had put her in their car to travel to the nearest hospital several miles away. I remained with our car, waiting for the sheriff to arrive. I had no idea how seriously June was injured or how long it would be before we were together again. By the time I realized I didn't even know the names of the men who had taken her away, June was gone from the scene of the accident.

Over the course of our married life, one of June's pet sayings to me was, "You take good care of me." I always enjoyed that vote of confidence. As I stood by our wrecked car and sobbed tears of shock and remorse, I kept muttering, "I didn't take care of her. I didn't take care of her. I failed." When the day came I realized she was dying from Alzheimer's, I relived those words again. It had been only two months since a nurse had asked me why I was going to so much effort to keep her going since she was dying anyway. My angry response was, "Not on my watch she isn't!" But, she indeed "died on my watch."

As I think back to those experiences, I can identify several losses:

- My belief that I could always protect June from harm.
- At the time of the accident, my sense of pride as a skilled driver was gone.
- My sense of security about our lives.
- My fantasy that I could always be in control of our lives.

I felt intense grief simply at having to admit that our life circumstances were not always in my control.

The car accident was not a major loss. No one died. June was not permanently injured. The other drivers' insurance paid for car repairs and medical expenses in both instances. We continued to travel by car as much as ever. Nevertheless, it was important for us to pay attention to the effect this experience had on our lives. Working through the minor losses we experienced gave both of us some measure of preparing for the worst loss we would ever face—the day that one of us died and our idyllic life together would come to an end. I did not have to deal with "why?" questions. I already knew the real question is "Why not us?" "Why not me?"

The failure to recognize the impact of minor losses is one reason people are often so poorly prepared when a major loss occurs. Reflecting on the way that smaller losses affect our lives can help us prepare for the inevitable major losses that everyone experiences.

If nothing else, paying attention to smaller losses helps us understand loss is a part of being alive. Look within yourself to reflect on your response to a smaller loss, and you will discover resources that will serve you well in times of major loss. Chapter 21 discusses more about preparing for loss.

8

Four Key Facts about Grief
Building a Foundation
for Recovery

Learning four key facts about grief will help you take control of it. Accepting these facts will help you develop the stamina and patience you need to endure the burden, stress, and duration of your grief. These are the four key facts about grief:

1. The way out of grief is through it.
2. The very worst kind of grief is yours.
3. Grief is hard work.
4. Effective grief work is not done alone.

These are the four axioms of grief recovery. They may not seem self-evident, but, like all axioms, they are true whether we like it or not. Learning to work with grief in these ways may feel strange and uncomfortable. These concepts may represent a whole new way for you to think about grief. But in time and with practice, you will find these concepts to be invaluable tools to recovering from your loss and moving on in your life.

1. The Way out of Grief
Is through It

This is the single most important fact for you to learn about grief. If you want to recover from your grief and grow through your loss, you must learn that there are no shortcuts to a good and full life after a major loss. The most useless bit of advice anyone receives when a loved one dies may well be "You will get over it." It is equally nonhelpful for the bereaved person to talk about "getting over it." There is no "over."

You have to live *through* grief to resolve it.

To talk about getting "over" any sad experience carries a sense of amnesia. June and I came to understand that we were "over" a quarrel not when we had kissed and made up, but when we forgot the quarrel ever happened. I have yet to meet the be-

> There are no shortcuts to a good and full life after a major loss.

reaved spouse or parent who wants to forget that a deceased loved one ever lived. Speaking personally, I found the exact opposite when June died. She had been sick for so long the images of her decimated body were all I could recall. I found boxes of photos June had stored in a closet. They were of happy, wonderful times. I put many of them up, posted others on Facebook, and put out things my artistic wife had made. All of these helped me to remember what she was like as a well person and all the things we did and places we went together. Those memories helped me get through the worst experience of my life.

Because grief work is so demanding, it's common to look for *any* way to get out of going through it. No one wants to face grief. No one wants to feel the loneliness and heartache that can persist for two to three years. The common tendencies we have when we experience grief are to

- Look for some way to avoid or lessen the pain.
- See how quickly we can get back to our normal life.

And, when neither of these work . . .
- Try to wait it out

How often have you heard it said that "Time heals"? It's one of the more popular myths that is simply not true. To say time by *itself* heals is like saying "Practice makes perfect." Practice does *not* make perfect. As competitive roller skate dancers, June and I learned that it is quite possible to practice a perfect mistake. Only perfect practice makes perfect. The truth is, only effectively working *through* grief heals the deep wounds and enables you to recover your balance in life. One woman showed up in a grief support group I was leading twelve years after her husband died. She had waited twelve years for time to heal her sorrow. It didn't work. When she came to the group she had the same two to three years of grief work to do as if she had started right after her husband's death. Time alone can put scabs on wounds and ferment wine, but it does not heal grief.

Time alone can put scabs on wounds and ferment wine, but it does not heal grief.

Two years after her husband's death, Maggie said to me, "I'll never get over it." We were in a grief-support-group meeting. As I turned to her, I said, "Maggie, you're absolutely right. You could work for the next fifty years and you would not get over Roy's death. Neither can you get under it or around it. But, Maggie, you can get *through* it!"

The only way to forget the pain of a loved one's loss is to forget the loved one. I have never yet met the bereaved person who was willing to give up the memories of a loved one to avoid the pain of that person's death. Now, I am one of those people.

When you lose a loved one, go through the pain of a divorce, or experience some other dramatic change in your life, you do not "get over" it. That person, place, or time of your life will always be a part of you and your personal history.

An old spiritual, although not written about grief specifically, certainly reflects this important truth. It says:

It's so high you can't get over it,
So low you can't get under it,
So wide you can't get around it,
You must go in through the door.

The more significant your loss is, the greater your sense of grief. You will not get over that loss, or under it—nor is there any way around it. You cannot wait it out. You have to go squarely through the middle of it. The good news is, you will come out on the other side with a life you can enjoy. Learning this truth is vital to your grief recovery.

If you have been through divorce, you know one of its great illusions is that divorce puts an end to problems between spouses. The fact is, all that often changes is that you no longer live in the same house.

If you and your ex-spouse fought and argued during your marriage, you are likely to fight and argue after your divorce. If you have children together, you will continue relating to each other for the rest of your lives. When your children are grown, there are their weddings to witness, grandchildren to love, and all the big events in their lives that they want both of you to attend.

Life is too short to spend those years continuing the battles that ended your marriage. The way to achieve peace is to go squarely into the grief that follows the end of a marriage. You can only do that by facing terribly difficult feelings. It has always seemed to me the first casualty in any divorce is the self-esteem of both spouses. This loss alone can knock you flat on your back emotionally. It isn't unusual to need a year or more to *begin* recovering a healthy self-image.

When one couple divorced after sixteen years, the husband was willing to go to a counselor. He worked his way through some very painful discoveries about himself. He learned that he had related to his wife and family in ways that contributed to the breakup of their marriage. He came out of the experience changed for the better. He is more patient and understanding. He does not take himself so seriously. He walks through life with a lighter step than before. He is married again and very happy. For all the sadness it caused at the time, he is able to look back and say that working through his divorce was a good thing. He is grateful it motivated him to grow and change.

His wife, who initiated the divorce, never seemed to face her feelings. She seemed to be trying to wait out her sadness. It didn't work. For three years after their divorce she continued to call on her ex-husband for money, household repairs, and emotional support. After he remarried, she moved back into the house they had shared for several years.

To "go through" grief requires stamina and incredible reserves of patience. At some point along the way, you will feel terribly sad, lonely, lost, angry—or all of these. To get in touch with such unpleasant feelings, you have to be convinced there is absolutely no other way out of your grief than straight through the middle of it. You must have a strong sense of purpose and direction.

It isn't unusual or abnormal to feel more uncomfortable after confronting your grief. It should be expected. To "go through" grief also is to "grow through" grief. And that is a positive experience.

> To "go through" grief also is to "grow through" grief.

Many times after one of our grief-support-group meetings one of the participants will call me to say, "I felt worse when I left than when I came in." The caller is often surprised when I respond, "Good for you! It means you're growing."

Feeling better comes a day, a week, or even a few months later. If you are working through a major loss and feel comfortable, it's a danger signal. It's time to check to see whether you are trying to skirt the flank, dig under, or get over your grief. It's a fact: You can't!

One more time: Going *through* the experience is the only lasting and healthy way *out* of grief.

Throughout this book you will find exercises that provide effective ways to handle the feelings that emerge as you move through your grief and establish a new life after your loss.

2. The Very Worst Kind of Grief Is Yours

Which grief experience is the worst? Is it more difficult for the widow if her husband suddenly and unexpectedly drops dead of a heart attack? Or is it worse if he dies a day at a time from cancer? Is it worse to lose a spouse to death or a marriage through divorce? Is the death of a child the worst of all losses? All of these are questions I've been asked many times. The truth is there is only one very worst kind of grief—and that is yours.

In one winter two disastrous events happened at the same time, each of which affected my life. First, a number of men were killed in a mining accident in another state. My sister called because she lived where it happened and knew some of the families. That tragedy made headline news everywhere. The other tragic event was having our fifteen-year-old cat put down.

Can you guess which of those events caused me to cry my eyes out? You guessed it—the cat!

There is scarcely any comparison to be made between the loss of human life and the end of a semicrippled old cat. But Samantha was my cat. I loved her. She was a permanent part of our history. Her loss was not an academic thing. I didn't look at television or newspaper accounts of her death and say, "That's too bad!" and go on to the sports page. She was mine. Her loss plunged me into grief.

I stood in the front room of our home as my wife drove off with the cat to the veterinarian's office to have her euthanized. I couldn't walk into that office and fall apart in tears. Everyone knows big boys, especially professional clergymen, don't do that sort of thing. So . . . I let my wife do it! I held Samantha briefly, tickling her under the chin in the way she liked so much, then carried her out to the car where June was waiting. As she drove off, I screamed and sobbed, crying out over and over, "I want my kitty. I don't want her to die!"

This was my loss and at that moment, as far as I was concerned, it was the worst thing to happen in the whole world. I didn't want anyone to tell me how great it was that she didn't suffer, or how far beyond a normal life expectancy she had lived.

I have known deeper times of grief—much deeper. My mother, father, sister, and brother have all died. The loss of June is in a category of sorrow all by itself.

However, at the moment my cat died, her loss was the very worst kind of grief for me in the whole world.

Think about your own experience. Perhaps you sold one home and bought a new one. You were excited as moving day approached, only to find yourself standing in the empty old house after the last box was gone, overwhelmed with a deep sense of loss and sadness. As one man said, "It is as if you have divorced your house."

> *The truth is there is only one very worst kind of grief—and that is yours.*

That feeling of sadness is grief. And at that moment, for you, it was the very worst kind of grief simply because it was *yours*.

The death of even the most aged family member hurts because the loss is yours. Rabbi Earl Grollman's father was past ninety. His health had been poor for years. He was an invalid confined to a rest home. When he died, a well-meaning friend said to Earl, "He had a long and good life. Aren't you glad his suffering is over now?" Earl says he replied in a voice that did not mask his anger, "You don't understand. *My daddy died!*"

Learn to acknowledge that your loss is worthy of grief. Whatever your experience is, you must endure your very real feelings of sadness and anger on the way to recovering a full life once more. If you are going to come out of grief a better person, you cannot be concerned about how you "ought to" feel on the way through it.

When Phyliss came to our grief support group, she had lost her daughter, son-in-law, and three grandchildren in a bizarre mass murder. That was a catastrophic loss. Two years later, her husband died of cancer. By contrast, Susan came only because her widower father needed her to bring him. A year later, he died. Susan continued to come alone after the funeral. One day she said, "I feel guilty for feeling so sad. My loss seems so insignificant compared to Phyliss's loss."

That attitude could have been a stumbling block to Susan's grief recovery. It was important for her to know that her grief was just as real as that of Phyliss.

It hurts to lose people, places, and things that were important to your life. The correct and appropriate response is grief. If you don't acknowledge your loss and begin to work your way through it, even small grief experiences begin to stack up. They become like bills waiting to be paid as they pile up interest.

> *As long as you tell yourself you shouldn't feel as you do, or pretend you don't hurt, the loss stays with you.*

As long as you tell yourself you shouldn't feel as you do, or pretend you don't hurt, the loss stays with you. Recovery begins when you admit that no matter what other tragedies exist in the world, at this very moment, the very worst kind of grief is yours.

You do not owe an apology to friends, family, or God for grieving the loss of anything or anybody. If others understand, that's nice. If they don't, that's too bad.

The way out of grief is through it. And, the way through it begins by acknowledging that your loss is worthy of grief, even if it's for an old cat.

3. Grief Is Hard Work to Be Done

Making your way through grief is called doing grief work. I never fully appreciated what that means until I immersed myself in other people's grief experiences. I came to understand it even more as I grieved June's death. There is no better way to describe the things that will be required of you than the word *work*. Grieving is work. It is the most difficult work any of us will ever do.

Viewing grief as work to be done will help you take an active approach to your grief. It will help you avoid trying to wait it out. It will help you refrain from looking to others to be responsible for making you feel whole again. There are some tasks that you just can't assign to someone else. Nobody can do the work of acknowledging the death of your loved one for you. No one else can take over the very difficult task of saying good-bye and releasing that person, that relationship, that part of your body, or whatever it is you have lost. You must do that for yourself.

The following image helps me understand the work dimension of grief.

Suppose you have had a group of friends over for a spaghetti dinner. It's been a delightful evening, but now your guests have gone home. You walk into your kitchen, and there sit the dishes. Those tomato-sauce-turned-to-glue-covered dishes are one of the truly ugly sights in the world!

Viewing grief as work to be done will help you take an active approach to your grief.

You're tired and in the mood for anything but washing dishes. You have two choices: You can leave the mess until morning. Or you can wash the dishes now, regardless of how you feel. If you leave them, the present moment is certainly more pleasant. In fact, the balance of the evening can be delightful, and your night's rest refreshing. But come daylight, *there they are*, uglier than ever!

Now the task is even more difficult. The pleasantness of the dinner party is forgotten as you face the same decision: wash them now or put off the gruesome task for another time.

If you choose to wash the dishes immediately after dinner, your guests might help you, if you're lucky. At worst, you face a tough evening of cleanup and go to bed exhausted. But come morning, the task is finished. You can go on to the new day basking in the memory of a good evening and the knowledge that your kitchen once again looks sparkling.

Grief work is much like that image. You have work to do at a time when you feel like doing nothing at all. Like those dishes, grief work can be put off. You can feel better for a while by avoiding some feelings and not talking about some things. But the day will come when you awaken to see that your feelings are still there, and things still need to be talked about with someone who understands and cares. One woman had not wanted to deal with grief when her husband died. She kept herself busy and did a pretty good "end run" around her sorrow. When a neighbor's husband died several years later, she found herself plunged back into her own loss. She came to the grief support group and faced up to the work she had to do. I'm glad to say that three years later she had established a new normal for her life.

The longer you wait to address those feelings, the more difficult and unpleasant grief work becomes. Grief is not an illness. But if you try to avoid grief work, you may well become sick.

> *About 25 percent of those who mourn experience a dramatic decrease in their body's immune system six to nine months after their loss.*

Dr. Glen Davidson's research showed that about 25 percent of those who mourn experience a dramatic decrease in their body's immune system six to nine months after their loss. That lack of immunity accounts in part for the higher rate of illness when we are grieving. The research also demonstrated that this immune system deficiency can be avoided.[1] If you do the work of grieving, including taking care of your physical and emotional needs, your risk for diseases will be no more than if you had not experienced a major loss.

The first thing you need is a support group with whom you can talk freely. See Chapter 19 for more about that. Then you must pay attention to the foods you eat, the amount and kinds of fluids you drink, and getting adequate exercise and sufficient rest.

It's hard work. There is much to do and only you can do much of it. But in other ways you need to share the burden of grieving with others who can help you, as you will see next.

4. Effective Grief Work Is Not Done Alone

One of the most hurtful myths you will hear about grief goes like this:

- Grief is such a personal experience that it should be kept to yourself.

Another is:

• Nobody else can help. You have to handle your own grief.

Nothing is further from the truth!

It is another fact of life and loss that effective grief work is not done alone. Your grief should never be a private affair. While it is true that there are things you must do for yourself, it is equally true that you need other people as much as you need air to breathe. You need to talk about your experiences and your feelings to people who will listen and try to understand.

You need to listen to others share about what's happening to them. There is more than comfort in such sharing. There is a valuable learning experience that brings the strength you need to endure the length and burden of grief.

If you keep your grief to yourself, you run an unnecessary risk of it becoming distorted. Mike dropped out of our grief support group after coming twice. He said he wasn't willing to come week after week and "cry in front of a bunch of women." The last I knew he was still struggling with blackouts and ulcers. He married again less than a year after his wife's death. His new wife came to see me several times to talk about his moodiness. Mike always refused to come with her.

Jane could never tell the group that her marriage had not been the idyllic romance she had wanted it to be. Neighbors and friends knew about the loud arguments and alcohol problems. But after her husband's death she talked about their relationship as if it had been made in heaven. After a few months, she became increasingly hostile and unwilling to share her feelings. Her participation in the group was limited to giving advice to others. In time, she dropped out altogether. For a while, she attended other grief groups in the city, none of which satisfied her. Four years after her husband's death, Jane was still a bitter, unhappy person.

You need to talk about your experiences and your feelings.

The saddest fact about Mike and Jane is their problems could have been avoided. You can move through your grief experience and come out a healthy person. To do that, however, other people must be involved in your life and your grief.

The Power of Shared Experiences

Of all the groups in the church, my favorite is always the grief support group. I can't imagine a more sensitive and caring group of people anywhere. Nowhere else have I seen the age barrier disappear more rapidly.

The more you talk about your grief work publicly, write about it in letters, and share in the grief of others, the more effectively you will adapt to your own loss.

There is something very special about seeing a young mother whose baby was stillborn and an eighty-year-old widow taking care of each other. Other mutual support groups can have much the same therapeutic essence. When people gather to talk about being a caregiver for someone with dementia or a permanently impaired stroke victim, they are talking about coping with major losses. The same is true for burn victims and people with prostheses for legs and arms.

Those who share such deep places together become a real help to others. They seem to know instinctively the right words to say to a newly bereaved person. They know the time to speak and the time when words are neither adequate nor necessary. The more social your grief work is, the better you will do with it. The more you talk about your grief work publicly, write about it in letters, and share in the grief of others, the more effectively you will adapt to your own loss. I don't mean to imply it's easy. It isn't. But, it is *necessary*. One grief support group I lead meets every Wednesday from four to five p.m. Afterward, all who wish to do so go to a prearranged restaurant and dine together. At times, as many as eighteen people will have this time of dining and fellowship. For some, it is the one meal in a week they do not eat alone. For others, it's just a good time of storytelling and laughter. Lasting friendships have formed over the years. Some, having spent this time together in addition to the group meetings, form a two-person mutual support pact. They share telephone numbers and are available for talking when needed. This postgroup gathering has become an integral part of the healing network.

Men and Grief

A few men still seem to have more difficulty than women sharing grief experiences in a group meeting. Some of this reluctance probably has to do with the masculine dread of emotionalism. Many of us have grown up with the silly notion that showing emotions is a sign of weakness and lack of character. The price for such foolishness has proven to be very high. The women in our grief support group are quick to remind any man who comes that big boys don't cry, but real men do.

Fortunately, most men, especially younger ones, have learned the truth of this before their losses. Experiences like being in the labor and delivery room and coaching a wife through childbirth have a softening effect on male emotions. Professional athletes are seen crying after losing a game or winning a championship.

Greg came to the group after his wife died of breast cancer. In the aftermath of her death, his relationships with his stepdaughter and sister-in-law collapsed. It became so painful that his tearful sharing in the group was more about this trauma than his wife's death. At times his anger seemed to block out the grief he needed to face and express. It took months for him to work past the heartbreak of these broken relationships and finally begin dealing with the loss of his wife. Attending the funeral of a friend broke the dam that had held back his grieving. He sobbed openly as he told us how much he missed her and how sad he was that she had died.

Men have the same basic needs for healthy grief recovery as women. This includes the need to be with others who have had similar losses and the need to talk openly about what is happening inside as the result of the loss.

If you are male and have suffered a major loss in your life, don't try to handle it alone. If you are too uncomfortable meeting with a group that includes women, a little investigation will uncover other men who share your feelings. Get together for breakfast or lunch on a weekly basis. Use this book as a guide for your discussions. Make a sign for yourself that has the same message as the one I have that says, "People and tears are welcome here." Remember that means your tears, too.

Careless Things People Say

Almost every divorced person and everyone who is widowed has had someone say something that can only be called careless and cruel. Bereaved persons are often rejected for crying and rewarded for keeping a bright smile, even though "faking it" inhibits their recovery. Divorced men and women find friends taking sides and making judgments at a time when the thing they need most is a friendly ear.

It is more than common for grieving people to hate the question "How are you?"

It is more than common for grieving people to hate the question "How are you?" The only acceptable answer to those who have not walked the path of grief is "Fine," when you are not fine at all.

Numerous widows have shared experiences with me of being forgotten by social or church groups after the death of their spouse. After her husband's death, Maggie gathered up the courage to go back to a bridge club they had belonged to for several years.

It was a difficult step. The bridge club was an activity she and Roy had always shared. When Maggie arrived, she was greeted at the door by a longtime friend who said, "My dear, don't you know this is for couples?"

It doesn't take more than one experience like that to convince you to keep grief to yourself!

You will find people, including some doctors and clergy, who are too uncomfortable with grief to reach out to you. Friends may avoid you because they don't know what to say. Co-workers may be afraid they will say something that upsets you, so they say nothing at all. You may yearn to hear the name of your spouse or child who has died and no one says it. It often seems that a conspiracy of silence develops whenever you are present.

Nevertheless, it is a fact that effective grief work is not done alone. It is vitally important for you to find a counselor or a support group who will listen, if friends and family aren't up to that task. Almost every community offers such resources simply because loss is a universal human experience. In Appendix B you will find guidelines for forming a grief support group yourself if one is not available.

I suggest you write down each of the four key facts about grief on a separate piece of paper or enter them in your smartphone. Choose one and write down how you are experiencing the truth of it in your journey through grief. Practice taking small steps to move through your grief. Remind yourself daily that your loss is the one you have to face and your grief is the appropriate response to it. Look at the task of grieving as work you must do, not something that happens to you. In modern terminology, be proactive in grieving. Find a support system. It may be two or three other people who have also had major losses. Try to find a support group that meets weekly. Attend once or twice to see if it can meet your needs and help you work through your loss.

The four key facts about grief are not complicated. They do provide a foundation for grief recovery. They are true.

9

Start Now!
Today Is a Better Day to Begin than Tomorrow

I keep a quotation by an unknown writer pinned to a bulletin board over my desk:

There will never be another now—I'll make the most of today.
There will never be another me—I'll make the most of myself.

It's a good motto for doing effective grief work. Today is the ideal time for you to start working through your loss. Tomorrow will not be a better day to face the task. The only one who can make the journey through your grief is *you*. Be assured: You will discover you are equal to the challenge.

> Tomorrow will not be a better day to face the task.

Doing grief work, in one sense, is a little bit like making love. Talking about it takes you only so far. And no one else can experience it for you. Admittedly, there is nothing pleasurable about grief. But if you learn the skills of effective grief work, you can emerge from your losses with a renewed sense of confidence and a good life to live.

If you have experienced a major loss, it won't help to wait for some other day when you feel better to start working on it. The potential risks to your health and the absence of joy from your life are prices too high to pay for postponing the task.

Helpful Exercises

This book contains exercises that can help you handle any loss in your life. They are well tested by people in grief support groups and the more than 100,000 who have purchased earlier editions of this book. Each exercise presents a task that focuses on a specific step to grief recovery. Not all the exercises will apply to you at this moment. However, all of them are worth your attention.

Doing the exercises will help you continue to move through your grief.

For instance, exercises on handling grief after divorce also apply to other losses. With minor adjustments, those that focus on death also apply to divorce or relocation. If the particular loss addressed doesn't fit your experience, it may apply to someone you know who needs your understanding and help.

Remember that you will not move through grief in an orderly, well-defined manner. A task that seems completed three months after loss may have to be done again many times. If this is your experience, it is not a setback—it is a perfectly normal way for grief to progress. Doing the exercises will help you continue to move through your grief toward recovery and the all-important new normal for your life.

Applying the Four Key Facts to Your Grief

As a warm-up to doing other exercises, copy each of the Four Key Facts about Grief (see box, page 119) onto separate pieces of paper. List one key fact at the top of a sheet, and then list the ways it applies to your grief experience. For instance, write at the top of one sheet, *The way out of grief is through it.* Under this heading, list what you can do to go through your experience and what behaviors to avoid that represent an

---

The Four Key Facts about Grief

For a full discussion of the Four Key Facts about Grief, see pages 101–115.

1. The way out of grief is through it.

2. The very worst kind of grief is yours.

3. Grief is hard work to be done.

4. Effective grief work is not done alone.

---

effort to sidestep your grief. For example, you could remind yourself to talk to someone about your loss every day. You could write a description of the way you feel right now. My preference is to hand write this one, but use a computer if you prefer that method.

Work with the four key facts until you are clear about the way each of them applies to your loss and grief. As you become more comfortable with them, you will be able to see more potential for a full and rewarding life after your loss.

Understanding and accepting these key facts about grief recovery is crucial to building a rewarding life after a major loss.

A Recent Life History Survey

This exercise is for everybody. It will help you identify loss experiences that may have seemed insignificant at the time they happened, but which could be continuing to affect your happiness today.

Take a survey. Get a piece of blank paper and a pencil. Answer the survey questions in the sequence in which they are presented. Answer every question before going on to the instructions that follow the survey. This one works very well on a computer.

1. List the most significant changes in your life during the past two years. Include positive experiences, such as a job promotion, new home, getting married (or having children married), retirement, or graduating from college. Negative experiences will include a death in the family, divorce, loss of job, surgery, serious illness or injury, moving from familiar surroundings, and business failure.

2. Diagram your moods over the past year: happy (contented); okay (some ups and downs); or sad (depressed, discontented). I found it effective and enjoyable to use Emojis to indicate my moods and feelings.

	Jan	Feb	Mar	Apr	May	Jun	Jul	Aug	Sep	Oct	Nov	Dec
Happy												
Okay												
Sad												

3. List any physical problems you have had in the last eighteen months.

4. Describe your outlook on life right now in terms of
   • A color
   • A taste
   • A smell
   • Touch
   • A sound

You might describe life as a dismal gray color, like a foggy, overcast morning. Or perhaps it is a good day, and life is the color of a rainbow. Life could taste bitter or rancid—or as sweet as a ripe strawberry. Life may have the odor of rotting meat, burn your lungs like acrid smoke—or smell like the freshness after a sudden rain. It may have the feel of gritty sandpaper or the softness of a baby's skin. Perhaps your life right now is as noisy as a Los Angeles intersection during rush hour, or maybe it sounds more like a clear stream bubbling over rocks.

Finding such ways to describe how life looks to you at a given moment is helpful in tracking your progress through grief recovery.

5. Write down the one thing in your life you would change at this moment if you could. (Describe the way you think it is and the way you would like it to be.)

Examine your responses. After you have completed the survey, read over your answers. Examine your responses by doing the following:

1. Ask yourself, "What losses did I experience in each of the major changes I listed?"

2. Choose which of these losses continues to make the greatest impact on your life. As you think about this loss, what feelings do you have? Refer to the list of feeling words in Appendix A for help in naming your feelings.

3. Check the diagram of your moods over the last year. Is there a correlation between your moods at various times and the loss you have identified? Focus on the saddest of your moods and try to remember what was happening at each of those times. Identify your losses in each of those experiences and name your feelings about them.

4. What was happening during your happiest moods? What feelings can you name about those experiences? In what way were you in control of your own destiny at those times?

5. Look at your list of physical problems. Is there a correlation between these problems and the loss experiences you have named? List the approximate time your physical symptoms were noticed. Measure back six months, nine months, one year, and eighteen months from this time. Note the events in your life around each of these times. Was a loss involved? If so, what was it? Is that loss still affecting your life today?

6. Do your physical problems keep you from doing anything you would do if you didn't have a limitation? If so, describe what you would do if you could. What words describe your sense of loss because you cannot do that particular thing?

Look at the words you used to describe your present outlook on life. Do you like these images?

- Is the color your favorite?
- Is the taste something you like?
- Is the smell pleasant?
- Is the touch pleasurable?
- Is the sound one you would like to hear again?

7. How do you feel about your answers in each category? Do they indicate a positive or negative outlook on life? If your outlook is more negative than positive, ask yourself, "What have I lost recently that, if it were given back to me, would make my outlook on life more positive?"

8. Think about the thing that you would most like to change in your life. Is it possible to realize that change?

You can't get back a loved one who has died, a divorced spouse who has remarried, a limb or organ lost to surgery or an accident, or a special time in your life. Recovering just about every other loss is possible, regardless of how improbable that recovery might be.

9. If the one change you would make is not possible, you have grief work to do. Identify the focus of your grief. Don't try to fool yourself or name a loss that feels respectable to you. For instance, if you are divorcing and it is not the loss of your spouse that hurts, but the loss of your children or self-esteem, say so. Focus your grief on that loss.

10. If the change you would make is possible, ask yourself, "Why haven't I already made that change? What is holding me back?" Does the change require the participation of someone else? Who? Have you talked with that person about it?

Knowing that for every change, there is a price to be paid, what is the price for the change you would like to make? Are you willing to pay that price?

Talking It Over

To get the most benefit from the survey, first go through it carefully by yourself and then share your findings with a trusted friend, family member, counselor, or clergy. The simple act of talking about your loss and feelings is an important step to recovery.

Your loss may seem so small that you are embarrassed to make an issue of it. If so, remember the second key fact about grief recovery: The very worst kind of loss is yours.

Pay particular attention to any correlation between your physical problems and a time of loss. You can spend a great deal of time and money treating physical symptoms and never get to their root cause if loss and grief are unacknowledged factors of your illness. If you suspect a connection, you need to see a counselor or clergyperson and a doctor who understand the relationship of grief and illness.

The simple act of talking about your loss and feelings is an important step to recovery.

Guidelines for Doing Grief Work

Once you have identified your losses, the next step is to begin the work of recovering your balance. The following guidelines will help get you started and keep you going when you grow weary of the task.

Trust that you will make it through your grief. It is a fact that experiencing grief means you have work to do. It is also a fact that this work has an end point. In the early going I can only ask you to take my word for it. You probably think your sadness will last forever. It won't. That will become evident to you later as you do the exercises I suggest.

Earlier I compared grief work to washing dishes. Once you have washed the dishes that work is finished until you use the dishes again. Grief work is like that. Once you have done the work required for you to regain your balance, it is finished until you experience another loss. The more you learn about grief, the better you can handle it.

The more you learn about your grief, the better you can handle it.

Nobody wants to be good at grieving. We are half-afraid that having such a skill would only attract more grief. We would much prefer to do without the grief experience entirely. Unfortunately, life doesn't work that way. Because you will not be spared from times of loss, it is important to believe that your grief has a purpose.

If your outlook on life is upbeat and healthy, you trust that life is fundamentally good. When you experience a major loss, that basic sense of trust is shaken. You will question whether life is not actually chaotic and unfair. In truth, sometimes it is!

Shortly after our marriage, my wife and I were awakened in the middle of the night in our third-floor apartment by a strong earthquake. We awoke feeling disoriented and scared to death. The room was swaying back and forth.

The sensible thing would have been to get up immediately and crouch in a doorway. Instead, we were paralyzed by fear and distrust of our environment. We lay in bed holding tight to each other until the movement subsided.

When a major loss occurs in your life, your sense of reality and security is shaken in a similar fashion. However, unlike experiencing an earthquake, you can't just lie low until the tremors cease. To get moving is a challenge, but being paralyzed by fear and distrust isn't going to help you recover your balance. You need to believe there is a purpose to all that is happening, and work with it.

That doesn't mean there is a purpose for your loss. If you believe your loss has happened to teach you some lesson or to punish you, the work of recovery will be more difficult than it already is. It is better to accept the fact that some things happen to us and our loved ones just because we are mortal human beings living in a mortal, frail world that is sometimes anything but fair. Some things, including tragedies, just happen. This world is dependable, and one of the things you can depend on is loss and grief.

A common question I hear from bereaved persons is "What have I done wrong? Am I being punished for something?" It's certainly an understandable question. It is also a foolish one for which there is not a good answer except no. Bad things happen to bad people and to good people and everyone in between. Loss and grief are not inflicted upon you or anyone else by design. They happen because you are alive in a mortal and imperfect world.

To grow through loss you have to learn that the fact of loss does not diminish life.

Be responsible for your own grief process.

No one can do your grieving for you. No one else can make your decisions or feel your feelings or cry tears that are essential for recovering from major loss. That's one reason it is so important for you to see grief not as an illness from which to recover, but as old-fashioned hard work that you must do.

Throughout the process of your grief work, you will do best if you maintain a personal responsibility for completing it. You will need to have the support of others, but the work to be done is yours alone.

The most difficult time to stay responsible for your grief recovery is when depression hits. When sadness is complicated by fatigue, and when things that normally bring joy don't stir you, it is hard to feel responsible for anything.

Depression is a way of taking time out from working through grief. You might say doing grief work is like lifting a barbell over your head. Perhaps you can lift it once, twice, or ten times. But there comes a time when the weight is too heavy and your muscles are too tired to lift it once more. At that moment you have no choice but to rest before trying to lift it again.

> *No one can do your grieving for you.*

Depression associated with grief can become so intense that you require medication. If it persists, you may need to be hospitalized. But even then, it is finally you who must choose to come out of the depression.

Because grief work is so intense, it is important to take a time-out now and then. It's okay to relax and allow some diversion to take your mind off of it. As one of those who has been there, I can tell you with certainty that your grief will be waiting when you return to it. By allowing yourself times of putting the work of grief aside, you regain emotional and physical strength for the "next round." If your time-out involves physical exercise, you gain the added benefit of improving your health.

Don't quit grief work too soon, however. This is an important point to remember. If you do take time out, have a plan ready for getting back to grief work—and then do it!

Don't be afraid to ask for help.

To ask for help is not to give up responsibility for your grief. It means you recognize that lifting yourself up by the shoestrings usually results in a hernia or broken shoestrings—it doesn't lift you off the floor!

Remember one of the key facts about grief recovery: Effective grief work is not done alone. You need others when trying to work your way out of the sadness and depression that follow a major loss.

The sharing that takes place in our weekly grief support group is just part of the group's value. A network of mutual support has developed between sessions that is extremely important. Some "veterans" have made themselves available to the newcomers for emergency telephone calls. We update and distribute a roster of grief-support-group members every few weeks. We put an asterisk next to the names of those people who are willing to be called at any time for support.

Because grief work is so intense, it's important to take a time-out now and then.

The security of knowing somebody is always available who understands grief makes the program work. Sometimes the simplest act counts the most. Two of our older widows were finding their evening dinner to be the loneliest time of the day. Neither of them was eating properly or regularly. One woman drives a car on a limited basis, the other not at all. By mapping out a route that kept them off the busiest streets, they were able to arrange for the one who drives to pick up the other to dine at a local cafeteria on a regular basis. Within two weeks I saw marked improvements in their energy levels and outlooks.

You should not be afraid to ask for help. It is equally important for the person you ask to understand the grief-recovery process. The best support you can find will come from others who are working through their own losses. You can find such people in every community.

I was a guest speaker at a church one Sunday. The minister announced that I would be available on the following Tuesday to meet with anyone who had experienced a major loss. Fully 10 percent of the congregation showed up for the meeting. Experiences like this have taught me that loss and grief are universal experiences. Given an opportunity to share and the promise of an open, accepting atmosphere, many people will respond.

If you look for others who are as eager as you are to work through loss and grief, you will have no trouble finding them. If you can find a leader who is trained in coping with grief and loss, that's a bonus. If you can't, just gather a group and use this book as your guide. You'll find more information about this in Appendix B, which gives you specific guidelines for forming a group and directing the first twelve sessions.

Don't rush it.

I am not known for patience. One of my dear friends, a ninety-two-year-old widow who "adopted" me after the death of her husband, called me "Reverend Buzz Bomb." It's a title that caused me to wince only because of its accuracy. I have always believed the best time to accomplish anything was yesterday.

When I was younger I walked fast, talked fast, and ate fast, much to my wife's disdain! I lived in the high-speed lane and wouldn't have had it any other way. Now that I'm older, I have slowed down only as much as my body makes me go slower. I now have sympathy with those of you who have problems being patient with your grief for a different reason. However, with all the compassion I can muster, I must tell you this: Grief work can't be rushed. It usually takes at least two or three years to work through a death or divorce. And, yes, it is no different for me.

It will take at least two or three years to work through a death or divorce.

Irene worked as hard as anyone I have ever known to get through the death of her husband. She said to me soon after his death, "Bob, I don't intend to let my grief own me. I intend to attack it with everything I've got and to seek all the help I can get. It may take others two or three years, but not me!"

She did attack her grief. Irene never tried to avoid any part of it, or any feeling that came with it. She was able to cry openly. She poured herself into helping others in the grief support group. She sought the help of one of the best psychologists in our city. I can't think of one thing Irene could have done that she didn't do.

Nevertheless, when Irene's journey through grief was finished, two years and nine months had passed. The process just can't be rushed. It will take more time than you think you can bear, but you can and you will. By the way, she is still a bundle of energy in her nineties.

More Things to Do

As part of your grief work, try these exercises. They will help you get closer to your feelings and will give you ways to talk with others about your grief.

After you complete the survey at the beginning of this chapter, share it with at least two others.

Write each of the following four statements on a 3 x 5-inch card. Concentrate on one of them each day. On the back of the card, outline what you think the statement means for your grief experience. Share those insights with four different people.

Here are the statements:

- I believe grief is essential to my healing and has an end.
- I will be responsible for my own grief process.
- I will not be afraid to ask for help.
- I will not try to rush my recovery.

10

Grief and Growth
Growing through Loss

You already know that grief is about losing. You need to know that it can also be about growing.

During the first weeks and months after a death, divorce, or any major loss in your life, you will need to be reminded many times that you will not always feel as you do now. You may think the pain of your loss will never go away. It may seem as if the feelings of sadness and emptiness will be with you forever. You may think you have smiled for the last time in your life. To have these thoughts and feelings is quite normal. The truth is, the pain will diminish, the sadness will leave, and laughter will return. If you work at it, the grieving process can become a time of growth.

The way through grief may not be a nice, neat stair-climb. Your path to recovery will have many ups and downs, twists and turns, but if you stay with it, you will emerge stronger than when you started. Some of the downs you can expect will come after several months, even a year or more. There is no magic time when you will have established a new normal for your life. If you know what to expect, you can avoid being harsh on yourself and adding to your own sadness. You can avoid the trap of thinking, "I am the only one who feels this way."

For instance, you may reach a point, perhaps six to eight months after your loss, when you feel better. You will begin to function more normally. You will sleep better, food will taste better, and you will perform routine tasks as you did before your loss. Days will go along fairly smoothly.

Hitting a low just shows how far up you have already been.

Then something will come off the wall and bite you. You may hear a familiar song on the radio, see a person walking on the street who bears a striking resemblance to your deceased spouse or have a vivid dream about the one who died. Perhaps you hear that your divorced mate is about to remarry or that someone has been named to fill your old job.

Whatever it is, your response is to have the roof cave in on your emotions. When this happens, it is common to think you have slipped and are starting your grieving all over again. That simply isn't true. You are exactly where you should be.

Many people have the same experience. A widow said, *"Hitting a low just shows how far up you have already been."* It isn't a setback; it's a sign of forward movement. Look at such upsets as mileposts along the way to grief recovery and as signs of personal growth.

I have led grief support groups for a very long time. It isn't uncommon to see folks come to the group for the first time eighteen months to two years after the death of a spouse or child.

The inevitable emotional upheavals are surefire signs that you are doing fine.

They will say, "I thought I was doing so well until one day I woke up feeling as if I were starting all over again."

When something like that happens to you, remind yourself that grief is not a bad word. It isn't something you shouldn't experience. There is no particular emotional place you have to be at a given time.

The inevitable emotional upheavals are surefire signs that you are doing fine. If you continue to face your grief and work through your loss, you will come out at the other end a stronger person than you have ever been. The one who will be the most surprised at this is you.

The following exercise is designed to help you see that grief is manageable. It lets you personalize your sense of loss by writing a letter that begins "Dear Grief." In the letter, you can describe whatever it is you would like to say to your grief, as though you were standing face-to-face. The exercise continues with a second letter, written twenty-four hours later. This letter is from your grief to you. It begins, "Dear _____ [your name]" and ends, "Sincerely, Grief." It describes whatever it is you think your grief is trying to communicate to you.

I have seen marvelous healing and growth begin with this simple act of letter writing. Four months after her husband's death, Irene wrote the following:

> Dear Grief,
>
> You are a rascal. You take our energy, our organizational abilities, and our brains and do strange things with them. I was prepared for the immediate grief and to feel the loss of my spouse for a long, long time. I was not prepared for the laziness, low energy level, and the stress.
>
> I am impatient with it all. You take so much out of us when we really need to be able to function well. I do not understand why.
>
> I must confess you've done good things for me also. I am more compassionate, understanding, tolerant. You have given me new ways to be of service, and God will show me those ways. Perhaps after I've had more time to look back I will feel different about you, but for right now you are not one of my favorite friends. I am a better person because of you and I must not lose sight of that.
>
> Sincerely,
>
> Irene

A day later she wrote this letter to herself from her grief:

Dear Irene,

I'm sorry I've caused you so much pain. Remember that your pastor said at the funeral, "Grief is the noblest emotion of all." It truly is the last gift of love you can give your husband, so experience it in a normal way. Let your own time frame happen.

I know you are working hard to get through this phase of your life. I commend you for that. But I also want to say, "Let go and let God." Just put it in God's hands. I suggest you read the verses on death in the Bible.

Remember, there is an atomic bomb of hope waiting to explode between the front and back covers of your Bible. I sense your excitement as you search through those scriptures. You may be truly amazed at what you find.

Begin to use your time more wisely. Get extra sleep once or twice a week. You'll be all right. Soon your energy level will return. You may even lose the weight you've been trying to lose for some time. In time you will walk lighter. You will sit lighter. You will feel great.

I am your friend. I am a part of life. There is a purpose for me. You will see.

Sincerely,

Grief

The attitude Irene expressed toward her grief in those letters was the key to her return to a full and productive life. She is again a person with a zest for living and an energy level that sparkles. She is positive, outgoing, and healthy. Irene has successfully handled a terrible loss. She has also been a great help to dozens of others at times of similar losses.

One Sunday Irene took me by the arm after church and said, "I have to tell you. It doesn't hurt anymore. I can enjoy the memories of our life together without having my enjoyment canceled by the pain of losing him. I am ready to live the rest of my life fully now."

That moment and the shine in Irene's eyes remains one of my all-time greatest memories. It became a source of hope for me when June died and an assurance that I too would be able to one day say "I can enjoy the memories of our life together without having my enjoyment canceled by the pain of losing her." By the way, one of those who attended June's memorial service was Irene.

Grief is always about losing. People like Irene have taught me that it can also be about growing and winning. The personal growth Irene experienced is possible for you too as you work through your losses.

I first began to connect grief and growth when I started meeting regularly with a group of bereaved people. As they talked about the many facets of their grief experience, I felt some of the incredible depth of sadness that accompanies such losses.

Growing through Loss

This is what it means to grow through loss:

- Growth means gaining a new love and reverence for life.

- It means shifting your attention from the ordinary to the quality elements of life.

- Growth is a greater awareness of our mutual need for each other and of the sacred dimension of life.

But something else was present, too. I saw those people laugh together at how forgetful one can become under the stress of grief. I saw new skills, talents, and compassion emerge from one person after another. A strong sense of unity developed among those people as they shared experiences with each other. "I didn't know anyone else did

I saw new skills, talents, and compassion emerge from one person after another.

that" became a motto for the group. It also was a source of comfort to me in the early stages of my grief when I felt disconnected and unable to concentrate on any task until it was completed. I found myself jumping from one thing to another to another.

A widow went back to school and is now enjoying the career she always wanted, but which she put aside for many years to be home with her husband.

A man who, in his own words, "couldn't successfully boil water," joined a cooking class at a community college after his wife's death. He now prepares gourmet meals for friends.

Several people learned they could do mechanical things they never thought possible before their spouse's death. There was a sense throughout the group that life had put each one to the ultimate test, and each was able to meet it!

Look at the box on page 133, which lists some of the ways it is possible to grow through loss. I have never seen this kind of growth happen as a result of winning a lottery, achieving success in business, or reaping a windfall of any kind. I see it weekly in persons who are working their way through loss and grief.

That doesn't mean grief is an experience to be treasured. None of us wants to feel the horrible emptiness and desolation that comes with a major loss. Yet we need to understand that feelings of grief won't hurt

Working through loss can also mean growing through loss. The depth of grief hurts, but it can be a creative hurt.

us if we face them and work our way through them. Working through loss can also mean growing through loss. The depth of grief hurts, but it can be a creative hurt.

When our first grandchild was born, our daughter-in-law and son chose to have her by natural childbirth. They went through training classes and when the time of birth came, he was with her in the delivery room as her coach. We waited outside the door with the other eager grandparents-to-be. Within a few minutes of our granddaughter's arrival, we were ushered in to see mother and baby.

Our daughter-in-law's first words were, "I'll never do it again this way; it hurt too much!" An hour later the memory of the pain was just a part of the total experience of creating a new life. By the next day it was something she had met and conquered. They have since had two more children by the same method. That's *creative hurt.*

The pain of grief can also be creative hurt. It is real and long-lasting, but it is not permanent. It passes. Not only does it pass, but it can help create new life along the way—yours.

Help from Others

The most helpful person to a newly widowed person is quite often another widow or widower. When a widowed person goes to see someone who has just lost a loved one, that person has something to offer that is special—his or her presence as one who "has been there and done that."

It shows, with a real and convincing quality nothing else has, that there is a way through grief and reason to hope.

> *The most helpful person to a newly widowed person is quite often another widow or widower.*

Over and over, I have seen one widowed person anticipate the exact day and hour that another widowed person needs to receive a telephone call and a word of encouragement. It is no coincidence. Once you have been there you understand what is happening, when it happens, and what needs to be done.

"I know how you feel" are words from one who hasn't a clue what grief feels like. They sound like fingernails across a chalkboard. They hurt instead of comfort. One who knows the experience of loss and grief firsthand will say, "I know something about how you are feeling," and that's completely different. It expresses a sensitive understanding

> *"I know how you feel" are words from one who hasn't a clue what grief feels like. They sound like fingernails across a chalkboard.*

that no one really knows exactly how another person is feeling—especially about something as emotionally loaded as a major loss.

Years ago, when the aerospace industry went through one of its many cutbacks, several men in our church lost their job. They were engineers and lab technicians who were well educated and who performed their job with skill. Being unemployed was the last thing on their mind until it happened.

An astute businessman saved the day for many of them. He gathered these men into a sharing-and-support group. They were free to talk about how terrible it felt to be laid off and how much their sense of self-worth was hurting. They didn't have to be strong with one another as they thought they had to do at home and in church. They gave each other acceptance and encouragement as one after another retrained for a new work field. About two years after it started, the group disbanded because it was no longer needed. All of them had learned new skills and were working in new fields.

No one could help them through it better than they could help one another.

Those men experienced grief as a result of losing their job, dreams, and a sense of self-esteem. No one could help them through it better than they could help one another.

My wife, June, responded to a mastectomy because of breast cancer by becoming a volunteer with the American Cancer Society. The program, Reach to Recovery, sends a woman who has had a mastectomy to visit another woman who has experienced the loss of one or both breasts or will soon. The notes and telephone calls that June received later made it abundantly clear how much it helped.

Once we were sitting in a restaurant when a woman walked up to the table. She pulled June to her feet and embraced her in a big hug. She didn't even look at me as she proudly pulled her shoulders back to let June see the silhouette of her reconstructed breast. She asked whether June would meet her new husband and brought him over to the table. Only after several minutes had passed did she look at me and nod a greeting. Before they left, she looked at me again and said, "You have a marvelous wife. I don't know what I would have done without her."

Take Inventory of Your Losses

What loss have you had recently? Think back over the past two years.

- When have you had periods of sadness?

- What was happening at those times?

- Make a list of your losses. Read it aloud.

- What feelings do you have as you hear yourself announcing your losses?

- Make a list of your strongest feelings. Read through the list of "feeling words" in Appendix A to express yourself more clearly.

- Have you had occasions when it seemed that other people were critical of or uncaring toward you?

- Have you had any illnesses?

- Are any of your family relationships more stressed than usual?

You can decide to grow through the most devastating loss in your life! A major part of the growing side of grief is coming to understand that, in the midst of a life-changing loss, we still have control over our own destiny. You may not be able to choose all of the circumstances of your life, but you can always choose your responses to whatever happens.

I urge you to begin now.

One way to begin is to take inventory of your losses. You might ask yourself the questions in the box above. All the questions refer to what can be considered signs of unresolved grief in your life. All of them are occasions of loss. You can also make them into occasions of growth.

To achieve the happiness you would like for yourself, pay attention to your losses and begin working through your grief. The process takes time to learn and will take a lifetime to do. Fortunately, a lifetime is exactly what we have been given for the task.

You can decide to grow through the most devastating loss in your life!

11

A Test of Endurance
Life after Loss Takes Determination and Time

O f all the challenges you face in working through grief, none is more demanding than the endurance it requires. It begins with 365 days of "the first time without," but it doesn't end there.

If your spouse or child has died, you can't bear to think recovering from that loss is going to take as long as three years. But rarely is it less and often it is longer.

No newly divorced person wants to think in terms of two or more years before life feels as if it is back on an even keel. It takes all of that time to recover from a lost love and broken dreams if you work hard at the task. The impact on children can last well into adulthood (see Chapter 14).

It's tempting for some widowed and most divorced persons to try to fill the gap of loneliness by getting involved with another person as soon as possible. You need to know that it often does not result in more happiness, but in greater sadness. You aren't ready for the emotional stress and may not make wise choices. If filling the empty places becomes a

> *Any major loss results in a permanent change in your life.*

substitute for working through your grief, it can also become a detriment to your physical health.

The length of your grief after any major loss will be considerably longer than you expect. Any major loss results in a permanent change in your life. You won't adjust to that change and move on without struggles that take a long time to overcome. It may well take three years or more to work through the various phases of recovery. To endure the time it takes, you must believe the rewards are worth the effort. Trying to rush the process is an exercise in futility—and can lengthen the time required for you to recover your sense of balance.

Grief Is Heavy

Fatigue is one of the most common symptoms of grief. Grief is heavy. Carrying its weight is tiring. For years people told me they were constantly exhausted in the first three to six months after a death or divorce. I found out they were right when my wife died.

It isn't that grief beats on you so much as it *leans* on you. In the early months, you feel its weight night and day without relief. It seems to wear you down by persistence.

> For years people told me they were constantly exhausted in the first three to six months after a death or divorce. I found out they were right when my wife died.

When Dick lost a business because of an unscrupulous partner, he spent a solid week in bed, too weary to bathe or get dressed. If you are so tired after a major loss that everything you do is an effort, you are reacting in a normal way. It's a heavy load and it takes an incredible amount of endurance to carry it. I have always been an energetic person. That changed when June died. I found myself so tired I couldn't keep my eyes open sometimes two or three times during the day. I did not have more sleep disturbance at night than usual, but those who do feel daytime fatigue just as much.

The stress of carrying the load of your grief may result in feelings of inadequacy and discouragement. You may have little interest in eating regularly or paying attention to the nutritional balance of your meals. If you are like most people, you will be dehydrated and you will not get an adequate amount of exercise. You may have trouble sleeping or staying awake.

Fatigue is a normal part of grief recovery. You may want to add this statement to the growing list of helpful reminders you post around your house:

Grief is heavy. To feel tired is normal. My fatigue will not last forever. I will endure until I win.

Grief recovery is hard work that requires a maximum of stamina and patience from me.

Whatever else you may call your movement through grief, you will surely label it an endurance contest of the first order.

Your Physical Health

Health problems are much more likely to develop after a major loss. The classic study done by Erich Lindemann in 1944 indicated that one's risk of developing coronary artery disease becomes 250 percent higher after the death of a spouse. Risks for developing cancer, high blood pressure, arthritis, diabetes, thyroid disease, and skin disease are similarly high for those who have suffered the loss of a spouse.

Subsequent studies, most notably those of Dr. Glen Davidson at the University of Chicago and Southern Illinois University, indicate an increased risk for migraine headaches, chronic depression, low-back pain, and blood-chemistry disorders. Widows and widowers are also at increased risk for developing alcohol and drug dependency.

The good news is, you do not have to become a victim of health problems. Your response to the grief that follows a major loss is in your control.

Developing Grief Fitness

Working through grief is a little like working out for physical fitness. Those who lift weights cannot start with the maximum weight they hope to lift. Those who jog or walk can't begin with a maximum distance. They have to work up to these goals a little at a time. In the same way, you don't start out handling grief in the way you will later. You grow into grief fitness a little at a time. It doesn't come easily, but it is the way to regain your balance in life after a major loss.

Over and over you will need to tell yourself, "I will not always feel as I do now." You will need patience with others and with yourself. You will need to remember that sometimes you will feel worse before you begin to feel better.

How to Take Care of Yourself after a Loss

Based on a ten-year study of 1200 people who had lost a close loved one, Dr. Glen Davidson recommends taking the following five actions to strengthen yourself for the work of grief recovery. In looking at more than one hundred factors, only these five were found to make a measurable difference in protecting health. The sooner you begin, the better!

1. Be part of a support group. Nothing is more important for your physical health than having a group of people to talk to about what you are experiencing.

There is a built-in healing power in a gathering of people who have all experienced a major loss. As one person tells of a particular struggle, heads nod in a knowing manner that says, "I understand because I've been there, too." The single most common complaint I have heard from bereaved people is the difficulty in finding someone who will listen with compassion to the stories of their losses. It is very likely that your need to talk about your loss will far exceed the willingness of most family members and friends to listen. Those in a grief support group will listen to you tell the story of your loss as many times as you need to tell it.

A grief support group does not require highly skilled professional leadership to be effective. Appendix B at the back of this book provides instructions for twelve sessions. This plan has worked successfully for many people, and it will work for you.

2. Drink an adequate amount of water. Under the stress and emotional upheaval of grief, you will tend to be dehydrated without being aware of it. Over the length of time required for recovery, this dehydration can weaken your immune system.

The ideal amount of water to drink is 2 quarts per day.

The ideal amount to drink is 2 quarts of pure water each day. It's a large quantity and, yes, drinking this much does have the expected result on your bladder. But it works! If you just can't get down that much water, do the best you can. One quart isn't as good as two, but it is much better than none.

Fill two 1-quart bottles with water and place them where they are easily reached in the front of your refrigerator. If your tap water is not pure, buy bottled water or get a filter. Some people find it helps to add a slice of lemon to the water. The main thing is to consistently drink as much as you can, up to 2 quarts a day.

Note: Soft drinks (regular or diet), iced tea, coffee, and alcoholic beverages are *not* substitutes for water. In fact, these can work against you, requiring an even greater pure-water intake.

3. Eat nutritiously. While it may be challenging, it is important to maintain a well-balanced nutritional plan while you are struggling through grief. Avoid junk food; high-fat foods; and excesses of sugar, caffeine, and alcohol.

The challenge for most of us is that eating is a social occasion. If you have to eat alone, food may not interest you during the early weeks and months after a major loss. It is common for people to

(Continues)

(*Continued*)

put off eating until hunger reaches the point of discomfort, then overeat the wrong kinds of foods. The best plan is to try to maintain your weight within five pounds of what it was prior to your loss.

Talk to your doctor or a recognized nutritionist to develop an eating plan for you—then stick to it!

4. Get adequate exercise. Exercise, within the boundaries of your own limitations, is helpful both physically and emotionally. Forty-five minutes of brisk walking does wonders for relieving the symptoms of depression—and it's free! If you have back, knee, or hip problems, walk in a swimming pool. The resistance of the water adds to the value of the exercise and supports your body while you are doing it. Stretching, swimming, weight lifting under the supervision of a personal trainer, and whatever level of aerobic exercise your doctor permits can all be of great benefit to you.

You will tend to exercise more regularly if you get someone to do it with you. The most difficult part of any exercise program is doing it when you don't feel like doing it. Usually you will feel better and have more energy when you are finished. Having a friend who will help keep you on track to do your exercise is a great help.

5. Get sufficient rest. There is no substitute for getting enough rest while dealing with grief. It is good if you can stay as close as possible to the sleeping pattern you had before your loss, if it was a healthy one. Because of the fatigue and stress involved with grief, it is even better to get additional rest in the form of naps for the first several months after your loss.

Sleep disturbance is very common after any major loss. On pages 231–233, you will find instructions for ways to help you stabilize your sleeping patterns. It includes a detailed plan to follow if you wake up in the middle of the night and can't get back to sleep.

It isn't uncommon during the first year or two to have times when you think the work is finished. Then something happens that plunges you back into the depths of anguish.

The first year after a death or any major loss is dominated by constant reminders. Every day is another "first time without" experience. The more significant the day, the more painful the experience. Birthdays, anniversaries, special family days, religious holidays, and typical vacation dates are among those that are frequently the most challenging.

Take things one day at a time, even one experience at a time. It may come down to enduring one more night of loneliness or one more meal across from an empty chair.

It helps to know the first year after a major loss is not going to be one of the best years in your life. But it doesn't have to be the worst year, either. After all, it has a purpose and a direction. You can come to the end of the year and know you have made a significant accomplishment just because you survived.

Passing the anniversary date of a major loss can be like a graduation day. People say to me, "I didn't think I could do it, but I did." I see a new sparkle in their eyes. They have endured the worst and survived. Often, anticipating the anniversary of your loved one's death is worse than the day itself. It helps if you are proactive about what you will do that day. Don't wait for

I didn't think I could do it, but I did.

it to come to you. If you plan to hole up in a corner and cry all day, that's okay as long as you plan ahead. It's proven to be a good idea to set a time, place, and environment for this memory cry, then plan for a meal out with a good friend or some other activity not by yourself.

The Lonely Year

The second year of grief calls for more patience with yourself than with anyone else. After getting through the first year, you may think life will return to normal. It doesn't. Many bereaved people call the second year of grief their lonely year. They say that surviving the first year proves

Many bereaved people call the second year of grief their lonely year.

you will make it. The second year proves how lonely it can be to make it without the one you lost.

It may seem as if you are starting all over again. You aren't. This is a good time to rejoin a grief support group if you dropped out.

Once the second-year crisis is past, you will be ready to start getting on with the reorganization of your life after loss. This doesn't mean there is no more grieving to do. It means you will have developed sufficient skills to handle your grief.

In time and with hard work, the good days will begin to outnumber the bad ones.

By the end of the third year, the pain of your loss should be diminished to the point where it finally seems manageable.

> *By the end of the third year, the pain of your loss should be diminished to the point where it finally seems manageable.*

Perhaps the most important growth that will come to you during grief recovery is the sense of confidence and pride that emerges. You have endured the very worst of all experiences and finished on top. You are a different person, a stronger person, and a better person than when you started. You have developed skills you never had and be well on your way to creating the all-important new normal for your life.

12

Beliefs that Help or Hurt
The Use and Abuse of Religion

Religious beliefs are a central element in grief recovery. If you are not a person who embraces religion, it makes a difference when a major loss occurs. If you do hold religious beliefs, it makes a difference what you expect from your faith.

People of faith need to know they do not have a pass to excuse them from major losses and the challenges of grief recovery. Nonreligious people do not necessarily have a more difficult time with grief recovery. Neither are they more susceptible to physical problems than religious people. The fact is that almost everyone has some sort of a belief system that is called into play when a major loss occurs.

My wife and I grew up as people who did not practice religion. Neither of our families attended church when we were children. As we became young adults, we were not antireligion. We simply gave it no thought.

It was two months after our marriage as teenagers when my wife's young brother was killed. He was playing with another boy in front of his parent's house and ran into the street. A car struck him, stopped, and backed over him. He died a few hours later.

When the news reached us, waves of shock and disbelief rolled over us. The first words out of our nonreligious mouths were, "Oh, God, not Ronnie! Please, don't let it be true."

Like many others, the fact that we never went to church didn't keep the name "God" from our vocabulary when tragedy struck. We were totally ignorant about the Bible and didn't have a clue what prayer was all about. We just knew we were hurting more than we had ever thought possible. We felt helpless in the face of this unthinkable loss. The sensation was as if we had fallen into a dark, damp, and deep well with no way to get out. We didn't know where else to turn, so we called out the name of God.

In the months that followed, we blamed God for Ronnie's death. We promised ourselves never to care about anyone so much again because God was so cruel.

We may have been disinterested in spiritual matters before our loss, but when confronted with death and grief, God was at the center of our thoughts.

Our experience was like that of thousands of other people. Several years later, I became a clergyman. I have officiated at more than a thousand funeral services. Time and time again, I have seen people going through the same challenges that we did—and asking the same questions: "Where is God?" "How could God let this happen?"

It isn't any easier for people of faith when they experience a major loss. In fact, people of faith usually ask exactly the same questions as everybody else at such times.

Talking about God and religion in times of major loss is almost universal.

- "I lost my faith in God when a car accident killed my wife and three of our children."
- "How can God allow such a thing to happen to an innocent child?"
- "Why did God take my loved one from me?"
- "My faith is all that held me together when we divorced."

- "Knowing my child is with God gives me the courage to go on."
- "My church was there for me and my family. I will always be grateful."

These statements all come from people who experienced a major loss. Every one of them expresses a normal reaction when life comes crashing down in a heap. Each of them expresses some form of religious faith.

The important issue for grief recovery is whether any belief system has a positive or a negative impact.

Spiritual beliefs can help you cope with major losses. They can work for you as you make your way through the process of grief and recover a sense of joy in your life.

Your beliefs can also be an almost insurmountable barrier to healing the deep wounds that have been inflicted upon you.

It all depends upon what you believe and how you practice your beliefs.

Dr. Howard Clinebell Jr., an internationally recognized authority on grief and loss, said a healthy religious faith and the support of a spiritual community have a unique ability to help turn *miserable minuses* into *positive pluses*. He affirmed that healthy religious beliefs can provide incredible strength for the task of grief recovery.

> *The important issue for grief recovery is whether a belief system has a positive or a negative impact.*

In her book *Living Through Personal Crisis*, Ann Kaiser Stearns says, "Faith is a powerful energy when it represents the trust that, with struggle, our sorrows can be overcome."[1]

However, religious faith can also get in the way of recovery. "Make a wish" religion is very popular. It is the kind of religious expression you see on some television programs. It's very "me"-centered. It assumes that the sphere of prayer is something like sitting on Santa's lap with a wish list for Christmas. If you are good enough, or, in this case, have enough faith, your wish will be granted—and you will avoid the grief and suffering experienced by the rest of the world.

This inappropriate, unhealthy religion looks for short, simple answers to complex questions for which there are no simple answers. It hopes for some magical way to either bypass grief or to resolve it quickly and painlessly.

If you look upon religious faith as an inoculation against the kinds of tragedies that happen to others, you will be unprepared when you experience a major loss—as you surely will. Faith in God is not a quick fix for sorrow and mourning. A reasonable expectation for healing the emotional wounds of grief is two to three years at the least. There is no shortcut through the process for people of faith. The requirements for healthy grief recovery are exactly the same for believers as for nonbelievers.

"Make a wish" religion ignores this basic fact of human life: **This is a mortal, frail, imperfect world in which the word *fair* doesn't always apply.**

Anna was the mother of two sons, both in their early forties. "Her boys" were the center of her life after her husband died suddenly from a heart attack. Anna could not believe her ears when she received a telephone call saying that one of her sons had taken his own life. The wounds from this terrible loss left a gaping hole in her life that was not even beginning to heal a year later—when her other son also committed suicide.

When Anna joined our grief support group, all of us wept with her as she related the pain and horror of her story. She had tried going to a church group in another city to find comfort. Instead, she was told that suicide was a sin and her boys were doomed to hell for eternity. She felt the unspoken question was "What was lacking in my faith to deserve such sorrow?" The pastor made it abundantly clear that he believed all losses were God's will to test people's character and faith. He told her that she should not question God's will, but accept it and pray for her own forgiveness.

There was nothing fair about Anna's losses. There certainly was nothing fair, helpful, or healthy in the response of that church and its pastor. Her grief wounds could have been deep, unresolved, and, perhaps, fatal if she had not rebelled against that kind of hurtful religion.

Anna's subsequent return to a good and satisfying life started with her coming to understand that this is, after all, a mortal, frail, imperfect world that is not always fair. That understanding enabled her to move beyond the "why?" questions and begin building a new life for herself. When our daughter, Jeanne, was in high school, we lived in a small community. There was a tightly knit sense of unity between the students, teachers, and parents.

Jeanne was one of seven song leaders who performed at sporting events and parades. During her senior year, one of the other song leaders was killed in an accident. She was riding with her boyfriend in an open vehicle on a mountain road. In a moment of carelessness, he lost control and the vehicle rolled, throwing out Jan and crushing her. She died instantly.

The funeral, held in the local mortuary, was packed with grieving students, parents, teachers, and community leaders. Everyone was in a state of shock. As we arrived, we passed small groups of teenagers huddled together, sobbing uncontrollably as they tried vainly to console each other. Again and again, I heard young voices asking why God would allow a tragedy like this to happen.

As the service started, more than two hundred pairs of tear-filled young eyes looked hopefully at the minister who was leading the funeral. When he began his sermon, I started to feel sick in the pit of my stomach.

He told those grief-stricken young people that Jan's death was a blessing. He said God was out walking in the heavenly garden, looking for the most beautiful flower to pick. Jan was chosen. He praised the young man whose mistake had caused her death for having such faith that he could smile and praise God that Jan was in heaven.

I wanted to stand up and scream, "NO!" I probably would have made matters worse if it hadn't been for my more-in-control wife. She placed her hand on top of my white knuckles, gripping the seat in front of me, and quietly said, "Not now. It isn't the time." She was right: this book has been a better place to express it.

Still, some of those young people left that place thinking they should not be too good, or they might be next on God's flower list. Others were encouraged to bury their grief and anger where it could fester and grow. Jan's boyfriend went on "praising the Lord" until the day he collapsed and wound up hospitalized to have extensive psychiatric treatment. Years later, I learned that at least seventy-five of those two hundred teenagers eventually required professional psychological treatment of some kind.

This experience and that of Anna remain for me the classic examples of the abuse of religion as a resource for grief recovery.

Letting Go of "Why?" Questions

Yearning for some rational explanation of tragic events is as normal as breathing. Asking "why" after a major loss is a common part of the grief recovery process, but it represents just one step along the way to wholeness. Recovery depends upon, among other things, letting go of the "why?" questions and turning to questions that begin with such words as *how* and *what*. "How do I go on with my life now that this has happened?" and "What can I do to recover a sense of joy and meaning in my life?"

> Whatever our religious orientation, the message is the same: Experiencing major losses, even though painful beyond words, is not optional.

Questions beginning with *how* or *what* imply an acknowledgment of the loss and an affirmation of survival.

When we experience a major loss, the only answer to the question "why?" is the one I've already given you: This is a mortal, frail, imperfect world in which the word *fair* doesn't always apply. The world is not perfect and life does not follow a perfect script. This is a world that operates by the laws of gravity and physics. Therefore, accidents do happen. It is a world in which human beings have free will. Therefore, mistakes will be made, people will be unkind and cruel, violent acts will take place.

We live near Tempe, Arizona, a high-energy, rapidly growing college town with a festive atmosphere. A young, single mother moved to Tempe from Chicago to get away from the dangers of her inner-city neighborhood. A month after she arrived, she stepped outside her apartment, holding her baby in her arms. A shot rang out and she fell to the ground, mortally wounded. A deranged neighbor didn't like the music she had been playing, and he shot her.

Trying to explain the "why?" of such an event is as foolish as it is meaningless.

Whatever our religious orientation, the message is the same: Experiencing major losses, even though painful beyond words, is not optional. There is no grand plan or purpose to every loss we face. There is neither a divine nor a demonic plot to "get us." It's just part of living in this less-than-perfect world. When people ask me what they did to deserve their loss I tell them, "You only did one thing—you were born and you didn't have anything to say about that."

Winston was driving in his car when he had a high-speed collision with an eighteen-wheel truck. For fifteen minutes he burned alive until a fire truck arrived. When he awoke from a morphine-induced coma after two months, his physical pain was beyond description. His emotional pain wasn't far behind. He said, "I was mad—mad at the truck driver, mad at the world, mad at God. How had I been named the delegate to suffer? I contemplated suicide daily. The hospital staff had to tie my hands down. Then the denial kicked in. I thought if I could dream in color for two months [as he did during the coma] and believe it was real, who's to say that being here like this wasn't just another chapter? This wasn't happening to me. I still dream of one day awakening from the nightmare into my old life."[2]

When terrible tragedies occur, be it a catastrophic injury to us, or the death of a loved one, our mind races as it tries to make sense of what has happened. Struggling with denial, anger, fear, and fantasy is a normal part of living the nightmare of a major loss. Healing begins when we confront reality and begin the work of grief.

Six years later, Winston said, "I had to take my grief by the horns. Complaining changes nothing. I am alive, I have family and friends who care for me, and I have a purpose."[3]

Those are the words and perceptions of a young man who has found the way to healing and a new normal for his life.

Beliefs that Help

Dell and Liz were active laypersons in their church. They held leadership positions that gave both of them high visibility. Both were equally well known in the community. People thought of them as the ideal married couple. When they announced they were getting a divorce, it came as a total shock to all who knew them.

Both of them felt they were not only failing at marriage and as parents, but were also betraying their church and friends. The church they belonged to was a large one and, at first, they made an effort to both remain in the congregation. It seemed possible that they could coexist with the many programs and multiple worship services, but it was not to be.

Dell transferred his membership to another church and soon was involved in the leadership of that church. Liz remained in her church where she organized a singles program that became a major tool for support and for church growth.

During the stress and conflict of their divorce proceedings, neither Dell nor Liz blamed God for their struggles. Both expressed strong faith in God's acceptance and found their hope for new lives among the people of their churches.

In time, both remarried and went on to happy and fulfilling lives.

Out of one couple's very real grief experience has emerged help and encouragement for others. Liz also developed a new career that has brought her much satisfaction. Both remain positive forces in their community.

Dell and Liz's faith was able to encompass something as challenging as divorce. The congregation was willing to enter into their loss and grieve with them without being judgmental. Because everyone involved practiced a healthy religious faith, something very good came out of a painful loss.

After her divorce, Liz married Wes. They were "soul mates" who enjoyed traveling to exotic places in the world or just sitting on their patio with a glass of wine. The wedded bliss ended when Wes was diagnosed with cancer and died some time later. Liz again turned to her faith and her church to work through her grief. She built another new normal for her life. She traveled with friends or her daughters, maintained the house she shared with Wes, and still pursued her career.

Five Ways Religion Helps

There are five very distinct, precise ways that a healthy religious faith, used appropriately, can be of tremendous help at a time of major loss.

1. Religion influences one's fundamental view of life. There are two different points of view from which to begin the task of grief recovery: For the nonbeliever, life is temporary and death is permanent. For the believer, death is temporary and life is permanent. These statements represent vastly different starting points for the task of grief recovery. The task to be done is the same for both, but the underlying belief system is quite different.

For the nonbeliever, death is the great canceled stamp on every achievement. One may have achieved many good things in life, but all that is canceled by death. To see life as temporary and death as permanent is to live by the motto "It was nice while it lasted, but it's all over now."

The permanency of death gives greater power to all the other losses in life. A well-known beer company ran a successful advertising campaign that said, "You only go around once in life, so grab for all the gusto you can get." The implication is we must get it now because there is no tomorrow. So, what if I invest all my life in a career—and am laid off? What if the marriage I thought would last forever ends in divorce? How do I face the inevitable decline in my physical strength that comes with age? How do I begin the process of grieving for my lost loved one?

I know there are answers for nonbelieving people because I see them recover from major losses. I must admit, however, that I don't know what those answers are. For June and me and our families, there were no answers and no hope until we turned to a faith in God.

For believers, the starting point of grief recovery is different. Death is not seen as the great cancellation. Death is no more than the ultimate nuisance in life. Because of my Christian faith I believe life is permanent and death is temporary. This does not in any way diminish the pain I feel when a loved one dies, nor does it make major losses any less real. June was a part of my life for sixty-nine years, sixty-four of those as my wife. Creating a new normal that does not include her physical presence is greatest challenge I have ever faced.

The believer looks at the experience of grieving as a dark valley through which we have to walk, just as the nonbeliever does. But for the believer the dark valley is not a box canyon. It is something through which to travel to get to a destination on the other side.

Death can wreak havoc in our life, but according to my faith system, neither death nor any other major loss has the power to cancel anything. I said that to a group of single parents and was asked, "What about divorce?" One lady said, "Those who lose their husbands to death are lucky. They can go to a grave and express their mourning and pray for the deceased. In my case, he is still walking around after our divorce and I only wish he were dead!" But even that woman had to admit that not all of her marriage had been bad. There had been moments of intimacy and times that were wonderful. The divorce did not have the power to cancel out those experiences unless she allowed it to.

I meet with people every week in a grief support group. Most are widowed, some have lost children, and a few, like me, had spouses who had Alzheimer's disease. These folks are able to express deep love and sentiment for their loved ones, even years after the person's death. They are able to relive precious moments and shed tears freely as we talk about the life they shared together. The dominant emotion, through tears and all, is that of hope. They know that only one phase of their connection is over; there is more that has just been interrupted.

2. Religious faith can provide the motivation required for grief recovery. Recovering from major losses takes a long time. Grief is fatiguing. It wears you down. Indescribable anguish can rip and tear at your insides, making the smallest responsibilities seem overwhelming. Sometimes just remembering a name or your telephone number is impossible.

Even while anguish pummels your feelings to the point of numbness, an oppressive, silent sadness leans on you, too, without ever seeming to let up. Under this kind of pressure, we need a

The first step on the path to renewed joy and vitality after a major loss is the most difficult of all.

source of motivation to begin the journey toward recovery. The first step on the path to renewed joy and vitality after a major loss is the most difficult of all.

This is the point at which joining a grief support group can be so important, but often taking that step is extremely difficult. Here, religious faith can play a major role and supply the motivation that is needed.

Jewish and Christian scriptures provide vivid images to help motivate us enough to take at least a baby step on the long road to recovery. The most familiar image is that found in the Psalms: "Yea, though I walk through the valley of the shadow of death, I will fear no evil." It is powerful imagery. It affirms that somebody has done it before. Nearly all newly bereaved people think they are the only ones to feel as they do. It also says that the path of grief is not a dead-end street but a well-marked trail leading to a destination and we do not travel it alone.

3. Religion is a powerful resource for overcoming anger and bitterness. Everyone who loses a loved one to death is angry. However, very few people express it openly. Some will vehemently deny being angry. Nevertheless, the signs of it are quite visible. Quarrels develop among family members, doctors and hospitals are criticized for not doing enough, people stay away from church, and efforts of friends to be helpful are rejected. The most difficult anger to talk about is that directed at the one(s) who died. Something inside says it isn't nice to be upset with a loved one who has died. But, like most parts of grief recovery, anger is not a well thought out, sensible response.

My parents died one day less than six months apart. Mom was fifty-four and Dad was fifty-seven. Both died of heart disease due to years of chain smoking and alcohol abuse. Their deaths came less than a year before I graduated from college, entered seminary, and changed careers from business to the ordained ministry. All classes for my bachelor's degree were at night while I worked full-time to support my family. I had looked forward to the day my parents would be there as I achieved a goal that took six years to complete. As I came to my big day knowing neither of them would be there, I realized, to my surprise, just how angry I was at them for dying. Fortunately, seminary for three years turned out to be a good place and sufficient time to gather and utilize the resources of Christianity for releasing anger and escaping bitterness.

It can be embarrassing, even humiliating, to talk about your anger when a loved one dies. I can tell you from experience that it isn't easy. If you have a religious faith of any kind, look to your scriptures and values for guidance. Hanging onto anger turns it into bitterness which works against everything you need to do to take care of yourself as you make the journey to grief recovery.

4. Religion is a great antidote for the loneliness that accompanies every major loss. One factor of grief that is common to all, regardless of the kind of loss experienced, is loneliness.

- "I am the only one who has ever felt this way."
- "Nobody else can understand my grief."
- "I am terribly lonely and I will always feel as I do right now."

To eat alone, watch a sunset alone, see some historic event on television alone, or just have a passing thought with no one else with whom to share it can cause fresh pain in each instance. Loneliness is the longest-lasting part of grief recovery. One widow of seventeen years said, "I have a good life with many friends. My days are filled with doing things I enjoy. But, the nights are still lonely."

Bereaved persons in the Christian tradition find there is great comfort in the words attributed to Jesus at the close of the Gospel of Matthew: "Remember, I am with you until the end of the age." I would interpret those words to mean loneliness is always an illusion. The statement means *that even if everyone else deserts me, I am not alone.* I may be in a crowd and feel all alone, but it's only an illusion. That belief is holding me together again in a time of personal loss. It doesn't make the pain of our losses any less, but it does make them bearable.

5. Your religious community can provide supportive strength. Never underestimate the supportive power of a religious community (church, synagogue, or fellowship). For all the failings of people in our churches and synagogues, there are no other groups who do so much at a time of major loss.

Funerals or memorial services held in the familiar surroundings of the bereaved person's regular place of worship offer a warmth not found in mortuary chapels. The simple act of providing food and a reception following the service—or taking food to the home—brings a sense of belonging and the assurance of being loved.

Ministers, priests, rabbis, and other professional religious leaders are the only people trained in grief counseling who do not need an invitation to reach out to people at a time of any major loss. Many times someone in our congregation has asked me to visit a neighbor or friend who has lost a loved one to death or who has gone through a divorce. In most cases, these are not people who have attended our church. They did not call to request my involvement; they just shared their sorrow with a neighbor or friend. I have never been refused entrance to a home when I have called. A doctor cannot do that and neither can a psychologist nor social worker. It is a rare privilege given to religious leaders, and with the privilege comes responsibility.

For all the religious community does, so much more can be done. Traditionally, congregations have been directly involved in supportive ways with bereaved people for about one week. With all that we now know about the length of normal grief recovery, it is imperative that congregations be involved for a minimum of two to three years. No other group in society is in such an advantageous position to be with people for the long haul. Providing grief support groups and divorce recovery groups, making contact on the anniversary of a death, and providing one-on-one contact to make reentry into church worship and activities easier are all ways that churches and synagogues help people through grief.

In some churches, a minister or layperson delivers a plant or flower arrangement to widowed persons on the anniversary of their spouse's death. Placing a silk rose in a green plant carries the message that the congregation hasn't forgotten and continues to care. In another church one of the pastors offers a booklet on coping with grief every month for a year.

Survivors are often challenged by a household responsibility that was carried out by the one who is now deceased. There are churches that keep a list of persons with skills in the most common areas of expertise, such as accounting, plumbing, electricity, automotive maintenance, cooking, and driving a car. When someone makes a need like this known, the church is able to refer the call to a volunteer, who provides the requested assistance.

Other churches have provided "shepherds" or other caregivers who are available to initiate contact on a regular basis to offer a listening ear. This has proven especially helpful to divorcing persons as well as to those who have lost a spouse or child to death.

In all of these ways, a healthy religious faith and a sensitive religious community can be of tremendous help in a time of major loss.

Three Things Religion Cannot Do

There are only three things that religious faith cannot do for us. Understanding and accepting these limitations is as important for grief recovery as using the things that faith does so well.

1. Religious faith cannot grant us immunity from loss. Practicing "fire insurance" religion (reading the Bible, attending services, tithing, praying, and doing good deeds for the primary purpose of avoiding divine "punishment") leaves folks ill-prepared to cope with the losses that are an inherent part of being a real person in this mortal world. Being persons of faith does not excuse us from our own mortality or that of our loved ones.

Those who pretend that the rules of life are different for people of faith face an almost certain sense of guilt when something goes wrong. We hear this point of view in such statements as "I wonder what he [or she] did to deserve that?" or "Somebody up there was sure looking out for you this time." I hear bereaved survivors question how God could allow their loved one to die when he or she "was such a good person who was loved so much."

It's vitally important to understand that death, divorce, and other major losses are not necessarily deserved or the result of God's taking time out from looking after us. The rain falls on the good and not-so-good alike. Good fortune seems to pour out on people without much regard to their morals or religious character—and so do major losses.

It's vitally important to understand that death, divorce, and other major losses are not necessarily deserved or the result of God's taking time out from looking after us.

In the early days of our religious experience, my wife and I belonged to a prayer group. We not only met to pray for ourselves, but also to pray for and visit sick people in their homes or in the hospital. A request came for the group to pray for a woman who was diagnosed with inoperable cancer. A tumor in her abdomen was the size of a grapefruit. She was given no chance for survival. Three members of the prayer group went to her home and prayed for her.

Upon her next visit to the doctor, the examination showed the tumor was gone. Needless to say there was joyful celebration, not only in her household, but also among members of the prayer group. They were sure God had intervened in response to their prayers and faithfulness. A month later, the woman died of a heart attack.

My wife and I were driving to a meeting at 2:30 p.m. on a clear, sunny Sunday afternoon. As we approached an intersection, the light turned green for us, and all cross-traffic was stopped. The intersection was empty. As we slowed, then proceeded through, we never saw the car that ran the red light and hit us broadside. Police estimated it was traveling at least 45 miles per hour at impact. Our car was totaled, but we escaped with only moderate injuries.

The response of some church members was "This can't happen to you—we can't get along without you." Others said, "God was sure looking out for you." A few days later, four teenagers were killed when their car went out of control and hit a light pole only a few blocks from the scene of our accident.

If we survived our accident because God was looking out for us, does that mean God decided not to care about those young people? If the woman whom the prayer group prayed for recovered from cancer because of their prayers, does it mean they failed to pray adequately for her heart? Or does God "draw straws" to see when we win or lose?

It seems to me to make much more sense, and to be much more in harmony with the basic tenets of the Judeo-Christian heritage, to say, "This is a mortal, imperfect, frail, and flawed world. Life is not always fair. Tragedy and major loss are as much a part of life as victory and times of joy. As a human being, I am subject to these realities. So are my loved ones. My one and only assurance from God is that I will never be deserted in any circumstance."

Such a perspective may not be comfortable, but it is real, and it provides a solid foundation for using faith in the most helpful way at the time of a major loss.

2. Religious faith cannot give us back our dead loved ones or our dead relationships. The one thing bereaved persons want more than anything else is to have their loved ones returned to them as healthy persons. It is the one thing that neither God nor we can give them.

Strange as it may seem, to acknowledge this fact up front with a survivor is always comforting. It says that we understand the enormity of the loss, and it lets the bereaved person know that we have no simple or pat answers. In the face of a major loss, every person needs compassion, understanding, a listening ear, and people who are willing to carry out needed tasks without being asked. To downplay the pain of a death or divorce with religious platitudes frequently only magnifies the sense of loss.

For the caregiver to acknowledge the finality of the loss is often the beginning of the journey to recovery for the survivor. Loss means gone at least for the duration of this life. The mechanism of denial is overcome when the survivor understands *and acts on* this excruciatingly painful reality. It is at this point that the most basic decision of recovery can be made: "I will live." That pledge will have to be renewed many times throughout the first year of recovery.

To acknowledge that our religious faith cannot bring back our dead loved ones is in no way a denial of life after death. I have no doubt that my wife, friends, and family members who have died are "okay" in that mysterious place we call heaven. While that affirmation gives me a certain sense of comfort, it does not diminish my sadness or loneliness at losing them. One thing is clear: I will not see them again in this life. That part of my history has ended.

Frequently people are told that their loved ones are in a better place. My personal and professional experience say that those are empty words of someone grasping at straws for something comforting to say. It does the opposite. It implies the bereaved person's grief should therefore be lessened and that can inhibit grief recovery and increase the health risk of the bereaved person.

We must understand that "loss" equals "gone for the rest of my life." The possibility for a full and rewarding life after any loss begins with this understanding.

3. Religious faith cannot provide a shortcut through grief. Every clergyperson I know wishes this were not true. We would give anything to find a pathway of faith that would take people from the point of their losses to a full recovery—and do it quickly. Unfortunately, such a shortcut isn't available to us. Some of us have to experience personal loss before we catch on.

It is another of those strange-but-true facts of grief recovery that religious faith serves us best when we start out understanding that the pain of grief will not be less nor will the path to recovery be shorter because of our religion.

Again, for the sake of the physical health of bereaved persons if nothing else, clergy and laity must never let people think that because they have prayed for them, the bereaved person's grief should be lessened. People who maintain a classic "stiff upper lip" and who come back to church without tears should not be publicly praised or held up as the ideal of faith. More often than not, those who are having the worst time—who weep uncontrollably and seem to need the most help—are actually doing the best job of grieving.

Trying to shortcut the grieving process is like giving someone with hypoglycemia a major dose of sugar. The person might feel quite high—for a little while—but an even greater crash will follow.

"We want you to know we will be with you every step of the way."

Divorcing and bereaved people need assurance from their pastors and congregations that their church will not desert them over the long haul of grief recovery. The church can provide support groups, special programs dealing with losses, and a bereavement-care team, and it can make the effort to *maintain* contact with those who have suffered a major loss for at least two years (three is better). In these ways the church can say, "We know this is a long, tough, and painful journey for you. We want you to know we will be with you every step of the way."

Religion and You

Religion and the religious community can be sources of strength and courage for you in times of major loss. But understand that loss and grief are a part of life for the believer and nonbeliever alike. All of us are subject to disappointment, heartbreak, and death. When we suffer a major loss it hurts—regardless of our faith or lack of faith.

When we suffer a major loss it hurts—regardless of our faith or lack of faith.

You will search for hope. The kind of hope that will serve you best acknowledges life will never be the same again, but insists that life after loss can still be full and good. The resources of religious faith can be strong motivators to reach for this hope. If you believe God has been present with human losses for a long time, you will be encouraged to try again when you want to quit. You will be able to accept new places, new stages of life. You will know that whatever challenges you face now, or in some future loss, you will not face them alone.

Personal Postscript from the Author

Twenty-four hours after June died, one of our granddaughters gave birth to her first child, a son. She, along with her husband and son, live in another state. I decided that going to see newly born Caleb would be good for me. Four days later, I left a doctor's office where I had some biopsies done and was driving back home to pack for a flight at three o'clock the next morning. My mind was rehearsing all I had to do so I wouldn't forget some essential thing, such as my boarding pass.

My thoughts were interrupted by the clear, unmistakable sound of June's voice in my mind, saying, "Bob, I'm fine. It's wonderful!" It startled me so much that I pulled to the side of the road. June had not been able to call me by name for two months before her death. It was her voice sound and her way of expressing herself. No conversation. Just five words I needed to hear more than anything to give me strength to do the grief work I have needed to do from that day until now. I share this as an obviously subjective experience because it has been my rock of hope. I hope it encourages you, too.

—Bob

13

Quiet Losses
Private Struggles Grieved in Silence

Author's Note: In the fourth and fifth editions of *Life after Loss*, this chapter was largely the work of my wife, June Deits. It was her special contribution to people who experience losses that seem more difficult to talk about with other people. Her insights came out of a series of personal losses that began when she was four years of age. They included being the victim of sexual abuse as a child, the loss of a breast to cancer, and the onset of memory loss that progressed to Alzheimer's disease and finally took her life. By sharing her experiences for as long as she was able to do so, June enabled countless men and women to break a silence they had felt compelled to keep. She called them quiet losses. In her honor I will try to faithfully share her insights so that her devotion to others can go on.

All major losses are worthy of grief. There is no such thing as an easy loss. If it doesn't hurt, it isn't a loss. You have already read in this book that the worst kind of a loss is the one that happens to you. That isn't a theory, it's a fact that is documented in thousands, if not millions, of lives.

However, the pain of a loss can be even more intense if you perceive that you can't talk about it. Experts call such losses disenfranchisement. June preferred to call them quiet losses. She said, "There are no sounds heard by the world around as you make your way through the dark valley of grief. The pain is excruciating, as with all major losses, but seems magnified because you think it must be kept to yourself. With quiet losses, there aren't any arms to reach out and hold you, or sympathetic shoulders on which to cry. The dominant word in your head is *shame*."

Throughout this book, I have been sharing real-life stories of real people, while carefully protecting their identity with fictitious names, unless they agreed to have their real names used. As June and I talked about this chapter on silent losses, we considered hiding her identity. However, precisely because these quiet losses are usually suffered alone, we decided not to do that. Therefore, instead of my writing about her experiences and covering her identity, June told them personally. Now, I need to tell you her story because it is as important as ever for you to hear. There are only a small number of photographs of June as a young child. In most of them she appears to be a typical happy child with a winning smile. There is just one that she said reveals what was really going on inside of her. This photo shows an incredibly sad little girl who is obviously deeply troubled. June said that even when she looked at the happy photos, what she saw was a little person wrapped up in a blanket of guilt and fear. No one seemed to notice that she cried when she heard music and bit her fingernails until they bled. Biting her nails continued until she was fifty years old.

> *The pain of a loss can be even more intense if you perceive that you can't talk about it.*

The Loss of Innocence

June was barely four years old when she was the victim of sexual abuse for the first time. Without a vocabulary to describe it or any understanding of the magnitude of the loss, her childhood innocence about sexuality was taken from her. For almost fifty years the events were buried beneath the level of her conscious mind. She "forgot" it ever happened—but it was always with her and impacted both of us after we were married.

One day, while she was driving the car, the memories started coming back. The images were terrifying and disgusting. She said later she had to pull to the side of the road to avoid causing an accident. It was that evening that she hesitantly told me what had happened. I could see that it was taking courage and trust in our relationship for her to open up. I held her, listened to her, and assured her she had nothing of which to be ashamed. Her parents later confirmed the reality of her memories.

Those reading this book who have been victims of abuse will understand. There are many of you who will. Studies indicate up to 50 percent of women and 40 percent of men have been the victims of some form of sexual abuse as children. This means there are millions who have suffered in silence. Doing so makes one of the most destructive experiences in life more painful than it already is.

It was always June's hope that as she broke the silence and talked about her experience, it would help others face their own past without fear. Perhaps if this applies to you, you, too, will decide to cease being quiet about your loss.

June's childhood nightmare began when a neighbor became a friend to her parents. They never suspected that his real motive was getting access to their daughter. June was thrilled when "the mister," as she was told to call him, first offered to swing her on his backyard play set. It was great to have the attention of this grandfatherly man. Soon, however, she came to dread her visits to his home. "The mister" would take her into a storage shed, hold her on his lap so she couldn't move, and warn her not to yell. She said his hands were rough and caused intense pain in parts of her body she barely understood. If she cried, she was told the pain was her fault. Sometimes these encounters took place in the kitchen of her parent's home while they were watching television in another room. If she cried, she was told she would be in trouble with her parents and they wouldn't let her live there anymore.

Eventually, her family moved to another neighborhood and the visits to "the mister" stopped. She had no outward signs of the abuse on her body. However, the emotional scars ran deep and plagued her life for decades.

Her body had become sexualized long before its time. The innocence of childhood was gone. As she grew, June said there always seemed to be a vulnerability about her that seemed to draw unwanted advances from male playmates and other grown men. She blamed herself and wondered what she was doing wrong. Her father was raised on a farm in Oklahoma and had only a seventh grade education. He was a good man but certainly not sophisticated. He once told June that she attracted men like an animal in heat. She was less than eight years old at the time.

We were married the day after June's nineteenth birthday. I was five months younger. We had not had sex before our marriage (although the idea crossed our minds every time we were alone). We were about as naive as two people can be, but we were in love and looked forward to life as a grown-up married couple.

From the beginning, our sexual relationship was a mixture of joy and frustration. If I walked up behind her and put my arms around her, she would freeze. Neither of us understood why my act of affection was repulsive to her. The same kind of thing was often true after making love. Neither of us had any idea of the dark memories buried beneath the surface of June's awareness. The only thing we knew was she dreaded any intrusion into her private space. She continued to chew her fingernails and often cried because she could not stop.

As the years went on, for all that was good in our lives, including being married, three children, and a large group of friends, it was obvious June was never content. She would sometimes talk about the sadness of her childhood. We did not talk about her reaction to sex because that would often lead to a quarrel.

It was as June approached her fifty-first birthday that the flashbacks came. Just breaking the awful silence of forty-seven years was its own reward. As her memories unfolded, I listened and cried with her for the innocent little girl who had been wounded so deeply.

The more we talked, the more I was able to help June see that it wasn't her fault. She was able to see and understand that she had done nothing wrong. With the silence finally broken, she discovered she was a normal person who was now ready to deal with a terrible experience in a healthy way.

Contentment didn't come overnight, but it came. The final step in putting the past to rest came when she stood before a thousand people in our church and shared her story with them. She subsequently repeated it many times in workshops and seminars across the country. The response was always the same. Women and men shook her hand or gave her a hug and whispered in her ear that they, too, were victims. They thanked her for opening the door to their memories and giving them the courage to begin talking about their experiences. Some told her that it was while they were listening to her that they faced their own experience for the first time. On one occasion, June and I spoke to military chaplains. At their request, June shared her story. Ten women chaplains and two men sought her out afterward to let her know they shared a common secret. Before we left she urged them to form a support group with each other so they could have a safe place to break the silence.

No Longer Silent

The loss of innocence is a terrible loss. The pain is excruciating. Those whose mind cannot cope with the emotional pain often do what June did: bury it below the level of consciousness. If that meant that it had gone away, it would be okay, but it isn't gone, and it surely isn't okay.

This hidden emotional wound diminished the quality of her adolescent and adult life. She could not explain her nervousness. She was ashamed that she could not keep from biting her fingernails. There never was a time when she felt totally contented or happy until the day she broke the silence. It was on that day that her healing began.

Over the ensuing years, she walked more lightly and laughed more easily than ever before in her life. She never bit her fingernails again.

June found it was essential for her own growth and healing to release the anger she felt toward "the mister" and her parents. She realized that he was an old man with a twisted personality and that her parents were too unsophisticated to know how to deal with it. It was clear that her father's sense of ethics would mean either he would actually have to shoot the man or move his family away. He did the latter, not out of cowardice, but out of compassion for his wife and children.

I heard June say in lectures many times: "My value as a person is not diminished by the tragedy of my experience. I am not less desirable as a woman or a wife. My life is good—very good. But first the silence had to be broken."

If you are reading this with more than a detached interest, my thoughts are with you. I learned from June that you start by facing the experience head-on. It often helps to put your memories and feelings in writing. Find at least one trustworthy person with whom you can share everything. Write yourself reminders that you did nothing wrong and nothing of your value as a person has been taken from you.

Here are some of June's discoveries:

- As you break the silence, you will find your emotional pain decreasing.
- If you listen carefully, you will find others who are also suffering in silence. You can find more healing together than any of you will find alone.
- Find a way to let go of your stored-up anger. It's hurting you far more than those at whom it is aimed.
- Don't be afraid to enjoy your first feelings of relief and joy. You deserve them.

Loss of Body Parts

The loss of innocence is not the only loss that can be difficult to share with others.

On Valentine's Day 1994, June lost her left breast to cancer. Until that time, neither of us considered how much the loss of a body part impacts emotions—or how difficult it is to talk about it.

Our awareness of the problem changed the day June's routine mammogram revealed a suspicious cluster of calcifications. I heard the news at the same time June did. I was also on the telephone when the doctor called to say the biopsy had revealed cancer.

Once the initial shock and disbelief subsided, we realized we had to make two decisions:

1. What kind of treatment should June have?
2. Who do we tell about this frightening development?

Telling our grown children was automatic. The challenge was to decide who else should hear about it. I was the senior minister of a church whose attendance sometimes exceeded 2,500. Because of the earlier editions of *Life after Loss*, we lectured and led seminars across the nation. We have been in contact with thousands of people who know us and care about us. We wondered just how private or public June should be with the news of her cancer.

It would be quite easy for her to keep the news secret. She could have whatever surgical procedure was required, and no one but our grown children and I would know the difference. We could make up a story about why June needed a little time off from public activity. No one outside our family would have to know that a symbol of her femininity, which was very important to her, had been disfigured. If she were fortunate enough to overcome the cancer, no one else would know at all.

June said cancer seemed like a "dirty" disease to her. We were aware that people who smoke or eat a high-fat diet are at higher risk for cancer. June told me she could just hear the whispers, "What has she done to get cancer?" She felt bad enough on her own because she thought her body had betrayed her.

Listening to her, it was clear that if she had broken a bone, contracted a virus of some kind, or even had a coronary problem, she would not have had the same desire for secrecy. They seemed to her like "clean" problems, even though some can be as life-threatening as cancer.

However, she had cancer, and had to deal with it and with her desire to keep silent about it. I told her that I would totally support whatever decision she made.

We learned very quickly that the only sensible treatment for her was the complete removal of her breast. There was a 50 percent chance of nonrecurrence if she just had radiation treatments, a 75 percent chance with a lumpectomy, and 90 percent chance with a mastectomy. Because the mammogram had discovered it early, the cancer was not invasive. There was no spreading of the cancer to lymph nodes or other parts of her body. She was, therefore, a candidate for an implant. This positive news actually reinforced her option for silence. Her body would not be disfigured, at least outwardly. Nobody would know except those she chose to tell.

June and I talked at great lengths in the days between the diagnosis and her surgery. She knew I would not think less of her with only one breast, but she let me know that she wondered if I would see her as sexually desirable as before. I assured June I would feel no differently. I told her I wanted her with me for the rest of our lives and it made no difference how many breasts she had. I think the turning point came when I reminded her that the primary purpose of the female breast is to nurse children. Since those days were decades into the past, I told her I wondered how many more babies she planned to nurse. It seemed to help put the challenge in a new perspective.

June always had a healthy attitude about the appearance of her body. She had thyroid surgery when she was twenty-six years old. There had been a faint scar across her throat since that time. It never bothered her. She had stretch marks on her abdomen as the legacy of giving birth to three children. However, losing a breast was quite another challenge. We both came to the conclusion that it is the connection between breasts or other parts of the body related to sexuality that makes it especially challenging to lose them. It also makes it more difficult to talk about it.

It wasn't just her physical attractiveness that concerned her. Her own sense of identity as a woman was involved. It was easy to understand that her breast was more than an appendage on her body. It was part of her identity as a woman. Letting go of it was not an easy decision for her—until she weighed the value of her life against a breast. She would later say that whatever sadness she would have at its loss, at least she would be alive to feel it.

In a typical June move, she wrote a personal letter headed "Goodbye, My Breast." She thanked her breast for being part of her for so many years and for the beauty it had brought to her body. She expressed gratitude for its function when babies were born and for the pleasure of feeling me touch it. She assured her breast that although an artificial mound would replace it for cosmetic purposes, nothing would ever take its place in her heart. I confess that when she gave the letter to me to read, I cried, not in sadness for the lost breast, but in awe of her courage and the tender love she had for it.

June knew it was time to break the silence once more.

She knew that if she was struggling with the challenge of cancer and losing a breast, so were others who were facing a similar struggle in silence. They deserved to have someone open the door to talking about it. June determined to be one who would do it.

On the Sunday before her surgery, I informed the whole church that June had breast cancer and would have a mastectomy. Following the service, she stood with me at the back door as usual as people were leaving.

One woman after another stepped up, took her hand, and said, "I am a ten-year survivor," "I am a twenty-year survivor," "I am trying to decide what to do myself." Men shared with her that they had been victims of prostate cancer, wished her well, and reminded her that life is more precious than any part of the body or any body function. To her great surprise, it was the men who were, if anything, most support-ive and encouraging.

There were some men and women who did not respond in helpful ways. Some people made an obvious point of shaking my hand, but walking around June as if she either was not there or breast cancer was contagious. Others touched her as though she was suddenly breakable. She said several people glanced in the direction of her chest, as if to see which breast was affected. Some of her friends just didn't want to talk about it. Women with whom she had shared in-depth conversations in the past now wanted no more than a minute to pass the time of day.

Such reactions were to be expected. June and I both knew that. Ei-ther of us could have been guilty of similar forms of rejection with other people in the past and never have known it. But rejections were a tiny minority. The vast majority of people with whom she shared the news of her cancer were very supportive.

On the day of her mastectomy the prayers of more than two thou-sand people were with her. She had arranged for a plastic surgeon to be present with the cancer surgeon so that a temporary, inflatable implant could be placed as soon as the breast was removed. She went into sur-gery at seven a.m. At seven p.m. the same day, she came home.

As soon as she recovered sufficiently, she formed a cancer support group for women. They met in one room while I met with the husband or boyfriend of the women in my office. Over the years that followed, we mourned the deaths of three of the women in June's group. It was comforting to know they did not have to die in silence.

June became a volunteer with the American Cancer Society in a program called Reach to Recovery. She visited other women just before or after breast cancer surgery. In addition to delivering a packet of help-ful materials, often including a temporary prosthesis, she was an agent of listening and encouragement. It was another way to help break the silence barrier. June was cheerful, looked great, and was very positive about the experience. On one visit she was alone with a woman about to have breast surgery. The woman was sobbing uncontrollably about how awful she was going to look. June opened her blouse and pulled up the left side of her bra and asked, "Does this look awful to you?" The woman said, "No, it looks fine," and stopped crying.

I took her with me when I visited people in the church prior to their cancer surgeries of any kind. They were glad to have me come and pray with them, but it was obvious the one they really wanted to see was June, so they could talk with a real live cancer survivor.

June and another breast cancer survivor started an annual "Daffodil Sunday" in our church. Daffodils are the official flower of the American Cancer Society, the first flower of spring and a sign of hope. There would be four thousand daffodils in the front of the church. People made donations to buy a few with money going to the American Cancer Society for research and patient services. The flowers were placed in honor of someone who was a cancer survivor, in memory of one who had died, or in gratitude if the one buying the flowers was a survivor. A list of these names were printed in the bulletin. Cancer survivors in attendance that day were invited to stand, if they are comfortable doing so. More than a thousand have utilized this means to break the silence of their own cancers. Over the course of several years, about $88,000 was raised for American Cancer Society. It was always June's goal to reach $100,000, but that was not to be.

June and I made presentations on the subject of "coping with cancer as a couple" many times. We saw it open the door for other couples facing cancer to talk more freely with each other.

All this came about because June made the decision not to keep her cancer a private matter. She said that in some ways, it felt as if she were making private parts of her body visible to the whole world. It took a long time for her to get comfortable when she looked in a mirror and saw one breast and one "mound." Nevertheless, she discovered there is life after the loss of a breast—or any body part. There is an end to grieving that loss. Healing comes as much from refusing to be quiet about it as from the defeat of the illness.

To keep silence is like having a wound that never completely heals. We have known people who lived with a colostomy or artificial limb who did everything they could to keep their "handicap" secret. There have been women who had a breast or uterus removed and men who lost sexual function due to prostate surgery. I knew of a few men who had one or both testicles removed. I can only imagine the fears and shame of these people because none of them ever talked about it.

June always tried to practice the old saying: "If life gives you lemons, make lemonade." We thought she was finished making lemonade after coping with sexual abuse as a child and having cancer, but we were wrong. There is no quota system to major losses. Having one loss, or two, is never a guarantee that there will not be more. That was June's experience.

In 2004, I realized there were times when June could not remember what someone said to her five minutes before. She accused me of not speaking loudly enough. I thought she might be having hearing loss, so scheduled her for a hearing test. It revealed that her hearing was normal for her age, except in the range of my voice. (I insisted that it was a selective loss!)

The real problem soon became clear. June was having memory loss. She could not remember conversations a few minutes after they took place. She could hear what was said, but could not retain it in her brain. She struggled with names and forgot plans we had made. I began making weekly schedules that June could carry with her at all times.

She felt stupid and foolish. She didn't want anyone to notice what was happening to her. The prospect of memory loss was more frightening than cancer: Cancer had the power to kill her, but not to humiliate her. When she faced cancer, there was a specific enemy and a well-defined way of attacking it. Dealing with dementia was totally different.

When former president Ronald Reagan was diagnosed with Alzheimer's disease, he said, "Now I enter the twilight years of my life." June was adamant. She did not want any "twilight" years! She said, "When I die, I want to go out knowing who is there and what's going on around me."

Richard Taylor, in his book *Alzheimer's from the Inside Out*, said, "Individuals have a cold, have cancer, have the measles. Alzheimer's has the individual."[1] It is a frightening prospect.

June's father died from Alzheimer's disease. What happened to him during his last years became her worst nightmare.

We tried in every way possible to keep her failing memory a secret. She avoided situations where she could embarrass herself, stayed close to me in group gatherings so I could cover for her, and resigned from areas of responsibility.

We decided that June should be tested to find out the extent of her memory loss and, perhaps, its cause. The days leading up to the tests were filled with anxiety and apprehension. She would wake up during the night trembling with fear and be unable to go back to sleep. Her imagination ran wild with horrible images of her father before he died. As we drove to Mayo Clinic for the two days of testing, waves of nausea ran over her. By the end of the second day, we were both exhausted from the stress.

When the results were in, it was clear that June's short-term memory was impaired. A normal score on one of the tests she was given is 25 to 30. June's score was 21. It's called mild cognitive impairment (MCI).

She began taking medication that had shown some possibility of helping. She also diligently worked mind exercising games on the computer.

However, they did nothing more than perhaps slow the steady progression of her memory loss. By end of 2008, her diagnosis was Alzheimer's-type dementia. *Dementia* means a crippling memory loss for which there are at least fifteen causes. Alzheimer's disease accounts for 70 percent of them. As of the day I am writing this, it is 100 percent fatal.

In 2009 June entered a clinical trial of an experimental drug. Over the next three years she received injections of the drug every thirteen weeks. The trial also involved multiple MRIs of her brain, PET scans, lumbar punctures, blood draws, and regular testing of her memory. As her dementia progressed, June continued lecturing with me. She still wanted to help people break their silence about losses that were more difficult to talk about. I shortened her presentations, printed them so they were easier to read, and stood next to her while she spoke so I could help keep her focused.

The final time she was able to lecture was in 2010. She struggled to read the pages and had tears in her eyes when she finished. I think she realized it was going to be the last time she could do it.

During part of this talk, she shared these experiences:

Bob and I are dancers. We have danced on roller skates competitively, danced ballroom showcases, and performed Argentine tango in front of an audience of a thousand. I can still dance tango socially because the follower is not supposed to anticipate the movements. But now, I can't remember the steps of other dances.

Anything that brings stress to my life seems to impact my memory skills negatively. Six months after the death of two of my closest friends, my back pain became unbearable. A series of tests revealed deterioration in my spine. I had two back fusion surgeries fifteen months apart. In between them, I had to take a narcotic painkiller which scrambled my thinking even more. At times I was disoriented and unable to perform even the simplest task without help. The pain was gone after the second surgery but the progression of the disease went on.

It is frustrating and frightening. As much as I abhor the thought of any "twilight" in my life, I see the specter of it looming before me. One thing is clear. Unlike my cancer, at this time there is no cure. Our hope is in the long list of treatments being tested here and around the world. In the meantime, I am doing everything I can to hold it back and function as normally as possible.

The last thing I want is for people to look at me as either stupid or a senile old lady who doesn't know what day it is or what meal comes next.

However, this is perhaps the ultimate "quiet loss," ranking right up there with AIDS in the desire to keep it hidden. But openness has become a lifestyle for us. I believe all losses, including this one, are more manageable if they are not kept under a blanket of silence. It is my hope that by sharing my experience with dementia, some of the 5 million people in the United States who have been diagnosed with it will find hope and comfort. Someone new is diagnosed with Alzheimer's alone every seventy-two seconds. No one should ever face the terror of "twilight years" alone.

As she concluded her lecture, the people stood as one and applauded her.

By the middle of 2012, Alzheimer's had reduced June to her worst fears. Her score on the memory test, on which she had scored 21 in 2004, was now 2. She could no longer carry on even the most basic functions of her life. In early 2013, I could no longer care for her safely at home and moved her to a memory care facility. It was the most difficult, gut-wrenching decision I ever made. I cared for her at the facility six to nine hours a day. Occasionally, I was able to take her out in her wheelchair to our favorite Italian restaurant. June responded positively every time. Sometimes she could talk there when that ability was lost everywhere else. The progression of Alzheimer's was like an invisible glacier that moved relentlessly with no way to slow it down or stop it. June's definition of Alzheimer's was spot on. She said, "*Fighting Alzheimer's is like trying to punch a cloud. You hit it and there is nothing there. Then, it swallows you.*"

From the beginning, June always insisted that when she died, she wanted to go out knowing who was there and what was going on around her. The strength of her will enabled her to achieve that victory. On February 18, 2016, she was lying on her bed with our three children and one granddaughter gathered around with me. She was seeming to be looking at something beyond us when Lauren, a granddaughter, leaned in front of her and said, "Grandma, look at me!" June turned her eyes to look at Lauren for several seconds, then looked away and was gone. She had said, "When I die, I want to go out knowing who is there and what's going on around me." That wish was fulfilled.

It is my hope, and I know it would be hers, that even from the other side of death, she will help you and others to break any silence that stands in the way of healing from grief.

Other Quiet Losses

I know a mother whose only children were two sons. They both told her they were gay on the same day. She agonized in silence that her dreams of grandchildren would never be realized.

The death of a pet can bring grief that is difficult to share for fear of looking weak or foolish. Well-meaning friends who suggest "get another one and get over it" don't help.

We have known people who moved from one state to another as a result of a job promotion. The deep grief they felt at leaving familiar places and people was masked behind smiling faces. They privately ask, "Who will understand my sadness when I should be so happy?"

Not everybody will understand. That's a simple fact of this real world. If you don't expect everybody to react sympathetically, you won't add to your disappointments. You can be sure that many more will support you than will be put off by your openness. Be sure you focus your attention on those who give support. Don't take your cues from people who don't understand your sadness.

June and I found the following exercise to be helpful. Try it. I think you will like it.

1. Identify a loss about which it is difficult for you to tell others.
2. Write down what you think would happen if other people knew about it. Read it out loud to yourself at least three times. Do you need to change anything?
3. Find someone with whom you can risk sharing your experience and ask them to read what you have written. Talk about your feelings.
4. Ask that person to help you identify the possible positive outcome of letting others know what has happened to you. How might other people actually be helped?
5. Choose the most appealing of these and experiment in pursuing that outcome.

Read the balance of this book and follow the guidance it gives for recovering from any loss—especially the quiet ones.

14

Children and Grief
It's a Big Hurt for Little People, Too

Try to imagine what it is like to experience the death of a loved one, the breakup of your family, or any other major loss as a child. If you can imagine these circumstances, you have some idea of how children grieve:

- You have all the sadness, fear, anger, and other emotions that adults have.
- You do not have the vocabulary to express the way you are feeling.
- Your limited exposure to life leaves you with little understanding of what is happening to you.
- You probably assume you are to blame in some way.
- The adults on whom you depend for daily care are distracted, upset, and seem to forget you.

When someone dies, children feel the loss as much as any adult. They just don't have the words to tell us about their feelings.

Remember that whereas adults internalize their feelings, children act them out. Their vocabulary may be limited, but their behavior can reveal volumes about their feelings.

When adults try to shelter and protect them from the experience, children turn to their own imaginations, which often suggest a situation even worse than the real one. Young children often assume they are somehow to blame for the loss. They are used to thinking in terms of blame for spilled drinks and broken toys. It's easy for children to interpret the combination of adult silence and sadness as disappointment in them. If a parent or grandparent dies, the child may think that all adults in his or her life will die. If their parents divorce, children may think it is they who are no longer loved.

Young children often assume they are somehow to blame for the loss.

As adults, we play a crucial role in the future lives of children after they experience a major loss. When the adults respond in ways that help the child face loss and work through grief just as we must do, there are no lasting emotional scars. When adults fail to respond in helpful ways, the effects may be seen for the rest of the child's life. Among these effects is the continuation of the problem to another generation. The child who carries grief wounds into adulthood will tend to be uncaring and unhelpful to others in times of grief.

Matthew and Lisa were six and eight years old respectively when their mother put them in the kitchen with bowls of cereal, went into the family den, and shot herself. The children found her body and called neighbors for help.

The children's father was wise enough to take them to a skilled counselor. She sat on the floor with Matthew and Lisa, helping them draw pictures of their mommy. Some of their pictures reflected their anger at their mom for leaving them. Others showed the fear they were feeling. Others depicted better times when Mom was happy.

Remember that whereas adults internalize feelings, children act them out.

On the day of the funeral, Matthew and Lisa placed some of their drawings in the casket with the body of their mother. They each added a small gift they had chosen.

Over the next several months, the counselor helped them understand that their mother did not die because she was angry at them. She assured them her death had nothing to do with their failure to pick up clothes or toys. It wasn't because they had been naughty or hadn't eaten everything on their plates at dinner. Mom was very sad down inside. She loved them and didn't mean to make them sad. Her death was a tragic event that she couldn't help.

Sunday school teachers in Matthew and Lisa's church were instructed to be prepared to listen to them carefully and to be sure they understood it was not God's will for their mother to die.

In time, their father remarried. Matthew and Lisa became happy in their new home. They formed a strong bond with their stepmother, who made sure they had pleasant memories of their biological mother. Today, they are contented, well-adjusted adults. The wounds of the past are healed.

When the adults in a child's life do not respond in appropriate ways, the results can be drastically different than Matthew and Lisa's experience. Rosemary was about the same age as Matthew and Lisa when her life was turned upside down. Her father, who suffered from chronic depression, was successful in taking his own life on the fourth attempt. Unfortunately for Rosemary, the adults in her life did not respond in a healthy way as happened with Matthew and Lisa.

When the adults respond in ways that help the child face loss and work through grief just as we must do, there are no lasting emotional scars.

Her mother became addicted to alcohol and drugs; withdrew from the support of family, friends, and church; and "went off the deep end." She entered into multiple sexual relationships and worked only sporadically. Rosemary reverted to bedwetting, lost weight, and couldn't sleep. She seemed frightened and insecure. The probability is high that Rosemary suffered emotional scars that damaged the quality of her life for many years and perhaps for a lifetime.

Telling Children about Death

To provide the opportunity for healing that children need after a death, adults can do the following five things:

1. Provide an open, honest atmosphere in which it is easy for children to ask questions and express their thoughts and feelings. This includes involving children in family discussions about the person, the death, and funeral plans. It may be important to sit on the floor while talking with younger children. Holding them on your lap and giving frequent assurances of their security and your love for them can ease many fears. Remember: While adults internalize feelings, children act them out. Watch for signs that tell you the children need your attention. A good rule of thumb is to treat any significant change in a child's normal behavior as a warning sign. The outgoing, happy child may become introverted and withdrawn. A child who loves hugs may no longer welcome being held.

2. Understand how children are interpreting their experience with death. I find that asking children specific questions enables them to tell me what they are thinking and feeling. I ask such questions as:

- Have you ever been to a funeral? What was it like?
- Have you ever seen or touched a dead person?
- If you go to the funeral, what do you think you will see?
- What else do you know about death and funerals?
- What would you like to know?
- What would you like to ask _____ [name of the deceased person]?

The fact that you are willing to talk matter-of-factly about these things is reassuring to children. It is helpful for you to sit on the floor or at a low table with them. It also helps to provide paper and crayons, a coloring book, or modeling clay to enable children to express themselves nonverbally.

3. Give correct and factual information as simply as you can. Dispel myths and the creations of the child's imagination. Do not use such phrases as "Grandpa has gone away," "Mommy is sleeping," or "God wanted him." Younger children take your words as literal, absolute fact. Children may interpret the statement that a loved one has "gone away" to mean that the deceased person wanted to leave them. If you say the person is "sleeping," they will wait for him or her to wake up. I have heard more than one child say fearfully that "if God wanted this person, God may want me next."

A useful and helpful statement to a young child (under the age of seven) would be something like this:

> When people die, it means their body is no longer working. Their heart stops beating and they don't breathe anymore. They don't have to eat or sleep. They are never too cold or too hot. Nothing hurts. They don't need their body anymore and that means we won't see them.

This statement has to be repeated many times on subsequent occasions because young children do not perceive death to be a permanent condition.

When her twelve-year-old brother was killed, Dawn, aged three, alternately understood that he was gone and expected to see him again. Michael's body was cremated and taken by the family to another state for burial. Dawn saw ashes in an ashtray at the airport and thought it was Michael. When the plane began its descent, Dawn began to cry, thinking the plane would land on Michael. When they disembarked, she was disappointed he wasn't there to meet them.

Each time the child expresses confusion, you need to repeat the same statement in the same way. Begin by saying, "Remember _____ [name] has died, and when someone dies, it means. . . ."

4. Help children preview what will happen at a viewing, memorial, or funeral service. Describe the physical setting and what the child will see. If possible, show the child a picture of a casket. Describe what the body will look like. If any marks or wounds will be visible, describe them as simply as you can.

Most experts agree that a child who is frightened about attending a funeral should not be forced to go. My experience is that children's anxiety is typically a reflection of the anxiety and fears of the adults around them. One of the most frequently asked questions is "Should children be allowed to touch the body of the deceased?" The answer is yes, if they want to and if they are prepared for it ahead of time. Children are naturally curious. How something feels is one way they determine whether it is safe for them. Try to describe the feel of the body in terms the child can understand. Tell them the person will feel cool instead of warm. Have the child touch your arm and compare the feeling to touching the arm of a vinyl- or leather-covered chair. A typical statement to make would go something like this:

> You may touch [name] if you want to. However, now that his [or her] body is no longer working, it will feel different. Instead of being warm and soft, it will feel cool and sort of hard. It won't hurt [name] if you touch him [or her] and it won't hurt you.

You may have heard horror stories about children having severe emotional damage done by touching or kissing a dead body. I have never encountered such a reaction, nor has anyone else in my acquaintance who works with death and loss. Such fears seem to reflect more of an adult anxiety about death. The key to all children's experience with death rests with the reaction and response of the adults around them.

5. Provide some means for children to say good-bye. The easiest and one of the most effective ways to do this is to have the children draw a picture that can be placed in the casket. Be sure to make a copy for the child to keep. If children are old enough, they can write notes that are also placed in the casket. Other useful expressions are photographs, especially of the child with the deceased person, recorded messages, toys, or articles of clothing. If the person has been cremated, these objects can be place in a niche with the cremains or burned and scattered with the cremains.

It is perfectly okay for children to see adults in tears. Just explain that you miss the deceased person, too, and feel very sad, too. Assure them of your love and that you will be here to care for them.

The Death of Pets

It is common for children's first experience with loss to be the death of a pet. Their sense of loss and grief needs to be taken seriously by parents and other adults. They need comfort and assurance. It's not a time for detailed explanations. It is also a mistake to replace the pet immediately. Children need to know it is okay to miss their pet. They may want to create some kind of a memorial to remember it and as a way of saying good-bye. Common questions are: "Why did my pet die?" "If I wish hard enough and am good enough, will it come back?" "Does death hurt?" It's important to answer such questions as simply and honestly as possible. When a new pet is acquired, let the child be part of the process. It helps them see that new pets do not just magically appear.

Age Makes a Difference

Children grieve and express their sadness in varying ways according to their age and development. It is not that young children do not grieve, they just perceive death and loss differently than adults or older children, and they respond differently. From infancy on, loss and grief are a normal part of human life.

Infancy

Infants show an understanding of loss well before their first birthday. They require physical touch and stroking for their development. Their two basic fears are loud noises and falling. Each of these is associated with a separation from the source of their security.

The first game many babies respond to is peek-a-boo. First eye contact is made with the child, then some object is used to block the infant's view. Momentarily the adult is gone, as far as the infant is concerned. Then, the object is removed and eye contact is reestablished, accompanied by the words "peek-a-boo." Frequently this contact is reinforced by some physical touch.

A great moment comes in the life of every parent and grandparent when the infant is able to control the game by controlling the object that breaks the eye contact. It is a sign of their security and assurance that the adult playing the game will be there when visual contact is made.

Preschool

Through approximately age four, children sense loss and sadness but cannot conceptualize death.

The fear of separation begins at about the age of one. After a death in the family, it is not uncommon for children to be afraid to be away from home or out of their parent's sight.

However, death does not seem permanent. It is more like taking a nap and waking up. The concept of time is limited. It may seem to a young child that death is only being "less alive." With the exposure of most young children to many hours of television, this understanding is reinforced by seeing cartoon characters in particular "dead" on one program and alive on another one that follows.

Anita was four when her grandfather died. When she and her parents arrived at her grandparents' house, her grandfather's body was laid out in a casket in the front room. Anita was told that she must stay in the dining room. She peeked around the corner and saw a room full of adults standing around her grandfather's body. Several were crying because he was dead, but she didn't know what that meant. She wanted him to get up and play with her, but again was told she must stay in the other room.

On the day of the funeral, Anita was not allowed to attend the funeral but was taken to the cemetery. When the casket lid was closed and it was lowered into the ground, she began to cry. She couldn't understand why they were all leaving Grandpa alone in the ground. She thought he would be lonely and cold in the dark. She wondered if he had been bad and somebody was mad at him. When it was time to leave, she tried to tell her parents that her grandfather had not kissed her good-bye, but nobody was paying any attention.

Anita still carried the memory of this sad experience when she became a grandmother herself.

Elementary School

Between the ages of five and nine, the understanding of death becomes clear to most children. They come to realize that pets and people die and that death is final.

Jasmine had just celebrated her fifth birthday. She and her ten-year-old brother, Karl, were at home with their father while their mother was at work. The two children were ready for school and their father went out to start the car to take them there. When Jasmine emerged from the house, her father was slumped over the wheel. She ran back inside to tell Karl that Daddy was taking a nap in the car. Karl knew something was wrong and called a neighbor, who called paramedics. Karl had died from a heart attack.

Jasmine ran from person to person, wanting to know when her daddy would take them to school. Karl retreated to his room, knowing their father was dead but not knowing how to tell his sister the bad news.

At the funeral, Jasmine watched her father's body intently. At one point, she tugged on the sleeve of my wife's dress and said, "I think I saw my daddy move. He's waking up now." June replied in a soft voice, "No, Jasmine, your father did not move. He is not sleeping, he is dead. It will be okay. Your mother is here to love and care for you. I will see you in Sunday School every week and will come to visit if your mom and you want me to." Jasmine leaned against her, took June's hand, and nodded in agreement. "Daddy's dead," she said.

General Guidelines for
Talking with Children about Loss

The most important insight adults can communicate to children of any age is that life goes on after a death, divorce, or any major loss. To do this, you must become more comfortable with your own grief. The many exercises in this book can help you.

In addressing the needs of children of all ages at a time of loss, you will serve them well if you

- Offer your acceptance of their feelings and behavior.

- Listen carefully without being judgmental.

- Assure them of their security in terms they can understand.

- Make sure they understand they are not to blame. Express your love and care for them in unmistakable ways.

- Act in ways that elicit the children's trust.

- Answer all questions as honestly as you can.

- Help them understand that circumstances will not always be like this and they will not always feel as they do now.

- Provide an atmosphere of stability in the midst of any changes.

Maryann Makekau is a wonderful source of inspiration and insight in helping children cope with grief. Her Little Pink Books are a treasure store of wisdom on a child's level. A few of her titles include *When Your Teacher Has Cancer, When Your Mother's Cancer Doesn't Go Away, When Your Dad Goes to War,* and *When Your Grandma Forgets.* I coauthored this lattermost book with Maryann.

Karl responded to his father's death in much the same way as the adult members of the family. His greatest worries were who would take care of them and would he have to leave school and go to work. Fortunately, Karl had adults around him who were willing to listen and to assure him that everything would work out in time.

Adolescence

By the time a child approaches adolescence, he or she has come a long way from the days of playing peek-a-boo. Death now has a social dimension in which concerns about the consequences are paramount. The death of the same-sex parent when the child is about twelve or thirteen years old seems to have the potential for lasting problems. It is wise to seek professional intervention when possible.

As adolescents move further into their teenage years, death raises philosophical questions about the meaning of life. It is a time when they feel immortal and death represents an intrusion of reality that can be terribly frightening. If one of their peers dies, it represents a special challenge to their sense of security. If that death happens to be the result of suicide, professional intervention is mandatory. Adolescents often become quite moody after a death, sometimes subjecting themselves to greater risks and impulsive behavior. Inviting teenagers to a grief support group or, better yet, forming one just for them is quite appropriate.

15

Losses in Later Life
Tarnish on the Golden Years

A young man said to me, "When you get older, losses hurt less. Right?" I answered, "Wrong!"

Because of this common but faulty perception, older people have often been denied the support and understanding everyone at every age needs when a major loss occurs.

Family and friends make the assumption that older people are more philosophical about death and other losses, and therefore it doesn't hurt as much. The theory goes something like this: *Older people don't expect a spouse or siblings to live forever or to remain physically strong and independent indefinitely. They know that nobody lives forever. They know they have to make adjustments in lifestyle as the impact of age hits them. Therefore, loss doesn't hurt as much as when you are younger.*

It's a great theory, except it has no basis in fact.

People married fifty, sixty, or more years almost breathe in sync. The license plate June and I had on our car for thirty years says 2NLOVE. The frame used to say "BobnJune, 2 hearts beat as one." When she died, I bought a new frame with hearts on either side that reads "June: 1933–2016, Bob: 1 heart beats for two."

It's an attempt, even if a feeble one, to tell the world how much I miss her and how difficult it has been to create some kind of a new normal for my life. June was very sick when she died. Alzheimer's is insidious in what it does to one's body and mind. When my logical mind is working, there is no way I would want June back as she was, suffering for my comfort. But, when the agonizing pain of living without her consumed me, I was sometimes not very logical.

Men and women in their nineties have shared with me how much they miss the touch of their deceased spouse and the simple act of talking to each other.

I am quite aware that there is a time to be born and a time to die. I am equally aware that our only options in life are to grow older or die. That doesn't mean it is fun to get old. I was in my fifties when a recent octogenarian told me, "Living past eighty is not for sissies." I laughed thinking she was joking. She wasn't joking and I don't laugh about it anymore!

When one spouse dies, the survivor's entire basis for making sense out of life is gone. Most men expect their wife to outlive them. If she dies first, he often thinks he's done something wrong. If anything, it is worse when a child dies before a parent. *This is not the way it is supposed to be. My child should be attending my funeral, not me attending my child's funeral.* That's a lament I have heard many, many times.

Widowed men and women in their seventies and eighties miss sexual intimacy as much as anyone else. They just don't talk about it.

Many times I have noticed older members of our grief support group suddenly walking with a renewed bounce in their steps. Inevitably, sooner or later, they reveal that they have a new boyfriend or girlfriend. Listening between the lines, it becomes clear that their relationship has become an intimate one. These are the same people who neither wanted nor expected to love another person after their spouse died. They often stay healthier longer than others. It is also interesting to note that those who survive the loss of a spouse and come out of it enjoying their independence most are always women. Women tend to wait longer than men before entering another relationship, if they do that at all.

This is another place in the grief recovery process where it is good to adopt the slogan "I won't always feel as I do now."

Loneliness, for many older people, is the most challenging and long-lasting result of a major loss. Ruby was a delightful, energetic eighty-year-old whose husband had been dead for seventeen years when I met her. She was active in her church and had many friends. Outwardly, she appeared to have no problems with her life as a widow. Ruby told me she had a good life, for which she was very thankful. But she also said, "Nighttime is the worst because it's then that the loneliness overwhelms me." She developed a relationship with Mel, another widowed octogenarian. Economic circumstances prohibited them from considering marriage. Their moral values would not permit them to live together. They maintained separate dwelling places, but dined together, went to church together, played cards together, and looked after each other in times of illness or other challenges. She said that once she and Mel got together, the evenings were no longer lonely. Ruby had two strokes from which she recovered the first time, but not the second. I could see Mel's health beginning to decline with her loss. He told me he was too old and Ruby was too good to ever find anyone else. He died three years later.

> *"This is not the way it is supposed to be. My child should be attending my funeral, not me attending my child's funeral."*

Older adults have fewer options for coping with loneliness than younger people. Some no longer drive a car, and many of those who do cannot see well enough to drive at night. Watching television, activities at church or clubs, and reading are the primary forms of escape from loneliness. However, even these activities don't always work. Married couples grow accustomed to talking about everything. A major part of their enjoyment of any event is sharing it with each other. Ann said, "I will be watching a good program on television and instinctively turn to Hal to say, 'wasn't that great?'—and realize he is no longer there." The same kind of thing happens when an old favorite piece of music plays on the radio, or there is a beautiful sunset. Ken, whose wife died after a series of strokes, said, "I miss just talking with her more than anything else." It is in these moments that the full impact of loss is felt and the loneliness feels like a crushing weight.

Many older couples help each other keep going and remain independent as long as possible as they grow more frail with age. Getting groceries, going to the doctor, or just getting out of the house was only possible by confronting the challenge together. Walkers, wheelchairs, and incontinence undergarments become a regular part of life. During the last four years of June's life I became quite skilled with vinyl gloves, Depends briefs, and all other personal needs she could no longer do herself (and I was sure I could do it better than Memory Care staff). The two greatest challenges to learn? Putting on her lipstick and bras! What I'm saying is that like other older couples, it all becomes second nature and a way to express love and care.

When either of them dies, the other not only loses a spouse and soul mate, but sooner or later the ability to live independently. For many, the word *hell* is spelled "nursing home." The disdain felt is so strong I've never been quite sure whether the onset of dementia is a cause or a result of facing life in even the best of such facilities.

Elmer lost his wife to cancer at the age of eighty-three. They had been married for fifty-seven years. He had cared for her at home for as long as he could. When she entered a hospice facility, he was there seven days a week. After her death, it became necessary for Elmer to move to an assisted living apartment. It was a beautiful place that offered endless activities and excellent meals. A few weeks after moving in, Elmer came to see me. He was noticeably upset and fighting back tears. When my office door was closed, he hesitantly confessed that he was missing his workshop and all his tools as much as he was missing his wife. His marriage and his shop work had defined the meaning of his life since his retirement. Now, both of these major segments of Elmer's life were gone. The pain he was experiencing was as great as anyone's at any age after a major loss. He died about two years later.

Earlier versus Later Losses

The process through grief is basically the same at every age. The concepts and exercises you are reading about in this book are equally applicable across the span of a lifetime.

There is really only one major difference between losses in earlier life and losses in later life. Losses in earlier life are usually *accidental*. Losses in later life are usually *incidental*—they go with the territory.

Children and young adults do die of cancer, heart disease, diabetes, or some other illness, but it isn't the norm. Deaths among younger people are more likely to come from accidents, suicide, or violent crime. Whatever the cause of death might be, during younger years it has an accidental quality to it.

It can be argued that no divorce is an accident. That's only partly true. People do not get married with the intent of it being a temporary arrangement. Every bride and groom whom I have known intended to be married just once and have it last for a lifetime. Rarely, if ever, does someone set out deliberately to undermine a marriage. In that sense, even divorce can be an accident.

Whatever the loss, if you are under fifty years of age, it seems like a big mistake that somebody should be able to rectify. It's an accident that causes permanent change. However, there is more time to adjust to the changes and to create a new life after any loss.

Among older adults, cancer, heart disease, dementia, and numerous other potentially fatal ailments happen frequently enough to be called normal. When we who are senior citizens say, "After sixty, it is patch, patch, patch," we are speaking from experience. When we say that living past eighty is not for sissies, we are not exaggerating.

The chart on page 200 shows the ever-increasing "loss curve" faced by people in later life.

In a typical family, parents are in their forties or fifties when their children begin leaving home. The dynamics are about the same whether parents are still married to each other or are divorced. The family structure of the past eighteen to twenty years is gone. Parents may outwardly

Losses in Later Life

Birth	40		50+	60–65		70–85	Death
	Unrealized goals		↑	Retirement		Death of siblings	
	Children leave home			Loss of feeling needed		Death of spouse	
	Decline of parents' health					Declining health	
						Loss of sense of usefulness	
						Loss of independence	

No longer ask:
　"How long have I lived?"

New question is:
　"How long do I have to live?"

Mortality issues become real

Quality of life in the future
　becomes of major importance

seem to celebrate their new empty nest, but it is still a loss—and can be a major one. This is also the era when careers are at their peak and the realization comes that some goals are not going to be reached. Parents may experience the death of their own parents during the same period of time. I was thirty when both of my parents died. My wife lost her parents when she was past fifty. The deaths of my parents fall into the "accidental" category. June's father was a victim of Alzheimer's disease at seventy-seven, and her mother died at eighty-three. The deaths of her parents were "incidental" to growing older.

Somewhere around our fiftieth year, we quit asking, "How long have I lived?" We now ask, "How long do I have to live?" This change in questioning, whether verbal or internal, represents a major change in perception. At this point, the question of our own mortality and that of our loved ones is no longer hypothetical but rather visceral. Quality of life issues rise to the forefront of our thinking. We are concerned with longevity, but we are more concerned with health and the quality of our life, however long we live.

There is, of course, the all-important matter of attitude, whatever your chronological age might be. Attitude can impact your health, fitness, and quality of life at any age, but its importance grows as you grow older. I know people in their thirties who look, act, and think old. I also know people in their seventies, eighties, and nineties whose lifestyle is anything but old.

Al was seventy-nine. He was physically fit and strong, with a physique that many men half his age would like to have. He was one of the best roller skate dance teachers in the United States for several decades. At seventy-nine he was still agile and skilled on skates, teaching even the most difficult dances for hours at a time. When a rare form of cancer took his life, Al was still not old by anyone's definition.

Frank made his first skydive at seventy-eight. At seventy-nine he rode a bicycle 30 miles down Mount Haleakala in Maui, Hawaii—and followed that up with a zip line journey above the trees in Kauai. When he reached his mideighties zip-lining was still a major source of fun. He insists that running with the bulls is not beyond the realm of possibility. Frank works out several days a week, controls his weight, plays golf and volunteers in numerous capacities. He is not old in thought or actions. June and I became great-grandparents in the same year we celebrated our fiftieth wedding anniversary. I also retired the same year. A year later our oldest child reached his fiftieth birthday. A year earlier we had the fiftieth reunion of our high school graduation class—complete with name tags showing our senior class photos. At the time of this writing our youngest is about to turn fifty-eight. Both of our sons are eligible for AARP. These factors tend to do away with any illusions I have about being young chronologically.

However, we danced the Argentine tango with enough skill to perform in public, taught it, and danced from midnight to six in the morning in Buenos Aires, and rode mountain bikes 10 to 20 miles at a time until Alzheimer's caught up with June. Sitting remains my least favorite thing to do. If it weren't for the various parts of my body that hurt most of the time, I would not admit to being old at all. My white hair is just another color, not a social statement.

However, whatever I may choose to think, there is no doubt I am getting older. Accepting this fact tells me that while I can continue doing many things, I can expect more losses in my life, with greater frequency, as time goes on. My losses will not mean that I am either unlucky or that I'm being picked on. They just go with the territory of later years. Understanding this helps me keep from making my losses worse than they are. It also motivates me to enjoy the moment, not to take myself too seriously, and to stay as active as I can.

Make a list of the facts of your life. Head one column "old" and another "young" or "not-so-old." How does your chronological age compare with your lifestyle age?

Factors of Normal Aging

I once shared leadership of a conference on aging with a physician who specializes in geriatric medicine. As she spoke about the factors of normal aging, it seemed almost eerie that such information was passed on so calmly. Every factor she listed raised another challenge about getting older. These are some of the *normal* aspects of aging:

- Reflexes slow down.
- Nerve function decreases.
- Muscles become more fibrous and less elastic.
- Vision declines—as does endurance.
- Memory acuteness and speed of comprehension lessen.
- Bones begin to lose fat pads—resulting in pain.
- Lungs don't function as efficiently.
- Food takes longer to digest, causing more intestinal problems.
- The protective coating in the gut decreases and dries out, leading to more problems with constipation.
- The colon tends to "droop."
- Skin gets spots and other blemishes.
- Hair turns gray and often thins.

- Body temperatures are not controlled as well—feeling uncomfortable is more common.
- Color perception changes, making it difficult to coordinate colors appropriately.
- Coordination declines.
- Sleep disturbance is more common.
- Sexual functions are inhibited by other body changes, such as dryness and decreased blood flow.

These are all considered normal factors of aging!

Every one of them represents a personal loss over which we have little or no control. Each of these losses has a negative impact on our sense of self-worth. A diminishing of self-worth is like a magnifying glass on any other major loss that we experience, including the death of a loved one, loss of independence, or relocation.

All of this is unique to losses experienced in later life.

Dr. Andrew Weil said in a lecture, "Aging isn't a disease. Rather, it's a natural breakdown in the efficiency of the body's normal maintenance and repair processes. Aging is simply living past our warranties." Sue is an example of someone who never paid much attention to her "warranty." She received her college degree in her seventies and was instrumental in getting her city to fund water wells in Africa. Three months after her husband died, she turned ninety. She celebrated by going skydiving for the first time. (See Chapter 5 on the importance of perception.)

Victim or Survivor?

Coping with losses in later life is another place where the most important decision we can make is to be a survivor, not a victim.

As it is with most losses, the circumstances present themselves without asking our permission. There is no question about avoiding losses associated with later life—we can't. But we can choose the attitude we will take toward those losses and the manner in which we will respond to them.

Living past eighty is not for sissies.

Choosing to be a victim means being passive and feeling helpless to do anything about the loss.

Choosing to be a survivor means being assertive and realistic without giving up hope. Survivors take responsibility for their own future. They face their challenges head-on.

Victims ask, "Why is this happening to me?"

Survivors ask, "How can I get the most out of life, regardless of the circumstances?"

Victims are dominated by fears, doubts, and frustration. They tend to be bitter and negative about life.

Survivors also have fears, doubts, and frustration—but they are determined to conquer them. They tend to be positive and upbeat about life. They give in to the factors of normal aging very begrudgingly. One man who was having increasing problems with joint pain was on the golf course when he said, "I can sit at home and feel pain, or be out doing the things I like to do and have pain. I'm not giving in as long as I can walk!"

Frank was a retired minister with a long history of heart problems. When his wife died, his family decided he should move into an assisted living facility. He was very sad about leaving the house he had shared with his wife for many years. His grief was compounded when he was forced to give up driving a car. Nevertheless, in a matter of weeks, he had become a voluntary chaplain to the other residents, visiting those who were alone and leading a weekly Bible study and worship service.

Losses come to everyone. In later life, they come more frequently. We can't avoid these normal factors of simply getting older. But we can make choices about how we will respond to them.

We can avoid allowing the facts of later life to overcome us. We will have losses, but that doesn't mean we have to be losers!

We will have losses, but that doesn't mean we have to be losers!

Getting older and experiencing the normal losses of later life cannot be avoided—unless you die young. You can choose to be a survivor instead of a victim.

A very energetic senior citizen said, "My one goal is to not stop living twenty years before I die." It's a worthy goal for all of us.

16

Making New Discoveries
Beginning with Loss—Ending with Life

It is uplifting and encouraging to talk with people who have made their way through grief! Those who have experienced a major loss and recovered from it remind me of explorers and adventurers.

Have you ever talked with someone who climbed a mountain, went on a jungle safari, or made a sky dive? Those who have conquered grief sound like people who have done such exciting and dangerous things. They will tell you not so much about what they have lost as about what they have *discovered*. Their life will not be lived only in memories of the past, but also in plans for the future.

If you have had a major loss recently, you probably can't imagine yourself thinking of anything else for the rest of your life. I assure you if you work through your grief in the ways I have been describing, you will not only think of new things, in time you will also sound like an adventurer. Jean is one of the adventurers. She was a young wife with a two-year-old child. Her husband died suddenly after open-heart surgery. For the next three years Jean worked hard at her grief. She was a regular participant in our grief support group. Jean learned stress-reduction techniques and sought counseling for a nutrition plan to strengthen her body for the task. At every step along the way of her recovery, she refused to take the easy way out. In the midst of her own struggles she became one of our most dependable volunteers to visit newly bereaved people.

As she looked back, Jean said the experience taught her she can do much more than she ever dreamed she could before Joe's death. Her family verified she is indeed more confident and self-assured. She purchased a brightly colored hot-air balloon and acquired her pilot's license, a dramatic symbol of the new life she had discovered after a terrible loss.

Jean would have gladly given up her new self in exchange for having Joe back. But because getting her husband back was not possible, Jean created a good life for her daughter and herself. If you met her and did not know her past history, you would never guess she is someone who struggled with grief for almost three years.

Whereas Jean was a very outgoing person from the beginning, Alice was quiet and shy. She was a contented homemaker and mother of two sons until her husband got cancer. After his death, Alice went through a dark and dismal time that lasted for almost two years. Like Jean, she refused to give in to her grief or to run from it. Alice is convinced that the Kleenex company must have added an extra shift of workers to keep up with her need for tissues!

Three years after her loss, she began working as a doctor's receptionist. She meets people easily, is considerably more forceful, and dresses in brighter, bolder colors. Alice says, "It's hard to admit I'm a better person today, because it sounds like I'm glad Larry died. Nothing could be further from the truth. I'd give anything to have him back. But I do like who I have become as a result of getting through my grief. I look back and I just can't believe I really did it."

Linda's best friend, Joan, was diagnosed with terminal cancer. Although Linda lived in another state, she quit her job and moved near Joan to lend support to her and her husband, Leonard. Joan's slow death was terribly difficult on both Leonard and Linda. Each of them tried to lend support to the other after she died. Linda felt that a part of her had died with Joan. She had fantasies of being able to take Joan's place in death and allowing her friend to go on with life. Her depression became deep enough that she sought the aid of a psychiatrist.

Her one ongoing contact with Joan was the relationship she had with Leonard, who seemed to understand her grief better than anyone else. Three years after Joan's death, Leonard presented her with a gold bracelet on Valentine's Day—and a kiss. It took another year of psychotherapy for Linda to get past her feelings of betraying her deceased friend by falling in love with Leonard. I had the privilege of performing their marriage ceremony.

Making Discoveries

Grief begins with a terrible and painful loss, but it can end with the discovery of new life. For all that is said in a negative way about grief, there is a positive side, too. Those who are willing to do the work required to take charge of their own grief, who stay committed to going through it, are surprised at their own strength in the end.

Kay and her husband were shocked when he was diagnosed with pancreatic cancer. She was devastated when he died just three weeks later. Kay would come to the grief support group in tears, go through a pile of tissues during the session, and cry most of the time until we met again. She put herself into the work of grieving with her full attention and energy, determined to be a survivor not a victim. The rest of us could see the slow but steady changes in Kay before she could. Three years later, she was a healthy, active person who had entered into a new relationship with a man she and her husband had known for years. She says that when sorrow comes now it is not deep and awful like crashing waves of an angry sea. It is more like rolling waves that are shallow and nonfrightening.

Jean, Alice, Linda, and Kay each discovered a strength of character within themselves they had never known before. Each emerged with a new sense of pride and self-confidence. Each knows she was put to the ultimate test in life and was equal to the challenge. None of them ever wants to experience a major loss again, but all of them know deep inside that if it should happen, they can handle it. This discovery alone has added a new dimension of happiness and security to their life.

Grief is not only a door-closer. Grief is also a door-opener.

You can make the same discovery. I believe each of us has a great deal more strength of character than we think. But it often takes some major event in our life to bring it out.

Grief is not only a door-closer. Grief is also a door-opener. A wise person said to me, "With God every time one door closes, another opens—but it is hell in the hallway!" It's true that you cannot get back a loved one who has died or a part of your body lost to surgery. You aren't likely to get back a marriage that ended in divorce or a dream that was broken. It is equally true, however, that life can still be good for you. Once you have faced your grief squarely and taken the necessary steps to get directly through the center of it, you will see new sources of happiness that you couldn't see before.

When my father and mother died, I made a discovery that has continued to enrich my life from that time on. *I learned how to cry!* Before their death I had always handled my sorrow with stoic reserve. In working through my grief following their death, I found I was actually healthier because I could cry. Tension and stress that were formerly stored in my neck and back were released through tears. My wife said I became a better husband. My family had a better father; my church, a better minister. When

Tension and stress that were formerly stored in my neck and back were released through tears.

June died I did not try to be tough. I cried every day, sometimes several times a day for months. Because I am free to cry, I am totally comfortable with the tears of others. This freedom opened many new doors to helpful counseling. But I didn't learn the effectiveness of tears in a textbook. I learned it in the laboratory of my own losses and grief, and by allowing myself to be immersed in the grief experiences of others.

Attitude and Expectations Are Important

As uncomfortable as the thought may be, one grief experience does not give you immunity from future losses.

Dan and Dora had two sons. Their younger son died from a virus that caused an inflammation in his brain. Shortly after his death they moved, hoping the new environment would help them adjust to their loss. Sometime later, a daughter was born. Their surviving son, Michael, was twelve years old when he was kidnapped, sexually assaulted, and brutally murdered. In the course of six years, these parents lost two of their three children.

Dan and Dora taught me many priceless lessons about courage in the face of overwhelming grief. They, like Jean and Alice, did not try to sidestep the impact of their second tragedy. In the early going after Michael's death, they faced their grief under the bright light of media exposure.

Because Michael's body was abandoned in the desert, they were unable to see him after the tragedy. To experience the reality of what had happened, they asked the police to show them pictures taken at the murder scene. Later, they visited the site where it happened.

Pictures of Michael were left up in their home. Conversations about him were carried on daily. Because of local publicity, the man who killed their son was put on trial in another city 200 miles away. When the trial began, Dan and Dora were there. Throughout the trial and afterward, they handled themselves with such openness and poise that they became inspirations to the entire community. A few months after Michael's death, a little girl in our city was abducted and killed. Among the first people to call the parents were Dan and Dora.

Working through the death of Kevin, their first son, helped prepare them for facing Michael's death. The most fundamental aspect of this preparation was they did not expect to be immune from tragedy.

Fortunately, not many of us have to face the kinds of tragedies Dan and

They did not expect to be immune from tragedy.

Dora faced. But all of us need to remember that the very worst kind of loss is always ours.

If we expect to suffer for the rest of our life after the death of a loved one, it will be more difficult to let go and move on to a new life. However, if we understand that the effective use of time will get us through grief, we have a foundation for starting the work and beginning the process. What you expect to discover after any loss plays an important role in your recovery from grief. Your attitude toward the new possibilities that emerge for you is equally important.

Creating a New Normal

When a loved one dies, a marriage ends in divorce, or we experience a life-changing injury, all that was "normal" in our life is destroyed. The long-range challenge in front of us is to create a new normal. One of the first ways widowed persons often confront this is deciding what to do about major holidays, such as Thanksgiving and Christmas. Trying to stay with former traditions for such emotion-laden times is more often than not an exercise in futility and frustration. Some people choose not to observe the holidays at all for two years or more. Numerous others found it easier to do something completely different than in the past. Some, whose traditions included large family gatherings, went on a cruise instead. If they did not have a family with whom to gather, others found a friend or two and traveled to some special destination away from home.

> The long-range task in front of us is to create a new normal.

The greatest challenge to creating a new normal for your life is acknowledging that significant parts of your former life are gone forever. It is not an easy task. You find yourself not wanting to admit your loved one has died or your marriage has really ended. It is a thin line between hanging on to important memories as a testimony to where you have been, while focusing your attention on creating new experiences—or trying to hang onto the past to avoid the reality of the present.

Ginnie, who introduced me to the term *new normal*, kept her husband's cremains in an urn on the headboard of her bed for two years after his death. At some point, she moved the urn to the top of her dresser across the room. A year or more later, the urn was placed on a shelf in her closet. About five years after his death, I met her in the memorial garden of the church and we placed his cremains in their permanent resting place. I saw the progression as an outward sign of healing and the new normal taking place in her life.

If you are ready to think about creating a new normal for your life, do this:

- At the top of a sheet of paper or on your computer write, "My normal life." Describe the activities, people, and conditions that made your life normal before your loss.
- List the parts of your "normal" that are now gone.
- What changes can you make that will begin creating a new normal for you?
- Pick one or two and list what you can do to make these changes.
- Begin acting on the things you have listed.

What Can Hinder Recovery

I often hear misguided statements like the ones that follow. The attitudes and expectations they represent are like barriers blocking the doorway to new discoveries.

- You never "get over" a major loss such as death.
- Time is the only healer for grief.
- If you love someone too much, your grief will be worse.
- Nobody else can help you with your grief.
- The death of a spouse is more painful than divorce.

- The death of a child is the worst of all losses.
- A slow death is easier to handle than a sudden death.
- Your loss was God's will and you should not question it.
- If you just keep busy, your grief will go away.

Not one of these statements is true! Confronting loss and grief is one area of life where popular opinion is worth less than nothing. To build a new life after loss, you must understand the facts of loss even better than you understand the realities of life.

Statements that reflect significant truths about the experience of loss do exist. I have collected some of the most significant ones in the box on the adjoining page.

Viewing loss and grief in these ways will help you put your life together again. You can't avoid major losses. Important people, places, and stages of life will be lost to you. Having one tragic loss doesn't mean you won't have others, but you can be assured effective grief work will open new doors as it closes old ones.

True Statements about Loss and Grief

The following are true statements. They represent important attitudes and expectations about loss and grief.

- You can get through a major loss of any kind.

- It takes time to be healed from your loss, and it also takes hard work.

- The better your relationship with one who has died, the more satisfying your grief work will be.

- Many people can help you work through your loss, especially others who have had similar losses.

- Grief that results from divorce is similar in many ways to grief resulting from death and is different in other ways. It is every bit as painful.

- It is never God's will for you to suffer nor for your loved ones to suffer or die. Death and loss are a part of this mortal life.

- If you keep too busy to face your feelings and avoid talking about them, you put yourself at a higher risk of illness following a major loss.

17

Significant Points along the Way
Mileposts on the Road to Recovery

Certain points in time after a major loss stand out with special significance. Chapter 6 includes a description of the steps you can expect to take on the way to grief recovery. The following are significant turning points along your way. It helps to think of them as signposts along the road, indicating you have come some distance and are heading in the right direction. Each one represents a time of discovering something new and being challenged to release a part of the past.

The Third Month

The third month after the death of a loved one, the filing of a divorce, or any major loss is often one of the most difficult times of all. By then all vestiges of shock and numbness are gone. The full impact of the loss is upon you. Many people have said this point was "the bottom of the barrel."

Enough has happened by this time that denying your loss is impossible. If your spouse died, you have had three full months of filing insurance papers, death certificates, and Social Security forms. You have eaten and slept alone for ninety days. If your child died, you know by now that you aren't going to get your little one back. If you have divorced you are fully into being a single person again. You may be a single parent for the first time. Your ex-spouse may already have a new love interest. The difficult adjustments of this step will persist for some time. But for some reason, the third month will stand out in your mind as the most challenging.

Lori was thirty-five years old when her mother died suddenly. They had lived in different states since Lori and her husband moved away shortly after their marriage. The two women had maintained telephone contact over the years and greatly enjoyed catching up on each other's news each week.

Ninety days after her mother's death, Lori came to see me because she found her thoughts dominated by suicide. She was certain her mother had come to visit her the night before. Her message to Lori was one of loneliness for her and the wish that Lori could be with her.

In the brightness of day, Lori knew her suicidal impulses weren't rational. At night they became more of a problem. I told Lori that what she was experiencing was a normal phenomenon for the third month of her grief recovery. We set up a series of counseling sessions and a procedure for her to call if a night became too difficult.

After meeting several times, I suggested to Lori that she write a letter of good-bye to her mother. (A full discussion of this exercise begins on page 247.) She was to tell her mother how much she loved her, how much she had enjoyed their years together and the special nature of their relationship. But now she had to let her go. Lori had to say good-bye so that she could go on with her life with her husband and family. She would miss her mother very much and would never forget her. She would show gratitude for all her mother had taught her by living a new life with its own fulfillment. After writing the letter, Lori was to read it aloud several times each day until she could get through it without breaking down. Then she was to bring the letter to my office and read it to me.

Lori was able to carry out that difficult task. It proved to be the key in enabling her to put away her self-destructive thoughts. As she faced the reality of her grief and understood more about what to expect of herself, Lori was able to move through it without further threat to herself. Please note: Some people have said they were not ready to say good-bye to their loved one by the third month. If you need to wait until later, do that. It's okay unless you are putting it off to avoid facing your grief.

If you are not already in some kind of a support group by the third month, try to find one. It is a time when talking with a professional counselor or clergyperson is better than the advice of inexperienced friends or family.

The Three-Month Mark

Make a note on your calendar about three months after you experience any significant loss. When some sign of your reaction to that loss occurs that you didn't expect, you can check the date and say to yourself, "Oh, it's about three months since _____, I'm due for something like this." That simple exercise can turn your normal grief reaction into a time of discovery instead of panic.

Six to Nine Months

This is a special time when you need to focus on the relationship of your body and emotions. Somewhere between six and nine months after a major loss, you could be quite vulnerable to the onset of a serious physical illness. Dr. Glen Davidson's study of bereaved persons indicates about 25 percent of them had a weakened natural immune system during this period. If possible, I strongly urge you to mark your calendar at the sixth month and to schedule a doctor's appointment for a physical exam. This is also a time when being in a grief support group is of maximum value.

When Pat's husband died, Pat was forced to close the home for runaway youth that she operated and move to a new state to find work. She had to say good-bye to friends with whom she had a long and close relationship. Ten months later, Pat developed a mysterious illness. She ran a high fever, suffered from exhaustion, and became too weak to walk without support. Tests revealed an immune deficiency of an unknown classification. In time, the disease disappeared as mysteriously as it had appeared. Pat is convinced that grief over her multiple losses lies at the root of this trying experience.

> *I strongly urge you to mark your calendar at the sixth month and to schedule a doctor's appointment for a physical exam.*

One Year

You don't need to mark the anniversary date of your loss on the calendar. The date of a loved one's death or some other major loss is etched into your memory. You will remember not only the date, but the time, the weather, the place, and many other details surrounding your loss.

The one-year anniversary date of a loved one's death is particularly significant. You will have done something you thought was impossible a few months earlier: You will have survived an entire year, three hundred sixty-five days, without someone who was as important to you as life itself.

Most people find the anticipation of the one-year anniversary is more stressful than reaching the date itself. Many people reach the anniversary date with a mixture of sadness and hope. You are reminded in a vivid way of how much you have lost and how much it still hurts. But you have made it through the year, and, if you allow it, you are more hopeful for the future.

> *Many people meet the anniversary date with a mixture of sadness and hope.*

After Lucy's husband died, those of us who knew her had a special concern. She didn't seem to be adjusting very well. She came to the grief support group a few times, then dropped out. She appeared to be losing weight and withdrawing from friends and neighbors. She could not dispose of her husband's clothing or a large collection of tools he kept in a metal shed behind their home. She had always taken great pride in her yard. Now it was in shambles.

As the anniversary date of her husband's death approached, we were worried. People in the grief support group worked out a plan to have two widows visit her on the morning of the anniversary date. I was to see her in the afternoon. Someone else would invite her to dinner that evening.

When the day arrived, the two women went to see Lucy. They found her out in the yard busily putting in new plants. The tools were gone, sold to a neighbor. The shed was now her garden-supply area. She wasn't home when I went to call because she had gone to a bridge club with a neighbor. At dinner she told her hosts that she had completed her responsibility to mourn and now it was time to get on with her life. The last I knew she was still a happy and well person who continued to find new ways to enjoy life.

Whatever your loss, make the anniversary a specific time you look forward to with at least as much hope as you give to looking back in sorrow. Mark the date in a special way. You'll find some suggestions for honoring the anniversary in the following box. As you begin the second year after your loss, it is time to focus your attention more on where you are going than where you have been. It is time to become fully life-oriented again.

The Eighteenth Month

This is the point at which you may find out your grief work isn't finished. By the time you are a year and a half away from your loss, it will seem as though the rough places are behind you. You are having more good days than bad ones. You probably have learned to laugh again.

You may wake up one day and it feels as if you are back at the beginning. Sadness returns. Tears flow like they did in the first weeks after your loss. Thoughts of what you have lost dominate your attention.

Marking the One-Year Anniversary

Make the decision to take charge of this important day. Be pro-active. Don't wait for the day to come to you. I suggest:

- If you work, take the day off. Have lunch or dinner—or both with a friend or friends who understand the significance of this day.

- Make a conscious effort to recall your loved one. Use photos and videos. It is okay to cry.

- Go back in your journal and read your entries for the year.

- Make phone calls or write notes of thanks to everyone you can think of who was helpful to you throughout the year.

- Using the exercise for goal setting on page 245, make plans and set goals for the coming months. Check how you are doing at creating a new normal for your life.

- If you are living in a new city or state, visit your old home area or call someone you know there.

- Begin studying your new area. Learn something of its history.

Nights that were finally tolerable get long and tough again. If you are divorced, you may have gone through eighteen months of sheer euphoria at gaining your freedom, only to have the bottom suddenly drop out from under your emotions.

Sadness returns. As bad as this feels, it's important to know you are responding in a normal way to a major loss. This is the time when some people turn to a grief

Phases of Bereavement

Reprinted by permission from *Understanding Mourning* by Glen W. Davidson ©1984 Augsburg Publishing House.

support group for the first time. Dorothy heard about our group from a friend. She walked in one day to say, "I thought I had this thing licked. I never did go through some of the things people told me to expect after my husband's death. Everything was going along fine until early this month. Now I feel like I'm headed backward." When I inquired how long ago Dorothy's husband had died, she told me it had been eighteen months.

Dr. Glen Davidson's study of bereaved people demonstrates the frequency of this return to a more intense level of grieving. The graph above shows that this intensity reappears between the twelfth and eighteenth months after the death of a loved one. The most important things to know about this bump in the road to recovery are:

- It is a sign of progress, not regression.
- It doesn't last long.
- The best way to handle it is to do what you would do if the loss were a recent one.

Beyond the Second Year

Once you have passed the second anniversary of your loss, your primary focus will be on adapting to the new life you are creating. Sometimes the greatest challenge is to admit you are ready to move on.

- You may struggle with a sense of being disloyal to a deceased spouse.
- If one of your parents has died and the surviving one begins to date another person or remarries, you may have a problem with anger.
- Parents who lose a young child to death often choose this time to begin planning for the birth of another child.
- For most divorcing people, the beginning of the third year is the time when the old marriage is finally put behind.
- You may begin to waver in your resolve never to be in a romantic relationship or marry again.

Beyond the second year you will find that the pain of your grief is not as intense as it had been. Special dates and occasions may still cause you to become emotional, but in general you will be better able to find out what life has in store for you now.

This is a time to begin making longer-range plans.

This is a time to begin making longer-range plans. It may be the occasion for a new wardrobe or hairstyle. It is a good time to give your loss meaning by using the coping skills you have learned to help others who are grieving.

The End of Grief

"You won't always feel as you do now." Do you remember my advice to post this message around your house in the early weeks and months after the death of a loved one? This is the time when you realize it is true. You don't feel as you once did. Grief does have an end. Now you know the light at the end of the tunnel is not an oncoming freight train. You have not been left with a lifetime of emptiness and despair. On the contrary, each of the special points in time that we have reviewed here are mileposts along the way to recovery. You are creating a new normal for your life and it is good.

You will not always feel as you do in the beginning, middle, or end of grief. If you enter into grief with an understanding of what to expect of yourself, you will find joyful surprises along with the sadness and disappointments.

Grief is not something to avoid. True, it is more difficult and painful than anything else you will face in life. It takes a long time to get through the experience. But grief can also be an unparalleled occasion for discovery of your own strength of character.

The person who drew me into my involvement with grief and loss was Frieda. When her husband died after a lengthy battle with cancer, I expected Frieda to fall apart. George had been one of those big, supermacho men who could do anything. He was a strong personality who dominated his family. Frieda seemed to lean on him for her support, and I wondered how well she would survive George's death.

However, from the beginning, I saw a new Frieda emerge. She became the guiding force in the development of our first grief support group. She helped one newly bereaved person after another see the need to gather together so they could help each other. She encouraged me to risk leading the group. Her open sharing of what she was experiencing week by week taught me my first lesson in understanding the process of healthy grief.

A little more than a year after George's death, Frieda announced to the group that she had remodeled her bedroom. Gone was the massive dark furniture that was characteristic of George. In its place she had a new bed with pink frilly covers, feminine decorations, and new wallpaper.

> *Grief is as much about finding as it is about losing.*

Frieda's grief was deep and her loss extremely hard for her to handle. But she gave it all she had. In doing so, she found a strength of character that surprised her more than anyone else. She continued to build a meaningful life for herself.

Frieda found what you can find. Grief is as much about finding as it is about losing. It is not an illness but a process of recovering your balance after life has dealt you a major blow.

Enduring the stresses and challenges of grief recovery calls for a discipline that can add a valuable dimension to your life. You can emerge from it considerably stronger and more compassionate than you have ever been.

18

Choosing to Live Again
Ways to Take Charge of Your Own Grief

As the weeks go by after a major loss, normal routines gradually will return to your life.

If you are employed, the need for income will take you back to work. If you are the parent of young children, you will find their lives go on and so do their demands for attention. Pets still have to be looked after and fed. Bills must be paid. Household tasks and yard work have not taken a vacation while you were in shock. June died at the time of year when income tax returns have to be filed. The accountant graciously filed for an extension to give me extra time to assemble the data, but it still had to be done.

Granted, nothing is the same as it was before you lost a loved one to death or divorce, moved to a strange new town, or faced the impact of a catastrophic injury. The tasks to be done may be the same, but you are not!

Work that was all but automatic for you may now seem impossible. The normal cries of your children may grate on your nerves. Routine household chores have become exercises in drudgery.

Your energy level will be very low. You may want excessive amounts of sleep, or lie staring at the ceiling night after night.

As you move beyond the first few weeks, the permanence of your loss comes home, and with that realization comes a new pain. The usual demands on your life call again for your attention. But now, the pain feels like trying to go through a normal day with the worst toothache you've ever had in your life.

One decision confronts you that dominates all others at this time: You must choose to live again.

Choosing to live again means taking charge of your grief. For the first few weeks much of your life was out of control. Chances are your grief owned you. Now it is time for you to own your grief and to direct the pathway of your recovery.

> Choosing to live again means taking charge of your grief.

You have been knocked off-balance—*flattened like a pancake* is probably a better description. And now it's time to get up again, recover your sense of balance, and get on with your life.

Giving Yourself Permission to Grieve

This exercise takes grief out of the category of "things that shouldn't happen" and makes it a symbol of your capacity to love.

If you have suffered a major loss recently, grief doesn't seem like something that requires permission. *Grief* for you is a dirty word; it describes something horrible. It's nothing to be proud of, and you wish it would just go away as quickly as possible.

I want you to give yourself permission to experience another kind of grief. With this exercise you are establishing a purpose for your sadness and taking charge of your own recovery. You will need an 8 ½ x 11-inch pad of lined paper and a pen or pencil. If you prefer electronic sites, use your iPad, tablet, or computer. Cell phone screens are too small.

Follow these steps in exactly the sequence listed.

1. Describe the loss that has brought you grief. How long ago did it happen?

2. Write as much as you want to about the importance of your relationship with that person, place, or condition that is lost.

3. Describe the pain and sadness you feel because of the loss. The list of feeling words in Appendix A may help you describe your feelings more clearly.

4. What is the impact of this loss on your total life? What else have you lost because of this loss?

5. Read your responses to numbers 2, 3, and 4 aloud.

6. What do your responses tell you about your affection for the person, place, or condition that was lost?

7. Considering the love you have for whomever or whatever was lost, and the impact of that loss on your total life, would any other response from you except grief be appropriate?

8. Write the following on a clean sheet of paper:

> The sadness I feel is a badge of honor. I wear the brokenness of my life at this moment with pride. These expressions of my grief testify to the importance of and the depth of my love for _____ [person/place/condition]. I am willing to feel the full impact of my grief as a final act of tribute and love. I will make my way through this experience and will not run from it.

9. Sign your name to the statement.

10. Make four copies. Keep the original for yourself and post it in a conspicuous place.

11. Send the copies to four other persons, at least two of whom are not family members. You may want to include your clergy.

Facing a Loss from the Past

If you described an event from the past by several years, you may not require the same amount of time to work through it. However, the grief you are experiencing is no less real.

As you read in Chapter 13, June was more than fifty years old when she first realized she had been sexually molested as a young child. For all those years, the trauma of that terrible event had lain in the recesses of her emotions, too painful to be allowed into consciousness. When the awareness finally came, a deep sadness and grief accompanied it.

Over the course of several months she dug into her painful feelings about her loss. There was no way to recover those lost years or the joy they might have held.

Using a method like the exercise you have just completed, June was able to work through the grief and take charge of her response to a deep wound in her life. She fully recovered her balance in relation to that event. She openly shared her experience to help other women and men deal with this painful loss. At the time of her death I received cards and letters telling me that her open sharing of that childhood trauma and the later loss of a breast to cancer opened the door to healing and wholeness.

Giving yourself permission to grieve is a great gift. It is an important step in recovering from a present or past loss and an important key to a full life after loss.

Keeping a Journal

Once you have given yourself permission to grieve, the next important thing for you to do is keep a daily journal of your journey through grief. It will be one of the most valuable things you do for yourself. Use a stenographer's notebook or a diary. Indicate the date and time of the entry at the top of each page. Include this information for each day:

- A significant event that happened
- The person who was most important to me today
- Changes I observe happening to me
- My plans for tomorrow
- Notes to myself

It's a good idea to write in your journal at about the same time every day. This establishes a habit and doesn't require you to think about whether you have made an entry. I found this especially beneficial during the chaotic early months of grieving.

The importance of a daily journal will only become evident to you some months, maybe even a year or two, down the road. The changes that mark your progress through grief come slowly. You may think you are making no progress at all and become more discouraged. At times like these, reading back through your journal will help you remember where you have been and how far you have really come.

The journal helps you stay in charge of your grief experience. It provides guidance for your sharing in your support group and helps you internalize the insights you gain there. There is also some indication that the regular use of a journal may help strengthen your immune system. For many people, making journal entries in the evening works best. Evenings tend to be a more reflective time especially when you are struggling with grief. By intentionally focusing on your grief at this time, you take charge of your experience. I call it *de-spooking the evenings*. It works! If you do write in your journal at night, do so at least an hour before you plan to go to bed.

It is a good idea to drink only herbal teas, decaffeinated coffee, or plain water while you work with your journal in the evening. Caffeinated or high-sugar beverages can interfere with restful sleep later. The same is true of alcoholic beverages.

How Journals Help

- Writing down the events of each day gives these events significance.

- Thinking about people who are important to you keeps you from further loneliness.

- Always noting your plans for the next day encourages a positive direction.

When you've finished writing in your journal, you may want to read or do some other activity that is relaxing before sleep.

If you have problems relaxing, the next exercises can be helpful. I like them because they are simple and effective.

An Exercise to Relieve Tension

This exercise is known as the 8–8–8 Breather.

Sit in a comfortable chair with your feet on the floor and your hands lying loosely on your thighs, palms down. Close your eyes. Do the following:

1. Gently blow out all the air in your lungs.
2. Slowly inhale while counting to 8. Allow your abdomen to expand while you are breathing in. Count: 1-and-2-and-3-and . . . up to 8.
3. Hold your breath to the same count of 8.
4. Slowly exhale while counting to 8 in the same manner. Relax your abdomen as you breathe out.
5. Breathe normally for about one minute.
6. Repeat this sequence several times until you feel your tension subsiding.

A Variation on Counting Sheep

This relaxation exercise can be done any time but is particularly helpful when you can't get to sleep or wake up in the night and can't go back to sleep, which is quite common after a major loss. It is my go-to activity when my mind is racing and I can't relax.

Lie down in bed on your back with hands by your sides. Do the 8–8–8 Breather exercise several times.

Close your eyes and look as far up inside your eyelids as you can.

Begin counting silently simultaneously from 1 to 100, and from 100 to 1. It is done like this: 100–1, 99–2, 98–3, 97–4, 96–5. . . . Keep looking up inside your eyelids.

As you continue to count, you will find your eyes becoming tired. Allow them to relax to a comfortable position.

At some point you will begin to have difficulty keeping track of the sequence of numbers. This is a sign your mind is beginning to relax and prepare for sleep. Don't force the sequence to continue.

When this happens, picture yourself at the top of a descending stairway. It is twenty steps in length and is of any design you wish. There is a landing halfway down.

Picture yourself slowly descending the stairs one step at a time. Count them as you go. One-two-three-four. . . .When you reach ten, pause on the landing. Then descend slowly the rest of the way.

You may not reach the bottom before falling asleep. *Don't fight it!*

If you do get all the way to the bottom, you will feel relaxed and at ease. Picture a room that is your own private retreat. No one else ever shares this space with you. It is decorated and arranged exactly as you want it to be. It is warm and comfortable. In this place you are free from all pressures and concerns. Allow yourself to be in this room for as long as you want.

Even if you do not fall asleep, you will be resting.

As a variation during the day, you can sit in a comfortable chair, fix your eyes on some small object or mark on a wall, and begin counting until your eyes grow heavy. Then allow your eyes to close, and begin descending the staircase. When you reach your room at the bottom, remain there as long as you wish. When you are ready to end the relaxation period, count your way back up the stairs. Your eyes will open near the top and you will feel quite refreshed and alert.

When You Just Can't Sleep

Sometimes, in spite of your best efforts, you will wake up in the middle of the night and not be able to go back to sleep. It seems to take only a night or two of interrupted sleep to get the cycle started, but it can take months to get back to normal. This exercise will help you reprogram your sleeping habits within a week or two.

First, create a daily calendar of the things you are going to do. Divide each twenty-four-hour period into four parts: mornings (after your usual waking time), afternoons, evenings (up to your normal bedtime), and nighttime (normal sleeping hours). Plan your time as follows:

Morning: List what you will do from the time you get up until you have lunch. Schedule your lunch at a specific hour and have it whether you feel like eating or not.

Afternoon: List what you will do after lunch until time for dinner. Also schedule that meal at a specific hour and eat it.

Evening: List the hours of the evening from dinnertime until bedtime. For example, if you eat at six p.m. and normally go to bed at ten p.m. your schedule would be:

> 6:00 p.m. Dinner
> 7:00 p.m.
> 8:00 p.m.
> 9:00 p.m.
> 10:00 p.m. Bedtime

Now fill in what you will do each hour of the evening. Do your best to follow through with each hour's plan. Remember, writing in your journal can be a productive activity that helps you relax.

Nighttime: List the time that you are waking most frequently during the night. Then list each half-hour from that time until your normal waking time. For instance, if you normally get up at six a.m., but now are waking each night at two a.m., your list would look like this:

> 2:00 a.m.
> 2:30 a.m.
> 3:00 a.m.
> 3:30 a.m.
> 4:00 a.m.
> 4:30 a.m.

5:00 a.m.
5:30 a.m.
6:00 a.m.

Each evening, write down what you will do in thirty-minute incre-
ments from the time you wake up until your normal rising time. **This
is crucial.** Give yourself tasks to do that are unpleasant. Clean cup-
boards or toilets, mop floors, balance your checkbook—anything that
you do not like to do! There should be no snacking and no lying in bed
staring at the ceiling.

If you go back to bed, use one of the relaxation techniques to fall
asleep again. Most people find that after a few nights of this regimen
they are sleeping until their normal rising time without further
problems.

Learning to relax is an important skill to master as you work your
way through grief and learn to live again. So is changing your attitude
about crying.

A Programmed Cry

This exercise is specifically designed to help you get rid of your fears,
fantasies, and reservations about crying. It can also help if you find you
cannot cry. You will probably use it more than once in the first weeks
and months after a major loss. It demonstrates clearly that your emotions do not have to be kept under a tight rein. If you have any health
concerns that you think could be affected by expressing your emotions,
check with your doctor before doing this exercise.

Preparation

You will be okay when you cry. However, to alleviate any unnecessary
anxiety, choose someone to be your caretaker. This person should know
what you are doing and be familiar with the circumstances of your
grief. He or she must be willing to be awake and ready to respond if

you call. Have your caretaker's telephone number readily available in case you need assistance.

Choose a room in your home that has sentimental importance for you. Supplies should include some large pillows, a full box of tissues, a music player, and photographs of the one who is gone. Do the exercise in the evening.

How to Cry

Turn the lights low. Turn on soft music. Select a station that plays sentimental music with few interruptions, or use recorded music. Set the volume to a comfortable level, as loud as you like.

Feel the impact of the mood you have created. Allow it to touch your sadness. Think about the person who has died or the dreams for a happy marriage that are gone. Or look at photographs of the people and places you left when you moved to a new city.

Remember the most intimate times. Think about your loss. Turn your feelings loose. Say what you are feeling aloud.

Put two chairs back to back. Sit in one and imagine the person or people you have lost in the other. Talk directly to the one you have lost. Say what you are feeling aloud.

As an alternative, you may want to picture God sitting in the chair. Tell God your feelings about your loss without restraint.

Hold a pillow in your arms and cry into it. Rock back and forth. Yell if you want to. Call out your loss. Feel it completely. Let your feelings go for as long as they want to come out.

Know that you are being healed by the release of all the pain and sadness. Don't try to hide your anger.

When you begin to feel better, allow that new feeling to emerge. Concentrate your attention on the positive thoughts you are having. Say those positive thoughts aloud.

When you are ready, turn up the lights. Turn the music low. Change its mood to something happy and bright. Put away the symbols of your weeping—the tissues, pillow, chairs.

Do breathing exercises, stretch your muscles, do some simple calisthenics, walk around, or run in place.

Drink a large glass or two of water. Make some herbal tea or have fruit or vegetable juice. Snack on fresh fruits or vegetables, crackers, pretzels, or popcorn.

Notify your caretaker that you are finished and ready to sleep. Take a warm bath or shower. Read a humorous book. Go to sleep.

As soon as possible, tell your caretaker about the experience. Tell your counselor or grief support group.

Record your experience in your journal.

You will find that most of your hesitancy and discomfort with tears are gone. From now on, you will be able to experience your feelings more easily and with less anxiety.

Many people have found this exercise to be like turning on the lights in a dark room. All the mystery and myth associated with the act of crying disappears. Instead of tears being a problem for you in working through your grief, they become a resource for healing. Once you are more comfortable with crying, you are ready to confront your grief in a more direct way.

Communicating with Your Grief

This exercise does for grief what the last one did for crying. It dispels the notion that grief is a six-headed monster that will "get you" if you mention its name. The task here is to communicate with your grief as though it has its own personality. You will talk to your grief and you will listen to your grief.

If your loved one has died, this is an especially helpful exercise about three to five months after the death.

You will write two letters. I suggest using whatever stationery you normally use for writing to friends or family. See pages 131 and 132 for examples. If you normally write on a computer or tablet, go ahead and use that device.

The first letter is from you to your grief. Use the following form:

Date, time:

To Grief,

Sincerely,

[your name]

Before you write, ask yourself, "If I could tell my grief what I am thinking and feeling, what would I say? What do I want my grief to know about its effect on my life?"

Be as frank as you can. Write the letter and sign it.

As close as possible to twenty-four hours later, but no less than that, write the second letter. This one will be from your grief to you.

Use the same format as the first letter, except address it to yourself and sign it "Sincerely, Grief."

Before writing, ask yourself: What do I think my grief is telling me? What does it want from me?

Then, as frankly as possible, write to yourself on behalf of your grief.

Put the letters aside for a day or two, then read them both aloud to yourself.

What do the letters reveal about your attitude toward the experience of grief? What new thing can you learn about yourself from the letters?

Find someone with whom you can share the letters and talk about your discoveries. If you are in a support group, this is an excellent activity to share with each other. I suggest you keep your letters with your journal.

About two years later, write the same letters again without referring to the originals, then compare your responses. You will be amazed that the same person wrote both sets of letters! You may find the second set sounds as though they were written by an adventurer rather than a person who is grieving.

If communicating with your grief is a problem, communicating with your friends, family, and co-workers will be, too. There aren't many people around who will be comfortable with your grief. Very soon after any major loss, including death and divorce, folks will want you at least to act as if you are choosing to live again. They will want you to do this long before you are ready for it.

Anthropologist Margaret Mead said, "When a person is born we celebrate; when they marry we are jubilant; but when they die, we act as if nothing has happened." Why? Because birth and marriage are occasions when loss is dominated by joyful gain. We know what to say and how to react in those occasions. But we see death as canceling every aspect of human joy. We don't know what to say to a bereaved person. We are terribly uncomfortable in the presence of someone else's grief.

About two years later, write the same letters again without referring to the originals, then compare your responses.

That's good to remember when it's our turn to grieve. When people stay away at the time we need them most, it's not that they don't love us. They just don't know what to say or do. They feel helpless.

The next exercise is designed to help you communicate with those whose support you need the most. This includes family members, friends, clergy, and doctors.

What to Remember about People Who Aren't Grieving

Type or write the following sentences on a card or piece of paper and carry it with you for the year of your grief experience.

1. I will not expect others to be better at handling my grief than I would have been at handling theirs before my loss.

2. People cannot be something other than who they are.

3. Most people want to help me. They mean well even when they do dumb and hurtful things.

4. Others, including professional people, will not know what is helpful to me unless I tell them.

5. I will be as patient with others as I need them to be with me.

Carry this information with you so it is readily available. You will want to read it for comfort several times each day because other people will do incredibly uncaring things quite innocently. For example, if your spouse has died, it won't be long before somebody:

- Asks how you are doing, and you will sense the only acceptable answer is "fine."
- Acts as if your deceased husband or wife never had a name. This will happen at a time when you want everyone to know that he or she was a special person who will always be a part of your life.
- Finds a way to avoid talking to you.
- Questions some decision you made about the funeral, burial, or events preceding the person's death.

If you understand that other people's poor reactions are not your fault, you will be spared one more burden from the load you are already carrying.

Things to Tell Nongrievers

Have the following statements typed or printed on good-quality colored paper. A quick-print store can do it for you. Almost every town has one, and it has all the supplies you need. Another option is to write the statements into your cell phone, computer, or other electronic device. When the need arises, text or e-mail the message.

My dear _____ [family, friends, pastor, employer . . .],

The loss of ____ [person, place] is devastating to me. It will take time, perhaps years, for me to work through the sadness I feel because of this loss. I will cry more than usual for some time. My tears are not a sign of weakness or a lack of hope or faith. They are the symbols of the depth of my loss and the sign that I am recovering.

I may become angry without seeming to have a reason for it. My emotions are heightened by the stress of grief. Please be forgiving if I seem irrational at times.

I need your understanding and your presence more than anything else. If you don't know what to say, just touch me or give me a hug to let me know you care. Please don't wait for me to call you. I am often too tired to even think of reaching out for the help I need. Don't allow me to withdraw from you. I need you more than ever during the next year.

Pray for me only if your prayer is not an order for me to make you feel better. My faith does not excuse me from the grief process.

If you have had an experience of loss that seems anything like mine, please share it with me. You will not make me feel worse.

This loss is the worst thing that could have happened to me. But I will get through it and I will live again. I will not always feel as I do now. I will laugh again.

Thank you for caring about me. Your concern is a gift I treasure.

Sincerely,

_____ [your name]

Alter this sample letter in whatever way suits your circumstances. If your loss was a death, ask for people to occasionally use the name of the deceased when talking with you. Give a copy to those whose support you need most. By putting thoughts like these in writing you will avoid much misunderstanding. People will know better what to expect from you.

With this letter, you also affirm in a strong way that you intend to be in charge of your grief experience and to grow through it.

Getting on with Life

Making the decision to live again after a major loss is not easy. It requires putting your willpower and thought-power ahead of some very intense emotions.

You cannot wait until you feel better and then decide to live again. You must make the decision intellectually because you know it is essential to your healing, and then wait for your feelings to catch up. They will.

The next chapter contains more exercises to help you carry out your decision and establish a high-quality new life after your loss.

Taking a Time-out

It's okay and wise to take an occasional time-out from the heavy business of grieving. To do so doesn't dishonor one who has died or indicate any lack of concern for the loss that has taken place. It does provide an opportunity, if only for a few days, hours, or minutes, to go through the motions of a normal life again. Your grief will not go away. It will wait for you.

It's okay and wise to take an occasional time-out from the heavy business of grieving.

The exercise on page 241 comes from a friend who is both a skilled bereavement counselor and a survivor of multiple major losses. It works wonders!

Fun Things to Do

Do one or more of the following on a given day.

1. Go to an ice-cream store and taste every flavor it has. (Tasting is free.)

2. Take a giant stuffed animal to a supermarket. Put it in your cart and push it around as you shop. You will be amazed and uplifted by the response of other shoppers.

3. Go to the classiest hotel you can find. Walk around as if you were staying there, being sure to window-shop the gift store.

4. Go to art galleries, antique stores, flea markets, or bookstores. Just "hang out" and browse.

5. Go to a mall. Measure the time it takes for you to walk it completely. When finished, treat yourself to a goody.

6. Go fly a kite.

7. Find a park with a duck pond and feed the ducks.

8. Plant a small garden. An herb garden in a pot works fine.

9. Create your own potpourri. Simmer and enjoy its fragrance.

10. Read poetry out loud. It's best done with another person—even over the telephone.

11. During summer months, put up a hummingbird feeder.

12. Take yourself on a picnic. If weather doesn't permit being outdoors, do it on the floor of your house, complete with picnic ware.

13. Play music that you enjoy. Turn it up loud and sing along. (It's good if you can sing, better if you can't.)

14. Take a child to the zoo or a carnival. Eat cotton candy together.

15. Start a humor scrapbook. Read the cartoon section of your paper and cut out the best.

19

Opening New Doors
Decisions that Make a Difference

Decision making is one of the most difficult challenges you will face as you work at recovering your balance and creating a new normal for your life. In the first few days after a major loss you operate like a robot as you face endless demands. You go through the motions of decision making feeling as if your head is in a fog.

Later, the numbness and shock wear off and you experience the pain of separation. Making any decision takes maximum effort. At first, the decisions are impossible to avoid: There is the paperwork that follows a death or divorce or the tasks of locating necessary services in a new town, or perhaps adjusting to life without one of your limbs. I found it difficult to fill out papers and notify people of my wife's death while sobbing profuse tears. The computer screen was blurred, my voice would not work to make telephone calls, and there were times when all I could do was double up in sorrow.

Still later, decision making takes on a new dimension. The pressure now is not so much what you *have to do* as what you *want to do*. You recognize it is time to move on. Your challenge is one of motivation. You may not feel like getting out of bed, getting dressed, eating, or leaving the house. If you are employed, your job can be a blessing as it requires you to get up and get going. This is a time when many people find volunteering provides the motivation they need to go on with life.

Carl found himself deeply depressed after his wife's death. He could not make himself go about any of his usual activities. Then a friend suggested he volunteer at a local blood bank. Having a responsibility to be someplace at a certain time and feeling a sense of satisfaction in helping others gave Carl the motivation he needed to get back into life. Frank's wife died after an eight year struggle with ovarian cancer. Frank responded by volunteering at the local MD Anderson Cancer Center. At the time of this writing he is still doing that after ten years.

Like Carl and Frank, you may find that the pain continues even with volunteer work. You are fairly sure the emptiness and sadness in the pit of your stomach and the ache in your heart will be part of your life for a long time. At least now you have a reason for living. As you give yourself to some task that benefits others, life is simply more bearable. Three months after June's death I faced the task of performing a funeral for a man in our church who had died of a disease very similar to hers. The challenge was to keep my own emotions in check while I took care of his family.

Six months after her husband died, Cindy came to see me in a new state of shock. A man in her office had asked her for a date! The fact that she now had a decision to make stunned her. She was single, but she didn't think of herself that way. Like most widows, she differed from divorced singles in that she saw herself as a married person whose husband was dead. Her divorced friends saw themselves as single and available to the right person. Cindy still wore her wedding ring. She hated filling out forms that required her to list herself as "single." (I understood Cindy at a different level after June died because I had the same dislike of listing myself as "single" and plan to continue wearing my wedding ring for as long as I live.)

For Cindy, the difficulty in saying yes or no to a date was that either answer acknowledged she now had decisions to make and a life to live without Hal. I think that's also the reason so many divorced persons are crushed by the news of their ex-spouse's remarriage. It drives home the fact that the past is really gone. It cannot be recovered, and life must now go on.

There comes a time in recovering from the grief of any major loss when you will seem to be standing in a large, cold room with no windows and many, many doors. You will know that you must leave this room sometime. It is not a pleasant place, but nevertheless, choosing a door isn't easy.

The room is filled with the memories and images of your past and the terrible loss you have experienced. You aren't sure that what waits beyond any of the doors is better. You hope so, but you can't see how life can ever be warm and cozy again.

To leave the room is to leave your past. You can take your memories with you, but that's all. One man noted that his deceased wife was no longer a relationship, but a memory. It was a painful insight, but also a freeing one.

Any choice you make will take you on to a new and different life that you have never lived before.

It's time to choose.

Earl Grollman says in his book *Time Remembered*:

It's a risk to attempt new beginnings. . . . Yet the greater risk is for you to risk nothing. For there will be no further possibilities of learning and changing, of traveling upon the journey of life. . . . You were strong to hold on. You will be stronger to go forward to new beginnings.[1]

An Exercise in Setting Goals

In your journal or on a separate tablet, put the date at the top of a page and answer these questions.

1. What tasks do I need to complete in the next seven days? If I didn't have to do these things, what would I *like* to do in the next seven days?

2. What barriers keep me from doing what I most want to do?

3. What resources do I have to overcome these barriers?

4. Whose help do I need to do the things I want to do?

5. What things would I like to do in the next ninety days?

6. What spiritual resources do I need to find or recover to help me go on with my life?

7. What would my life look like one year from today if I could have my way (realizing I cannot have my loved one back or other loss taken away)?

Choose one goal each from your seven-day, ninety-day, and one-year lists. Write down each of these goals and indicate how you will know when you have reached each of them:

Seven days
Ninety days
One year

Select one spiritual resource you would like to find or recover. Make an appointment to discuss this goal with your minister, priest, rabbi, or other spiritual leader. If you do not belong to a religious community, ask a friend for a referral.

Make a diary notation on your calendar to check on your seven-day goal one week from this date.

Begin working on each of the goals you selected no later than one day after the date on the top of your questionnaire.

> By setting short-, medium-, and long-range goals for yourself, you begin to open the doors to your future.

Keep a record in your journal of your progress on each of the goals you selected. If you accomplish one, choose another from the same category. If it becomes obvious that a goal is unrealistic, choose an alternate. If a new goal surfaces, go for it!

Share your goals and the dates for completion with a friend who will hold you accountable.

At the end of the first week, set a new goal for the next seven days.

Continue this procedure for at least the first year.

By setting short-, medium-, and long-range goals for yourself, you begin to open the doors to your future. Whether you reach all of the goals doesn't matter as much as working on them.

The important thing is that you are beginning to make new choices for your life after loss.

The next step is a painful one. I want you to know that up front, before you begin the exercise. It is also a very important step to your continued recovery.

Writing a Letter of Good-bye to the Past

Saying good-bye is never easy. Whether guests go home or you leave favorite relatives after a visit, the time of parting has an element of sadness to it.

To say good-bye to the life you shared with a deceased loved one, a marriage relationship that ended in divorce, the places and people you called home, or parts of the body you once had hurts beyond words.

However, before you can open new doors for your life, you have to close the doors that now lead to the past. It doesn't mean forgetting the person or memories any more than you forget your friends when they go home after dinner at your house.

To say good-bye acknowledges you will no longer share this mortal life with a person, place, stage of life, or part of your body anymore, other than in memory. If a loved one died, that person is forever frozen in time for you and will get no older than the day he or she died. You will. It was always a source of good-natured humor between June and me that she was five months older. Five months and fourteen days after her death, I became older than her and always will be.

My mother was fifty-four when she died. My dad was fifty-seven. I am now thirty years older than my mother. Now, there is a strange

> *If a loved one died, that person is forever frozen in time for you and will get no older than the day he or she died. You will.*

thought! My wife's brother, who was six when he was killed, would now be in his seventies. In my memory, he will always be six.

Writing this letter is an act of lovingly releasing a part of your life that will always remain important to you in memory, but which you must now leave behind as you live in the present.

It is important to say good-bye as you part temporarily from folks you care about. It's even more important to say good-bye to the life you had with those you will not see again in this life. It is just as important to bid good-bye to lost places and dreams.

Because you can't say good-bye in person to the one who has died or the marriage that has ended, another alternative is to write a letter. If you are like most people who have done this, it will be the most difficult letter you have ever written. It helps to remember this is also one of the most important letters you will ever write. Most people have either passed an anniversary of the person's death or getting near to it before being ready to write this letter.

To begin, think about whomever or whatever was lost to you that is the source of your grief. Go back to your journal and look at what you wrote in the exercise called "Giving Yourself Permission to Grieve" (page 226).

Use your favorite stationery for this letter. If you don't have a supply, buy some as though you were writing to someone very important. Use a good pen. This letter deserves the best you've got. No pencils or notebook paper, please. It's better if it is in your handwriting than done on a computer.

> *This letter deserves the best you've got.*

Address your letter as follows: If it is to a deceased person, use the salutation you used in life with this person. If it is to a marriage that is now over, address the focus of your loss, as if it were a person. That may or may not be your ex-spouse. It may be your mutual friends, the traditions surrounding the holidays, or the effect on your children. If it is to a place, address the letter as if it were to a person. When June and I sold a mountain cabin we had for twenty-four years, we wrote to "Our Dear Mountain Home. . . . " She wrote "Good-bye, my breast" after her mastectomy.

If it is an unfulfilled goal, a business failure, or a stage of your life, address it in a personal way.

After addressing your letter, immediately acknowledge that this is a letter of farewell to the past, not to the memory of that person.

- Express thanks for specific things you will remember. If you are writing to a deceased loved one, give your permission for that person to be dead and your faith that he/she is in heaven.
- Share your hopes and vision for the life you will live after your loss.

Sign the letter in whatever way is appropriate for you. Wait about one day and then read your letter aloud to yourself. If you need to add something or make changes, do that. Read the letter aloud several times each day for several days. When you can read it all the way through, even with tears, read it aloud to a friend, counselor, or clergyperson. If you are in a grief support group and are comfortable, you might choose to read the letter to the group.

Read the letter aloud several times each day for several days.

Keep the letter with your journal and other written exercises as an example of a historic moment along your journey to recovery.

Ken wrote the following as part of his letter after the death of his wife:

My darling Mae,

You and I always had our Lord with us. If it weren't so, I don't know what I would do now. That is what sustained us through your illness and now my faith and trust in my beloved Lord is what sustains me. The great void your death has left in my life is still a gaping hole. How can a "we" become an "I"? How can an "us" become a "me"? How can an "our" become a "mine"? Because of God, I believe there will always be a "we" and an "us" and an

*"our" in my heart. By faith I can release you to the love and care
of our Lord until we will meet again in his Kingdom.*

Ken

This letter helped Ken release his attachment to Mae and move on to a new life for himself that in time included another wife.

Martha's loss was the marriage she thought would last forever. After eleven years, it was over. She and Brad had shared a common dream for the first few years. As they struggled through a career change for him, she worked to help support them, sacrificing her own vocational goals.

She imagined that once he was established in his new career, it would be her turn to return to school. When the day came that Brad had a good job with a promising future in front of them, Martha quit her job and enrolled in night school. Brad was furious. He wanted her to work until their debt for his education was paid off. Their fights over money spread to the subject of having children. He was ready. She wasn't.

Outwardly they looked like an ideal couple. In private, the words between them grew ever more harsh, and the happy times became rare. It all ended when Martha came home unexpectedly in the middle of the day to find Brad in bed with another woman.

After the divorce became final, I suggested Martha write a letter of good-bye to Brad and their marriage. At first, I think she was sure I had lost my mind. In time, Martha did write the letter. Here is an excerpt:

Bradley,

As I write this letter to say good-bye to you, I refuse to add the word "Dear." I don't think I will ever forgive you for what you did to me, although I'm told this anger I feel will be more costly to me than to you. It's hard for me to remember that the first six years of our marriage were so good. I think it's knowing that once I loved you so much (and I think you loved me too) that hurts the most. It feels as if something inside of me has been murdered. I feel so

*sad and so angry, all at the same time. My only hope is that one
day I will be able to remember the good times without having my
thoughts dominated by the ugliness of the last two years. I am
trying to put my life together again. I have started going to
church again and that gives me some peace, at least for a little
while. I am going to night school and doing well and that helps
me to feel better about myself.*

*I don't miss you and all the hassles, but I do hate being alone so
much. I can't even stand the thought of getting involved with
another man. He'd probably turn out to be like you. Maybe
someday. First, I will get to know me and what I want much better
than I do now.*

*I believe there is a good life for me in the future because I believe
I am a good person.*

*Brad, this is hard for me to say, but thanks for the early years.
Our picnic breakfasts in the park and laughter we shared about
our first little apartment are memories I want to keep.*

*Good-bye. I hope you will remember some good things about
being with me, too.*

Martha

By reading her letter aloud several times, Martha was able to identify her anger and begin the process of releasing it. Over the next several months she was able to see more of her own failure in the marriage. In time she received a college degree and she is now doing well in her career. When I last saw her, Martha was still single.

Using the Resources of Religion

Regardless of whether you have been an actively religious person in the past, religious resources are important for you now. The resources that religion offers best are hope, comfort, a community where you are loved and cared for, and a sense of some greater meaning to life. You will benefit from all of these as you begin to open new doors to your life.

Grief is not first and foremost an intellectual experience. Philosophical religious concepts won't help you. This is no time for theological debates about the "right" kind of religion. What matters is that you find a religious expression helps you through grief. Read Chapter 12 again.

> *The resources that religion offers best are hope, comfort ... and a sense of some greater meaning to life.*

I urge you to find the clergyperson and church, synagogue, or mosque in your area that has the best program for grief support. Whatever the religious orientation of the group, it will help you.

Starting a Grief Support Group

The best support system while working through your grief is a group of people who have also experienced loss. One new door you can choose to open is organizing and starting such a group. It may sound difficult, but I assure you it isn't.

A grief support group doesn't require a highly trained, professional leader to be effective. It is an added bonus if one is available, especially as the group gets started. You may be able to find a counselor who will act as a referral resource if someone in the group shows signs of distorted grief.

> *Loss and grief are such common experiences that announcing almost anywhere that you are forming a support group will produce the people you need.*

Loss and grief are such common experiences that announcing almost anywhere that you are forming a support group will produce the people you need. A group doesn't have to be larger than three or four and should not exceed eight or ten people without a trained leader.

When someone's grief becomes distorted, the group provides a loving atmosphere in which it is okay to urge that person to seek professional counseling. Some people are hurting enough that the pain issues forth in language others do not want to hear. Usually, a nonjudgmental request made in private is enough to help alter profanities.

The exercises I have described in this book are useful as group activities. All of them have been tested over a minimum of twenty-five years in groups I have led.

Your church or synagogue can be an excellent source of people for the group. Your pastor, priest, or rabbi may provide a meeting place and perhaps help with leadership.

How long should you have a support group? The answer is, as long as you feel the need and until you have opened all the doors to new life that you want to open. A grief support group should plan to meet for a minimum of twelve sessions on a weekly basis for one to one and a half hours per session. I prefer holding the sessions to one hour. It allows ample time for sharing significant feelings and issues. At the same time it requires staying focused and not rambling on about subjects not related to a person's loss and grief. At times there have been as many as thirty people in a group I was leading. It can still be done effectively in one hour, but it is a good idea to have a co-leader sitting across the room who can see the signs of someone needing to talk and invite them to speak.

I personally like the ongoing model, in which people can attend for as long as they wish. This model also provides a ready-made referral place for newly bereaved persons. I make it clear that group members can "graduate" themselves any time they feel ready, but are always welcome back.

Remember, the entire first year after a major loss is dominated by experiences of "the first time without." For at least that year you need all the support you can get.

A support group also gives your own loss meaning because you are using your experience to help others. That's no little thing!

Appendix B contains a more detailed description of how to call a group together and what to do during the first few sessions.

Turning Your Loss into a Creative Hurt

When you get involved with the grief of other people, you should know one thing: Sharing in the grief of others is like playing in the mud. You can't do it without getting some on you!

At times, you will be sure you have all you can carry with your own grief. You won't see how you could handle that of anyone else in addition to your own.

However, there is a marvelous mystery about grief: The more you share in the grief of others, the more in charge of your own grief you will become. It won't be any less painful. But it will seem considerably more manageable.

The more you share in the grief of others, the more in charge of your own grief you will become.

When you share your struggles and discoveries with others and listen to their stories, you will find your pain becoming a creative hurt—an experience you can learn from. It will have purpose, meaning, and a dignity that you didn't sense before.

The people I know who have most fully established a new normal after a major loss are those who gave the most of themselves to others who are also grieving.

Jeanne lost her husband of forty-nine years after a brief illness. She was past seventy at the time. They had no children. Shortly after Alan's death, Jeanne began pouring her life into the needs of others. She befriended a young mother whose husband committed suicide, cared for a sister until her death at age ninety-three, and became the source of hope for another widow who was struggling with a drinking problem. She was past age eighty-five when she volunteered at a community food bank and served on the council for a preschool.

Mary, widowed many years younger than Jeanne, became a volunteer in the surgery waiting room of the hospital where her husband died. Dorothy, whose husband was a victim of Alzheimer's disease for several years before his death, filled the loneliness of her life by volunteering at a local school. She worked as a teacher's aide with first graders who dearly love her attention.

Al poured himself into volunteer work at his church after his wife's death to cancer. He sang in the choir, helped in the office, and led the personnel committee.

The opportunities and the needs are end-less. It's another step on the path to recovery that's often difficult to take, but the rewards are plentiful. I can't diagram an exercise to tell you how to turn the pain of your grief into a creative hurt. I can only tell you that the op-portunities are there if you will open the doors before you.

A creative hurt—a painful experience you can learn from.

Another door that is always before you some time after a major loss is the need to forgive someone. A failure to open this door can block your ability to release the past and move fully into a new life.

An Exercise in Forgiveness

Two almost surefire spin-offs of grief are anger and broken relation-ships. It is as true in the case of a death as it is with a divorce. It is a factor in relocation and other major losses.

I believe you can make the following assumption: *If you have experi-enced grief, there is someone you need to forgive.*

It's possible, of course, that there is someone who needs to forgive you. But that is *his or her task*. Your need to forgive is *your* task. Grant-ing forgiveness is another way to open a door in your life and move forward.

Begin with this survey, using a clean piece of paper. At the top, write the name of a person with whom you have had conflict or from whom you have felt alienated since your loss. Write down your answers to the following questions:

If you have experienced grief, there is someone you need to forgive.

- What is your relationship with this person? Is he or she a family member or friend? How long have you known this person?
- Do you blame this person in any way for your loss? If so, how?
- Are you angry, resentful, or hateful toward this person? If so, why?
- What is happening to you because of the break in your relationship with this person?
- Can you forgive this person and express your forgiveness? If you are able to forgive, write down a date on which you will offer your forgiveness. Also note if you will express it in person, on the telephone, or by letter or e-mail.

Granting forgiveness is never easy and can be especially difficult when grief is involved. You may think you would be disloyal to the one who has died or disloyal to your own principles if there has been a divorce. You may feel vulnerable or fear looking weak.

If your anger is still unresolved and you are unable to consider forgiveness, continue this exercise, using another piece of paper. Answer these questions:

- How is your self-esteem being affected by your anger? In what ways are you being robbed of energy? Is your sleep being affected?
- Write down the name of a trusted friend, counselor, or clergyperson. Share this survey and your struggle to forgive with this person.
- Determine why you are not able to forgive. Find the deeper reasons for your hurt and anger.
- Write a letter of forgiveness to the person whether or not you feel forgiving. Write as if you want to forgive. Place the letter in an envelope and put it in your journal. As you make your journal entry each day, read the letter aloud to yourself. Make changes in the letter as your feelings change. Stay with it until you can begin to feel forgiving.

Do not mail the letter or act on it until you are sure you are fully ready to forgive. I suggest choosing an occasion that has special meaning on which to act on your forgiveness.

Please note: If the person you need to forgive is deceased, write the letter as if you could send it to them. Read it out loud to yourself and one other trusted person. Find a ceremonial way to destroy it. Some people have found it helped to dig a small hole in the ground and burn the letter in it. Afterward, they covered the ashes with the removed dirt and smoothed out the surface.

Reaching out with forgiveness will bring more healing to you than to the one you forgive.

The Importance of Touch

During those first few days after your loss, when shock and numbness have shut down your emotional system, nothing will communicate caring to you quite as much as the touch of another person. Over the course of the ensuing months, you will appreciate those people who don't try to find the right words to say but are present with a touch on the arm or a timely hug.

The touch of another human being counts more when you have experienced a major loss than at any other time in your life except birth. I learned this while on call to a local hospital. My staff and I were providing supplemental pastoral services to the one full-time Protestant chaplain. The first emergency call I received was to the infant intensive-care unit.

A baby had been born prematurely and wasn't making it on his own. When I arrived, the newborn was hooked to special machines that helped him breathe and monitored his every function. After some time it was clear that he simply was not developed enough to survive.

The time had come to make the decision to unhook the life support. I held hands with the parents as the wires and tubes were removed. We took the baby to the mother's room, where each of us took turns holding him, stroking him, and crying while he died.

I had never had that experience before. At first it seemed cruel to me to subject the parents to holding their dying baby. It took only the first few seconds of my turn to hold the child to realize the wisdom of the experience.

He was not a fetus or an "it." He was a real person, worthy of love and worthy of grief because he was dying. It felt good to hold him and cry and tell his parents how beautiful he was. The mother and father unwrapped him from his blanket, admired each finger and toe, and gave him the only caresses they would ever be able to give.

I talked to those parents several times over the next months. They mourned their son in an appropriate way, but they were also proud of him. He was theirs. They had touched him. He had touched *them*.

I had touched him, too, and been touched by him. He became a permanent part of my life for as long as I live. In some way I will never understand fully, I am a better minister and a more compassionate person because of that baby who lived in this world only a few hours. I know it happened because we touched.

I'm telling you this in the hope you will be motivated to touch and be touched, even at those points in your grief recovery when you are most inclined to withdraw. One of those times is often about the third month after your loss. Another is between the ninth and twelfth months. Another is at or near the eighteenth month.

You may think that touching or hugging is no more appropriate at these times than I did in that hospital. I want you to know it is not only appropriate, it is great for you!

I now close every session of our grief support group by gathering the people in a close circle where we hold hands as we have a prayer. I think the touch is as vital to our well-being as the prayer.

I also find myself hugging widows, widowers, parents who have lost children, those who come for counseling because of divorce, and everyone who has suffered a loss and comes to talk to me about it. I haven't met most of them before the occasion. I have never been refused or put off.

Dr. Leo Buscaglia taught that hugs are good medicine for whatever ails us. They can be lifesavers when we are struggling with grief.

Making Peace with Grief

This exercise requires the help of a friend with a pleasant, soothing voice. Its purpose is to help you become more at peace with your grief and feel freer to open the doors to a new life. You will need a recording device.

Ask your friend to record the following message, reading it exactly as it is written. The narrator should speak in a soothing voice at a moderate rate of speed. Wherever three dots appear (. . .), it means to be silent for about three seconds before going on. The easiest way to time the silence is to count slowly and silently *one-and-two-and-three.*

Before you listen to the recording, please take a moment to get relaxed. Sit upright in a comfortable chair with your feet on the floor and your hands held loosely in your lap. Take off your shoes, remove your glasses, and loosen any tight clothing. Be sure you will not be interrupted by the telephone or other distractions.

The narrator will record this message, which you will play back on the recorder:

> . . . Please focus your attention on your breathing. Notice how breathing slowly and rhythmically helps you relax . . . Take a few deep breaths . . . Very good . . .
>
> Now take what we will call a peaceful breath. It's a special kind of deep breath that will tell your body and mind it's time to be at peace. The peaceful breath is taken like this:
>
> Breathe out all of the air from your lungs. Inhale slowly through your nose to a count of eight . . . Blow the breath out forcefully through your mouth.
>
> You will note a sensation of tingling after two or three peaceful breaths . . . That is your sign that you are relaxing deep inside.

Continue to breathe slowly and deeply, breathing in through your nose and out through your mouth. As you do this, close your eyes, if you have not already done so . . . Good . . . Now, with your eyes closed, turn your eyes as far to the left as you can, as though you were going to look out your left ear. Keep looking to the left as hard as you can . . . You may notice that your eye muscles and eyelids have become quite tense . . .

That's good, because I want you to experience the difference between tension and peacefulness. When I count to three, allow your eyes to come back to the front and feel the tension disappear. One . . . Two . . . Three . . .

Feel the soothing peacefulness around your eyes and in the back of your neck . . . Continue to breathe slowly and deeply . . . In through your nose, out through your mouth . . .

Begin to relax all the muscles in your face . . . around your eyes . . . in your cheeks . . . your forehead . . . your scalp . . . down to your mouth and chin . . . You may find your mouth dropping open a bit . . . That's fine . . . Keep breathing in the same manner . . . in through your nose, out through your mouth . . .

Allow your neck muscles to relax . . . Your head is tipping forward . . . You are feeling the relaxation and peacefulness moving to your shoulders . . . across your back . . . down to the middle of your back . . . down to your lower back . . .

Allow this same peacefulness to flow through your arms to your hands and fingers . . . down each leg and into your feet and toes. Continue to breathe slowly and deeply in through your nose, out through your mouth.

You may become aware of your heartbeat . . . Some people say they feel or hear the blood moving in their arteries. Whatever you are feeling is your body's way of being relaxed and at peace . . .

Start back at the top of your head and do a peacefulness checklist . . . Can you find any place where you are still holding tension? . . . If so, allow that tension to leave . . .

As you continue to be relaxed and at peace . . . Perhaps it's the most peaceful you have felt in a long time . . . Concentrate again on your breathing . . . Say to yourself with each exhale, *more relaxed* . . .

When you are fully relaxed . . . Take time to enjoy the feeling . . . Allow your body to enjoy the sense of peacefulness . . . Let it into your stomach and intestines . . .

As you are in this very peaceful, relaxed state, allow your grief to join you . . . It is not the hurtful, painful thing it was . . . but a natural part of life . . . You are at peace with your grief as you are with your natural body. Continue your breathing . . .

Allow your imagination to create a new life for you as you would like it to be in the future . . . See all the possibilities for you. Focus on your wish for yourself . . . As you breathe, tell yourself with every breath, *I will fulfill my dream* . . . Add anything else you want to say to yourself . . .

As you end this exercise, you will find that you are as refreshed as if you have had a restful sleep . . . You will be relaxed and yet full of energy . . . You will have a new sense of well-being and a new resolve for your life . . .

You can come back to this very peaceful state any time you want to by using your peaceful breathing . . . Now, breathing in an easy, normal way, as I count backward from five to one, you will open your eyes and be fully alert . . . Five . . . Four . . . Three . . . Two . . . One. . . . Very good!

You can play this recording for yourself as often as you like. It is the most effective anytime after the ninth month after your loss.

By the time you reach the point of opening new doors for your life, you not only deserve a sense of peacefulness, but also the right to spoil yourself just a bit.

The suggestions in the following box are made to help you take care of yourself. Your imagination may inspire you to add others to the list.

It's Okay to Live Again

Some actions are relatively simple but carry strong symbolic images of opening new doors:

- Change your hairstyle to something quite different.

- Make it 100 percent your choice!

- Consult a professional wardrobe stylist or personal shopper. Buy some new clothes in your best color or shape.

- Go on a trip you have wanted to take but couldn't because of responsibilities you no longer have. Because June needed my care several hours a day, especially when she had to live in a memory care facility, I never was gone unless I was ill. Six months after her death I went on a two-week journey by myself to do whatever I felt like doing at the moment.

- Remodel one room in your house to suit you. Sometimes just paint or wallpaper and a few accessories can do wonders.

- Change your mealtime routine, including the time. Many widowed persons find that sitting in their spouse's place at the table eases the loneliness.

20

Your Own Best Friend
Completing the Journey

Nobody likes to lose. Losing always hurts, whether it is a little loss and a little hurt or a loss that changes your life and hurts beyond description.

If you are a normal, healthy person, you want to be a winner. You grew up liking success stories. You were taught to believe bigger is best, more is better, and getting is much more fun than losing.

Somewhere along the way you had a minor loss. It was one of those disappointments that can "ruin" your life for at least forty-eight hours. A well-meaning friend asked, "What did you do to deserve that?" You were pretty sure you must have done something.

Now you have had a major loss. You have never before known this much sorrow. Your life has been permanently changed. Grief has become your constant companion. It has drained your emotions and robbed you of energy.

You have experienced grief for only one reason. You are a real, live, mortal person in this altogether too mortal and frail world where things happen that aren't fair. You don't deserve the pain or exhaustion, the emptiness, sadness, or frustration that accompanies grief. I hope you know by now that God is not responsible for your loss. There is not some divine justice system that has punished you for your mistakes.

As long as you are alive, you will experience loss from time to time. Some losses will be small and you will soon forget them. Other losses will change the course of your life.

As long as you are alive, you will experience loss from time to time.

When you pass the anniversary date of a major loss in your life, there is at least one good thing to say: *You made it!* This seems especially true when your grief is due to death or divorce.

It is finally up to you whether your major losses destroy you or help you grow into a stronger, better person. No one can make you grow through loss, but nothing can keep you from it either. When you say, "I made it through this year," you will be acknowledging the greatest accomplishment of your life.

Somewhere between the first and second anniversaries of your loss you will discover a new best friend—yourself. You have been in the depths. You have faced the worst experiences in your life. You have endured more emotional pain longer than you thought you could. You have made decisions that a few months earlier were unthinkable. In the midst of your own pain, you have reached out to others who were also

Somewhere between the first and second anniversaries of your loss you will discover a new best friend—yourself.

grieving. Please know that I have been in these places, too, and have a new appreciation for just how difficult the challenges are.

Now you are beginning to look at the possibilities of a new life. You didn't ask for a new life. You didn't want it. But now that it's here, you will make the most of it. As you think about the new normal you are creating, it seems to offer its own joys.

In spite of the ongoing loneliness, you are regaining your balance in life. Having gone through the most difficult places along the way of grief recovery, you know yourself better than you ever did before. As you build your new life after loss, you need to be especially aware of your current strengths and weaknesses.

The exercise "Best Friend–Worst Enemy" should help you identify both more clearly. Refer to the following box for this exercise.

As you continue to work through your loss and grief, the tasks before you in the second year will not be as crushing as those that are behind you. Your most difficult period will probably be somewhere around the eighteenth month, when some of the old sadness and impatience may return. I will remind you again: It won't last. You now also have your newly found best friend self to help you past this bump in your road to recovery.

If you are recovering from the death of your spouse or a divorce, most of your energies will be devoted to finding ways to shake off the loneliness. Other major losses can leave you facing the same task. Here is a three-word formula for success: *Release . . . Reorient . . . Reconnect.*

Release

It is painful to release the emotional ties to that part of your life that is lost, but you will never fully recover your balance until you do. This is never easy for anyone, but probably more important and difficult to do if you are younger rather than older. How you see yourself will depend more on your perception than your chronological age. (See Chapter 5.)

- It may seem disloyal or sinful even to think about enjoying life after your spouse has died.
- If your life was dominated by caring for your spouse for a long time, the sense of freedom you now have may be difficult to celebrate.
- Your load of disillusionment after a broken marriage may be overwhelming.
- It's rough to let go of sentimental attachments to the place where you spent a significant portion of your life.

Best Friend—Worst Enemy

Divide a sheet of 8 ½ x 11-inch piece of paper in half vertically by folding it or drawing a line from top to bottom. This is another exercise that can be done on a computer.

On the left side at the top, write "Worst Enemy." On the right side, write "Best Friend."

Now, reflect on the following statements:

- There is some way in which each of us is our own worst enemy; likewise, there is some way in which each of us is our own best friend.

- As our own worst enemy, we create inner conflicts and make it more difficult to do the things we want or need to do.

- As our own best friend, we bring special skills, gifts, and qualities to whatever we are doing.

On the left column, list the ways in which you are your own worst enemy.

On the right, list the ways in which you are your own best friend.

Examine both lists. In what ways can your "best friend" help your "worst enemy"?

Could your worst-enemy traits be helped by a professional counselor? If so, seek that help. Share your lists with your grief support group, clergy, or counselor.

Nevertheless, this letting go of the past is essential to moving on to a future life after your loss.

One image that has helped many widowed persons is to pretend the circumstances are reversed. That is, pretend you are the one who has died. If that were the case and you were aware of your spouse's grief, what would you wish for him or her? Would you wish for a lifetime of sadness, depression, and loneliness? Not at all! The two of you have spent years caring for each other. You would wish for your spouse to be happy again. Try to imagine your spouse wishing the same for you.

Think about your loss. Is it now time for you to release your emotional attachment to whomever or whatever was lost? To the marriage that is never going to be fulfilled? To a stage of life in which you found special meaning? To your body as it was? To some other loss?

Several months after his wife died, my brother called me to say he had come to realize that he no longer had a relationship with Mary, but a memory of her.

> To release your attachment doesn't mean to forget or to deny the importance of that part of your life.

Rhonda and Bill had both been married before. They were good for each other during the brief time of their marriage before he died of cancer. She took care of him at home until the end, using her professional nursing skills to enable him to die with dignity.

Alan and Margaret lived in the same community as Rhonda and Bill. They had shared life together for more than forty years before she died of cancer. Her deterioration was extremely difficult for Alan to accept. He called in hospice volunteers who helped with nursing and gave him much-needed moral support. I was holding hands with both of them when she died.

In time, Alan and Rhonda were able to come to the point of realizing they had done everything they could for their loved ones.

It was time to let go and move on. I'll always remember the day Alan called to say he and Rhonda wanted to be married. I have never enjoyed performing a wedding more.

To release your attachment doesn't mean to forget or to deny the importance of that part of your life. It doesn't mean you do not love your deceased child or spouse or parent. It means you understand this person will not be a part of your present life, but will live only in your memories. You are ready to release your attachment so you can move on—to open new doors to a life for yourself.

Use the exercises "Writing a Letter of Good-bye to the Past" (page 247) and "Making Peace with Grief" (page 259) to help you facilitate this release.

Reorient

The next step in reaching out to a new life involves giving yourself permission to begin reorienting your interests and activities in new directions.

You will not overcome loneliness by thinking about solutions. You will not release an attachment to the past by waiting for that attachment to subside. You overcome loneliness by becoming concerned about other people. Once you discover that you are your own best friend, you can share your friendship with other people. You will be surprised that you can let others into your heart and caring. You don't just think about it, however: you do it.

> You overcome loneliness by becoming concerned about other people.

Those people I know who have done the most to eliminate loneliness from their life after a major loss are the most involved in helping other bereaved people, community service, devotion to family members, and developing new friendships.

Releasing your attachment to the past is also a "doing" behavior, in which you reorient your attachments to the present. For a widow or widower, that might mean a new relationship with a person of the opposite sex. For the parent who has lost a child, it might mean focusing attention on another child in the family, having a baby, or adopting a child. In a new city, it means developing loyalties to local sports teams, joining civic groups, and getting to know the special features of that community.

The suggestions in the section "It's Okay to Live Again" (page 262) are simple but effective ways to begin opening doors to new experiences.

Try them, or use the suggestions to help you think of others you could try. Another good approach is to think of something you wanted to do before your loss, but could not. Do that thing now.

Susan always wanted to go on a rafting trip through the Grand Canyon. Her husband, Jim, would have no part of it. The subject was the source of more than a few family fights. When Jim got cancer, Susan forgot all about the raft and the river. She devoted all of her energies to Jim and their remaining time together.

About fourteen months after Jim's death, Susan took their two sons on a river trip through the Grand Canyon. It was a difficult decision for her, and she had moments of tears and sadness during the trip. But it was the turning point in her grief recovery. She went back to school, has a good job, and along the way, had her first date, much to her sons' amusement.

Richard and Janna were married for ten stormy years. They were in counseling almost from the beginning, but to no avail. Whatever else they could do in life, they could not seem to be nice to each other. They tried separating, but felt so strongly drawn to each other that they moved back together again. They fought over everything, including money, how to raise their child, and what to do on Saturday evening.

Finally, they separated again, but neither one could seem to initiate a divorce. Even living apart did not prevent them from quarreling. In time, each of them began living with a different partner. Richard and his new girlfriend had a child, but still he could not break the emotional tie with Janna. His life was in chaos. He used drugs, drank too much alcohol, and wound up in trouble for failure to pay taxes.

It was a matter of years until Richard could work through the loss of his marriage to Janna. The day finally came when the divorce was finalized. A few months later, he and Rebecca were married.

With the ties finally broken, Richard was ready to have his life go in a new direction. He paid off his debts, quit abusing his body, and saved money for the down payment on a house. Some years later, Rebecca sought a divorce. This time he handled it in a healthy way. His subsequent marriage to his third wife finally seemed to bring all the pieces together. He is happy in his marriage, successful in his career, and fulfilled in his life.

Whatever your loss, the time comes eventually to focus on the way your life is now, rather than the way it had been before your loss, and to head in a new direction. Make a list of things you can do now that you could not do before. Make an effort to begin meeting new people. As you do, write down your feelings about the experience in your journal.

Reconnect

Reconnecting is the final step. At this point in your life, you have reoriented your emotions to things in the present. You are able to love another person in marriage, if that is a possible alternative for you. You do not feel compelled to visit the gravesite of your child, although you may place flowers there on holidays, birthdays, and other special dates. I remember very clearly the occasion almost three years after we moved away from our home state for the first time. From the time we moved, going back to our former state always felt like going home. Our sense of loss was so great we often shed tears as we crossed the border returning to our new state. This time, almost three years after our move, we realized that returning to our new state now felt like going home.

We paused at the border and shed a few tears at the realization, but these were tears of joy.

I can't tell you when or if you will be ready for another marriage, another child, a different job, or a new city. Perhaps you will never choose any of those. The important thing is for you to be able to do these things, if you want to.

When you have released the past, reoriented to the future, and reconnected to the present, you will still have problems simply because you are alive, but loneliness will not be one of them.

Loss and Sexuality

If you are widowed or divorced, the issue of sex is a significant factor in your new life after loss.

I find that those who are widowed have a more difficult time talking about sexuality than those who are divorced. A part of this may be the relative ages at which people are widowed or divorced. It is not that widowed people in their sixties, seventies, eighties, and older are not interested in sexual contact. They come from an era when the subject of sex was not discussed in public—and certainly not with their minister!

If you are a woman who has lost your husband to death, you are one of the 11 million widows in the United States. There are about twice the number of new widows each year as widowers. Because of this, most older men are married; most older women are not.

After listening to both divorced and widowed people talk, it seems to me that those who are widowed remain celibate longer than those who are divorced. Most of that has to do with the sense of loyalty the widowed person has to his or her deceased spouse. In addition, a crazy cultural "rule" in our society says it is more appropriate for a divorced person to satisfy the desire for intimacy than is a widowed person.

That seems particularly strange when you consider the widowed person has usually come from a relationship where there was more of a fulfilling intimacy for a longer time than the divorced person.

Both widowed and divorced persons say that casual sexual encounters are a bigger problem for them than the frustration and loneliness of abstinence.

Finding ways to sublimate sexual energy is helpful for many people. Anything that is artistic, creative, and social will use some part of your sexuality in creative ways. A few brave people have said openly that masturbation relieves tension for a while but does nothing about the need for the intimacy of talking with, holding, and caressing another person.

If you have a safe place to talk about the issues of sexuality after loss, do that. It needs discussion in groups and with counselors. There are no easy or pat answers. Being judgmental or moralistic with yourself or others serves no useful purpose.

In her excellent book *Beginnings: A Book for Widows*, Betty Jane Wylie speaks for widowed and divorced persons when she says, "The limits of your behavior lie within you and not in the acceptance of society around you."[1]

Money Matters

Money is part of the pathway of your recovery. It may seem like a big jump from sex to money, but both are issues of particular importance to those who are widowed or divorced.

When I asked a group of widows what they would most like to tell young couples to prepare them for the loss of a mate, they responded unanimously with concerns about money matters.

If you are widowed or divorced, your income level has probably declined. If you are a woman, you may have had to find a job for the first time in years. If you are a divorced man with children, you have learned the expensive facts of child support and keeping two residences.

Chances are, you need to know more about budgeting and the use of credit cards than you needed to before. If your spouse kept the checkbook and paid the bills, take a class in bookkeeping. Community colleges and online programs are a good source of help (some websites even offer free courses, so look around for the one that fits your needs). Some churches offer counseling by a member who is an accountant. If you have not had a line of credit in your own name, build your own as soon as you can. Make a small purchase you can easily afford and pay it off promptly. Doing this is one way married people who are not employed can prepare for the possible loss of their spouses. Since June was not employed for many years, we got a credit card in her name and slowly built up a sizeable line of credit. If I had died first, she would have had credit already established.

Nutrition and Your New Life

Nutrition and physical fitness are vital components of your recovery. Far too little is said about the roles of food and exercise in grief recovery. The more I learn about and experience the importance of these factors, the more I understand why some people are able to handle their grief so much better than others.

Rey came to see me because he was depressed. He was not adjusting well to career setbacks and personal disappointments. He had been to psychologists and psychiatrists. He had taken medication for depression and been in group therapy for social maladjustment. None of it was helping. He was feeling worse.

Knowing the highly skilled nature of the treatment he had already received, I didn't want to see Rey. I tried to refer him to a psychologist, but he refused. I made an appointment with him not knowing what to try next.

When Rey came in and we began to talk, something he said triggered my interest in his diet. He was a bit rattled that I wanted to talk about the things he ate instead of his emotional problems. He was more rattled when I asked him to see a local nutritionist before we talked further.

The next day he called me in an excited and hopeful voice. Testing had shown he was suffering from hypoglycemia—low blood sugar. In extreme cases it can dramatically affect moods.

That was surely the case with Rey. By changing his diet, his depression was gone in less than two weeks. His ability to relate with others returned to normal. He was able to work at adjusting to his losses with a new energy and determination. None of the former problems have recurred.

Rey could have gone through therapy for years, taken medication, and still watched his self-esteem sink steadily lower. All he needed to begin a whole new life was a change in the foods he was eating.

It is as important for you to pay attention to your nutrition throughout the length of your grief recovery as it was for Rey. You may not have a blood-sugar problem, but what you are eating or not eating can have an effect on your energy level and ability to cope with the stress of the grieving process.

A diet complete in all the necessary nutrients is crucial to maintaining your health during the long and stressful time it takes to work through a major loss.

Maintaining an appropriate weight is the first step. We each respond to stress differently. Some people tend to eat more when stressed, and consequently gain weight, whereas others become disinterested in food and therefore lose weight. In either case, if the gain or loss is more than 10 percent of your usual weight, it is likely that you will be lacking essential nutrients, and your energy to cope with stress will be decreased.

To help conserve energy, prepare simple meals using casseroles and one-dish meals or choose from entrées and dinners that are well-balanced but not too high in fat or salt. Use your blender, Crock-Pot, microwave, or toaster oven to save effort. Let friends or relatives help if they offer to prepare a dish or meal for you. Occasionally take advantage of a local restaurant's home-delivery service or eat out. Avoid fast food. Use whatever means works for you. Just be sure not to skip meals or rely on only a few foods for all your nutrition. A wide variety of foods and adequate quantities are the cornerstones of a good diet.

Fluids are also very important. Your body needs water to keep all the systems working properly and to keep essential nutrients in proper balance. Beverages that are high in caffeine or sugar or contain alcohol can act as diuretics and therefore lead to further dehydration. Drink them in moderation. Plain water is the best fluid you can take!

What you are eating or not eating can have an effect on your energy level and ability to cope with the stress of the grieving process.

Getting all the needed nutrients from the food you eat is one of the most positive things you can do for yourself. It will be more difficult to ensure that you get all the important nutrients if your diet includes large quantities of high-fat or high-sugar foods. One of the best things you can do is to consult with your doctor or a nutritionist and seek help in setting up an eating plan at least for the first year. There are many online sites that offer guidance for healthy eating. The problem with these is that no one is monitoring you to see if you are following them, so if you can, seeing a professional will help you to pick a plan and stick to it.

Physical Fitness

I also urge you to get whatever amount of physical exercise you can tolerate. Walking is one of the best exercises and a great resource for combating depression. I had been away from our local intergenerational health center for three years due to the large amount of time I was spending in caring for June. One of the first things I did after her death was go back and begin working out again. I started walking just 1 mile every day on the track or treadmills and slowly increased it over time. I also began working with light weights and doing guided stretching. The effect on my strength and mood was significant immediately.

It's always a good idea to have a checkup by your doctor before beginning any strenuous exercise program. Two months after June's death I checked with my doctor because I was having shortness of breath. An EKG and blood work revealed significant changes in negative directions in several areas compared to similar tests six months earlier.

> *Walking is one of the best exercises and a great resource for combating depression.*

Most cities have health spas or clubs. Sometimes health plans offer their members exercise classes through hospitals at a slightly discounted rate. If you can afford the cost, a health-club membership or exercise classes make an effective social as well as fitness contribution to your stamina for grief work.

Getting on with Life

One of the great discoveries of the journey from loss to life is that you can be your own best friend as you make your way along the pathway to grief recovery.

The exercises I have suggested provide ways you can help yourself regain a zest for living and a deep sense of happiness. It isn't easy and it doesn't come quickly. But you can emerge from the depths of your loss as one who is on top of life.

One day you will sense it is time to leave the past and get on with the present and the future. When that day comes, you will have completed the journey and finished the work. You will be a whole person again with a normal life.

21

Preparing for Loss
A New Dimension in Wholeness

"There is no way to prepare for the loss of a loved one." You have heard this said many times—you may have said it yourself. However, regardless of how many of us believe there is no way to prepare for loss, it isn't true!

You can prepare for losses, including the death of a spouse, child, parent, sibling or friend; divorce; moving to a new city or state; retiring from work; children leaving home; major surgery; catastrophic injury; the loss of a job; and any other major change in life.

If you have not experienced a major loss, you need to know you are not helpless before the prospect of such an inevitable event in your life. If you have experienced a major loss in the past, you need to know this doesn't guarantee you won't face other losses in the future. Even if you weren't prepared the first time, there is no reason not to be prepared now.

Marge, whose husband had been ill for many years, described her anxiety about his declining health. She said, "I feel like an ant in the path of an avalanche. Everything is out of control and rushing toward me. All I can do is wait for his death because I know it's coming. I don't talk about it because I don't know anything I can do about it. I wait in silence."

Breaking the Silence

The first thing you can do to prepare for loss is break the conspiracy of silence surrounding it. It's okay to talk about death. A superstition many people have says, "If you talk about something bad, it will happen." I think most of us realize that is a silly notion—but still we keep silent. The truth is something bad is going to happen sooner or later and we are far better prepared if we have talked about loss and grief before it happens.

A widow said to me, "Bill and I never talked about death. He always believed if we talked about it, one of us would die." They didn't talk about death, but he died anyway at the age of eighty. His widow was left with many things she had never told him and a deep sense of guilt to compound the pain of her grief.

> *The first thing you can do to prepare for loss is break the conspiracy of silence surrounding it.*

Sometimes the pathway of grief does not follow an anticipated pattern. She had unsuccessfully tried to care for his plants for two years after his death because of a sense of loyalty to him. She had meant to tell him she couldn't garden like him because of her arthritis, but never got around to it; she had been afraid he would be upset because she was planning for his demise. Finally, she had the plants removed. Their unwillingness to talk about aging and death left her totally unprepared to cope with his death and take care of herself. It took another two to three years of therapy and medications to get her through the depression that consumed her. Really sad— and unnecessary.

Preparing for Loss Is Preparing for Life

Preparing for loss is not a morbid activity. It is not to become a pessimist about life, but an optimist who is also a realist. It is not to say, *Bad things will happen if I think about loss*. It is to say, *I can get through any loss in my life successfully*.

By preparing for grief, you will not avoid its pain or the steps through grief described in this book. I know of no way to get under, over, or around the heartache that comes with the death of a loved one. The same applies to going through a divorce or any other life-changing loss. Preparing for loss means strengthening yourself for the task of taking charge of your grief and working your way through it. It isn't easy or fun. It is necessary and possible.

Preparing for loss is to say, **I can get through any loss in my life successfully.**

As soon as you decide you can do things to prepare for life's inevitable losses, you have begun to take charge of your own destiny. Taking charge in this way can be a new and positive experience in itself. You will no longer feel as vulnerable or helpless as you did before. The unforeseen, unpredictable circumstances of life won't have the same power to terrify you.

I remind every couple who comes to me for premarital counseling that every marriage ends in one of two ways, death or divorce. I know of no other options. It helps to give newlyweds a realistic frame of reference for all of their planning and relating.

I was having a day of fun with my grandchildren when the telephone interrupted me with a call from a family whose three-year-old daughter had been killed in an accident. Tragic events do happen in this world! You can't always avoid them. But you can be prepared to face the grief that follows such losses.

Preparing Your Body for Grief

Physical health is as important as mental health in working your way through a major loss. Good nutrition, physical exercise, adequate fluids, and sufficient rest are all important during mourning. They are equally important as a means of preparing for grief. Whatever your age or physical limitations might be, you can achieve an optimum level of health for you personally with surprisingly little effort.

I suggest checking with your doctor to find the best dietary plan and level of exercise for your particular situation. Don't wait until you experience a loss to take care of yourself.

Nobody Does Grief Work Perfectly

In my experience, those who have unrealistic expectations of themselves do not handle loss and grief very well. If you are a person who always demands just a little more of yourself, you will add unnecessary frustration and guilt to your grief. Nobody does grief work perfectly. It is a time of slipping and sliding, of three steps forward and two back, of doing your best and discovering there is always more to do. Even "experts" on grief like me slip and slide with all the rest of you.

Before you experience a loss is a good time to look for any unrealistic personal standards you may have and work on changing expectations of yourself. Learn to be more patient with yourself *before* you have to face the challenge of grief.

Even if you have not already experienced a major loss, work through some of the exercises in this book. Ask yourself how you think you would respond to the death of a loved one, relocating to another area far from familiar sights and faces, or a divorce. Getting in touch with your feelings about the possibility of such events is a way of beginning to prepare for losses that are unavoidable.

> *Getting in touch with your feelings about the possibility of such events is a way of beginning to prepare for losses that are unavoidable.*

Loss and grief are not enjoyable experiences for anyone, but they happen to all of us at some time and usually more than once. You can prepare for loss in the simple but important ways I have outlined here.

Perhaps the greatest benefit of preparing is not what preparation does for life after loss, but what it does for life *before* loss. You will live with more confidence and less fear. You will know that you have more than good luck going for you. The quality of your life will be better.

Doing good things for yourself physically, mentally, and spiritually will add greater energy and enjoyment to your life.

People who successfully make their way through grief have a newfound sense of strength and self-esteem. They have faced the unimaginable and conquered it. They know that one loss does not give them immunity from other losses. Having made it through once, they also know that if necessary, they can do it again. By preparing yourself for the inevitable losses that come to all of us, you can gather some of that strength and self-esteem before any major loss confronts you.

The final thing I would like you to do before closing this book is take a fantasy trip that can be a healing journey. The images it presents will seem as deep and impossible as recovering from the worst loss you can imagine. But you can follow the fantasy and make the journey. You will come out of it feeling some of the inner peace that can be yours when the pathway through grief is completed.

As you read the words that follow, allow your imagination to take you through the experience it describes.

The Secret Box

You are in a meadow. It is a beautiful, green place with wavy grass and a scattering of colorful flowers. The sky is blue overhead with just a few puffs of white clouds. (Close your eyes for a moment and create this scene in your imagination. When you are ready to go on, open your eyes and continue reading.)

You walk through the meadow and come to a crystal blue lake. There is a short, sandy beach, so you take off your shoes and feel the grainy sand, warmed by the bright sunlight.

You walk across the beach to the water and wade in a short distance. Now you can feel the coolness of the water as compared to the warmth of the sand. It is very pleasant. (If you like, take a moment to close your eyes again and let your imagination take you into this scene. When you are ready to continue, open your eyes and read on.)

This is the amazing part. You walk farther into the water, feeling it come up around your knees, then your waist. The lake bottom is very smooth and sandy, with no rocks or weeds. You continue to walk into the cool, clear water as it rises to your chest, then your neck.

The great thing about a fantasy is that we are not limited by the usual constraints of our physical world. So, you continue walking into the water until you are under the surface! Wonder of wonders, you can breathe the water as though it were air, and you do not float. The sights around you are beautiful and you feel secure and elated. The water is cool and refreshing around you and, as you breathe it, you know why fish are so energetic. (You may want to lay down the book again for a moment and close your eyes to get the full effect. When you are ready, go on reading.)

As you walk deeper, the light grows dimmer, except for a very strong beam of sunlight that pierces the water at the very center of the lake.

As you approach that place, you see a small box lying on the sand. It is shaped like a small pirate's chest, is made of dark wood, and has a brass handle.

You pick up the box and open it. The light from the sunbeam illuminates the contents so you can see them clearly. You know what is in the box. (Close your eyes so that your imagination can see it very distinctly. When you are sure you know what is there, open your eyes and continue reading.)

You close the box and carry it with you out of the water and up onto the shore. As you walk toward the meadow, a figure appears. It is a man. He walks toward you. Though he is a stranger, you are drawn to him. He smiles, and you know you have nothing to fear.

As you draw near to the stranger, you are surprised because you feel completely at ease. You say nothing, and the man says nothing. You are standing very close, and you just look into each other's eyes.

Without a word, you hold out the box, and the man reaches out and takes it. You look at each other for a minute longer, then he nods, and you turn and walk away.

You walk back through the meadow feeling the warm sun on your back and a gentle breeze around you. You walk more lightly than you have in a long time. You know inside that life is really good after all. And you are healed.

When you are finished with this story, put down the book. Stand up and walk around for a minute or two. Notice that you feel a little bit lighter than you did when you began reading.

Life after Loss

Earlier, I suggested that talking with someone who had recovered from grief was like talking to an adventurer. I said those who conquered grief talk more about what they have found than what they have lost. Their lives reflect the events of the past, but are focused on the future. Death and loss do not dominate their thoughts. They have a sense of joy that is more solid than most people's because they know there is nothing life can deal that they can't handle. They are compassionate people. They have more patience than most folks. They have a reverence for life and a deep appreciation for human relationships.

It is my hope and prayer that when you have made your way through your grief as you have through this book, others will think that talking to you is like talking to an adventurer.

May your life after loss be full and rewarding with times of surprising joy!

Appendix A

Words that Describe Feelings

It is not easy to put feelings into words. The task becomes more difficult when our feelings are very strong either positively or negatively. We commonly say, "The sunset was beautiful beyond words," or "I love you more than words can say." We also say, "There are no words to describe the pain I feel because of his/her death."

To be able to put our feelings into words is important even though it is difficult. Describing our feelings of grief is an act of healing.

The following words describe feelings. As you write in your journal or work through the various exercises in the book, refer to this list often. Find the best word to describe the feeling you are trying to describe.

Happy

carefree	exhilarated	lighthearted
cheerful	glad	merry
content	hopeful	peaceful
ecstatic	joyous	relaxed
elated	jubilant	serene

Appendix A

Angry

annoyed	frustrated	outraged
bitter	fuming	seething
burning	furious	wrathful
cross	infuriated	
enraged	irritated	

Sad

bleak	dreary	joyless
brokenhearted	flat	melancholy
depressed	forlorn	miserable
discouraged	hopeless	mournful
dismal	in the dumps	unhappy

Fearful

alarmed	hysterical	scared
anxious	panicky	shaky
horrified	petrified	shocked

Tense

breathless	paralyzed	tense
hollow	stretched	uptight
immobilized	taut	weak

Hurt

aching	distressed	pained
afflicted	injured	suffering
crushed	lonely	tortured
cold	offended	

Courageous

bold	daring	proud
brave	determined	reassured
confident	encouraged	secure

Eager

avid	excited	intrigued
creative	fascinated	keen
earnest	inquisitive	sincere

Doubtful

defeated	pessimistic	unbelieving
hesitant	powerless	uncertain
hopeless	suspicious	wavering

Tired

burned out	heavy	subdued
exhausted	lethargic	weary
fatigued	spent	worn out

Appendix B

Forming a Support Group

Forming a grief support group is fairly easy to do. Because major loss is such a universal human experience, you will have little difficulty finding people who are willing to participate.

One of your first tasks will be to decide what the focus of the group will be. Will it be just for widows and widowers? Or will it also include those who have lost children, parents, or other loved ones? Will it focus only on the grief that follows death? Do you want to address the needs of divorced persons? Do you want the group limited to people in your church or other place of worship?

If you are going to be the one to form the group, reflect on your own situation and needs and start from there.

Be assured that once you have penetrated people's initial anxiety about meeting with strangers, you will find a positive response.

Churches, synagogues, clubs, fraternal organizations, PTA groups, and your own circle of friends are all good places to seek participants for a support group; if you live in an area where it is impractical to get a group together, consider starting the group online. Giving the page a straightforward and descriptive name will help others to find you. Available websites include Compassionate Friends and Caring.com (several types of groups). Skype and video technologies offer ways to connect.

You can call a group together in several ways. The following have all been used successfully:

1. Ask your minister, priest, rabbi, or imam to publish a notice in his or her newsletter about the formation of a support group. Ask people to

submit their names. Include your name and telephone number for additional information.

2. Put a notice in a club or fraternal group's newsletter. Offer to let the group meet at your home or arrange for another place.

3. Consult a local psychologist about offering a six- to eight-session series on grief and loss. Often, a counselor or psychologist will do it free of charge for potential referrals.

4. Talk to friends about getting together to support one another in times of loss and to share past experiences.

5. Publish a notice in your local newspaper or post fliers in markets, drugstores, and other public-display places, announcing the formation of the group.

Whatever approach you take, be specific about the group's purpose, the length of time it will meet, and cost, if any.

It is always good to put an end date on the initial series of meetings. This encourages people to be regular in attendance and provides a "safety valve" in case anyone has emotional problems that are too severe for the group to handle.

Have each participant get a copy of this book to use as a guide.

Groups should consist of at least four people, but no more than ten without a trained leader.

Unless a professional counselor is called in, it is important that whoever calls the group together leads the first series of meetings.

If the group is not led by a trained professional, its purpose will be different. Untrained persons should not attempt therapy with members of the group. However, providing a setting where people can freely share experiences and feelings and find a network of others who care is extremely helpful. A self-help format requires only that the leader understand the principles of grief recovery explained in this book.

The fundamental principles for a self-directed group are these:

- Feelings are neither right nor wrong. The leader must be as accepting of anger and frustration as of hopefulness and joy.
- It takes a long time to work through loss and grief.
- Review the steps of grief recovery in Chapter 6.

If you have questions, contact Bob Deits at rdeits@cox.net.

Session One: Telling Our Story

The first session is especially important. People often feel uncomfortable and anxious about what is going to take place. It is important for the leader to establish an atmosphere of relaxed security. If a professional counselor is not present, there are several ways to do this:

- Provide a comfortable, "homey" setting. Soft (not dim) lights, comfortable chairs arranged in a circle, easy-to-read name tags, and isolation from other distracting noises all help to establish the kind of setting that is needed.
- Children should not be present because they are too distracting. Childcare may have to be provided at a different location.
- Refreshments, if any, should be restricted to light beverages until the session is completed. Alcoholic beverages can be a problem. Avoid them.
- At least one full box of tissues should be within easy reach at every session. (I keep five full boxes on hand and deliberately set one out on a table or empty chair as each session begins.)

Begin by reminding everyone of the group's purpose. Have each person give his or her name and tell why he or she is coming to the group. All the participants should describe the loss they have experienced in as much detail as they wish. Encourage them to use the names of deceased or divorced persons.

It is important at this point of the group's life together that others just listen and not give advice. The group leader may have to enforce this at first. It is common to hear repeatedly, "I thought I was the only one who felt like that." It helps if the leader calls attention to the common ground of the group's experiences.

The main goal of the meeting is for people to tell their stories and to know they have been listened to and understood.

The group should meet for no more than ninety minutes and should end on time. Using prayer at the closing is a matter of personal choice. If prayer is used, it should be short, affirming, and not "preachy."

It is good to create a roster of the group and have a printed list of names, addresses, and telephone numbers ready for each participant at the second meeting.

Session Two: Four Key Facts about Grief

The setting should be prepared again as it was for the first meeting.

- Be sure the box of tissues is clearly visible and easily reachable.
- Use name tags again if group members do not already know each other or if new persons are joining.

Have each member of the original group introduce him- or herself to the newcomers and briefly tell his or her losses. Then the new people are welcomed to share their stories.

Present the "Four Key Facts about Grief "as described in Chapter 8. Take time for group discussion on each one and how various members are experiencing it. Don't rush. You may take up the entire evening with just the first one: The way out of grief is through it, because there is no way around it.

It is quite possible that tears will flow during the discussion. Always affirm to the group that crying is normal, appropriate, and healthy. I kept a sign in our meeting place that read, "People and tears are welcome here."

If time remains, ask people to describe the particular issues they have faced in the past week. Keep in mind that where people are in their grief process will determine the focus of their sharing.

In closing, ask people to identify themselves if they are willing to be called at home by others in the group. Urge group members to put a mark by these names on their rosters. The support that group members sometimes give each other in these informal, between-sessions contacts is often as helpful as the meetings themselves. It is not unusual to see lasting friendships develop in this way.

Session Three: Moods and Feelings

Begin the session by asking whether anyone has anything to share with the group. There may be a tendency to sidetrack onto issues not directly related to the individual's grief recovery. For instance, if someone is in the stage of blaming others for the loss, that person may take up excessive time talking about those others instead of his or her own feelings. If this occurs, it is the task of the leader to bring the focus of conversation back to the immediate experience of the group members. Do it gently. It is tempting for people to talk about the experience of others who are not in the group. It may have nothing to do with grief and loss. Again, it is the task of the leader to bring discussions back to the personal experience of those present as it relates to their grief and loss.

Pass out paper and pencils. Have the members of the group diagram their moods over the past year according to the instructions beginning on page 120. Ask them to describe their feelings at the moment in terms of a color, taste, smell, touch, and sound.

Have each person write an answer to this question: If I could change one thing in my life right now, what would it be?

Give everyone adequate time to do these two assignments. When the answers have been recorded, go around the group and discuss one question at a time. Try to draw out feelings and more detailed descriptions if anyone gives only superficial, brief responses.

Before closing, give each person the following "homework" assignment:

- Purchase a stenographer's notepad and label it "Journal."
- Record each day for the next week: a significant event that happened; the person who was most important to me today; feelings of which I was most aware today; plans for tomorrow.
- Note date and time of day of entries at top of page.
- Bring journal to the group next week.

Session Four: Keeping a Journal

Begin this and all subsequent sessions with the same invitation to share that was given in Session Three.

Ask for sharing about people's experience with keeping a journal. It is common for some group members to have either "forgotten" (repressed) the assignment or completed only part of it. Be sure to acknowledge that this is okay and they can try again.

Ask those who are willing to share some portion of their journal entries. You may want to ask them to choose a particular day and share the entries from that day.

Ask the group members to continue keeping a journal for the rest of the group sessions. They should add the following notations:

- Changes I observe happening to me
- Notes to myself

As the group moves into more personal sharing, it is natural for some people to report feeling worse at the end of the meeting than they did when they arrived. Assure participants that this is normal and a significant sign of growth. It is not a sign of slipping backward, but of moving forward. It is not a negative occurrence, but a necessary, positive one, even though it is uncomfortable. It will pass, and they will feel much better if they stay with the process.

If people drop out at this time, try to maintain contact and help them establish some other support base.

If any group member seems to manifest the symptoms of distorted grief as described on pages 90–92, encourage that person to seek the help of a professional counselor or psychologist.

Close the session in whatever way has become appropriate and effective for your group.

Session Five: Growing through Loss

After any open sharing, review the following guidelines for growing through loss that are described in some detail in Chapter 9:

- Believe that your grief has a purpose and an end.
- Be responsible for your own grief process.
- Don't be afraid to ask for help.
- Don't rush it.

Discuss how group members are experiencing each of these guidelines. In which areas are they having the most problems? In which areas do they seem to have a good grasp on their grief?

To close, lead the group in doing the 8–8–8 Breather exercise (page 230). Repeat the sequence several times. When finished with the exercise, join hands in a circle and give one another words of encouragement for the next week.

Session Six: The Influence of Religion on Grief

After giving an opportunity for open sharing, ask the group to talk about the positive and negative ways religious faith has affected their grief experience.

It is especially important, when dealing with the subject of religion, that people's individual views and feelings are recognized. Some people are very angry at God. Some cannot express that anger; some will deny it altogether. Others may have abandoned their faith as a result of their grief. Still others will look to their faith as the foundation for trying to put life back together again. You may find people who are convinced that God is punishing them. Others may tell you that God has taken their loved one. Whatever a person's feelings might be, the most helpful thing the group can do is just listen. Avoid getting into philosophical discussions about the presence of evil in the world, why tragic things happen to good people, or whether God punishes people through grief experiences.

Ask group members to keep their sharing personal and to accept the sharing of others, even if it is quite different from their own experience.

At the close of the session, do the 8–8–8 Breather exercise (page 230). Repeat the sequence several times. If the group is open to it, close the meeting by joining hands in a circle and offering a short prayer of gratitude. I ask directly, "Would you be comfortable if we had a prayer before we close?" I find that people will give an honest answer if an open and accepting atmosphere has been established during the session. If some wish to have prayer and others do not, allow those who do not to exercise the option of excluding themselves. The prayer should be brief, positive, and hopeful.

Remind everyone to keep writing in their journal on a daily basis. You may want to review the instructions from Session Three.

Session Seven: Coping with Forgetfulness

Begin by asking participants to share something significant from their journal writing of the past week. After all have had an opportunity to share, ask whether anyone is having problems with forgetfulness.

You can be sure that many are experiencing this.

Locking keys in the car; misplacing house keys; losing a cell phone; and forgetting appointments, telephone numbers, and people's names are common after a major loss. Assure the group that such behavior is a normal part of the grief experience for many people and that it passes with time.

If a person's car doesn't have electronic door locks, encourage them to keep an extra set of car keys in a magnetic box somewhere under a fender or to have an extra door key kept separately from the rest of their keys. It's a good idea to have a trusted neighbor keep a set of house keys. Even the most familiar and frequently used telephone numbers and addresses should be written down and kept in a visible place.

Ask these additional questions:

- Has anyone here wondered whether you are the only one having these kinds of problems with grief?
- Do you find that routine tasks have become more difficult to do?
- Do you ever wonder if you are going crazy?

You will find that most people in the group have experienced all or some of these symptoms of grief. It's called fragmenting, and it's totally normal in the first three to six months after a major loss. Those who have moved beyond this stage will remember when it happened to them. I have talked with people whose loss was more than five years old and they had never told anyone about the fragmenting symptoms. Just talking about them and discovering that other people experience similar symptoms often helps lift a heavy weight from the shoulders of bereaved people.

One of the beneficial spin-offs of this sharing is the common bond it can create among those who are divorced and those who are widowed. Often, if widowed and divorced persons are in the same group, a certain amount of tension exists among them. Exercises such as this one help relieve that tension by focusing on reactions to loss and grief that are common to both.

If time permits after the discussion on forgetfulness, ask the group to talk about any problems they are having with nongrieving people. This is another subject that brings grieving people closer to one another.

Have the group review the section in Chapter 18 that addresses the subject of relating to nongrievers (pages 236 to 239).

As a homework assignment for the next week, ask the group to focus on forgiveness in their journal writing.

- Who do you need to forgive for failing to respond to your loss in a helpful way?
- Do you blame anyone for your loss?
- Do you need to forgive yourself for anything?

Sharing on this forgiveness will open the next session of the group.

Close by joining hands in a circle and having members of the group give expressions of the unity they feel with the others as a result of their experiences together over the past six weeks.

Session Eight: Sleep Issues

Open the session by asking the group to share on the forgiveness issues they focused on in their journal during the past week.

Next, ask the group to respond to these questions:

- Who has been a significant person in my life this week?
- What did this person do for me?

After this sharing is completed, ask if anyone in the group ever has problems going to sleep, going back to sleep if he or she wakes up during the night, or getting up in the morning. (By this time in the life of your group, the subject of sleep problems may have already come up.)

Have people share their experiences. You may find wide variations between people. Some have no problems with either sleep or feeling fatigued. Others will have problems with both of these symptoms. Again, there is great value for the participants in hearing other people's experience.

Many times, what a person eats and drinks will result in more energy during the day and better rest at night.

Tell the group the following story about Hazel:

Hazel could not sleep after her divorce and subsequent surgery for a leg injury suffered in a fall. She was growing increasingly irritable, performing poorly at work, and gaining weight. Her leg was not healing. She went for counseling to find out what was wrong with her emotionally and spiritually. After a few minutes of gathering information, the counselor asked her to describe what she did during the evening and what food and drink she consumed after dinner—which she normally ate at about six p.m.

Hazel reported that she grew increasingly anxious as the evening went on. At first she felt a vague nervousness, but after her failure to fall asleep on a couple of occasions, she focused her anxiety on that.

To relieve the discomfort and to occupy her mind with other things, she would begin working crossword puzzles at about nine p.m. She drank hot chocolate and ate cookies while working on the puzzles.

Without realizing what she was doing, Hazel was stimulating her body with sugar and caffeine while she stimulated the analytical portion of her mind with the crossword puzzles. There was no way she was going to be able to fall asleep within hours of that kind of activity and food intake.

The counselor suggested she change the hot chocolate to decaffeinated herbal tea and the cookies to raw vegetables or a dish of oatmeal with warm milk. He also suggested she substitute a book of poetry or photographic artwork for her crossword puzzles.

Within three nights, Hazel had returned to her normal sleep patterns. She also visited a local nutrition counselor for guidance on possible vitamin supplements. Only a short time later, her leg began to heal.

Focus the balance of sharing on people's response to the story of Hazel and what it says about their own experience.

As a homework assignment, have each person prepare a daily calendar for his or her next week. The daytime hours should be divided into three sections: morning, afternoon, and evening. Have group members list what they plan to do during each of these periods of time for the next day.

The calendar for nighttime hours after their normal bedtime should be listed in half-hour intervals. They should list what they will do during each half-hour of the night until their regular time of rising, should they wake up in the middle of the night or not be able to go to sleep.

I suggest listing tasks that the person does not like to do and usually puts off as long as possible.

This schedule should be filled out each day and followed as closely as possible. Announce that the opening sharing for Session Nine will be focused on each person's experiences with the calendar for the week.

Close the group in whatever way has become most comfortable for the participants.

Session Nine: Grief Statements

The first order of business for the session is to have everyone report on his or her experience with the daily calendar. Take enough time for each person to share his or her successes and failures. Assure people that whatever happened, it was okay and they can continue to use the exercise for as long as they wish.

Pass out a clean sheet of lined notebook paper to each person. Dictate the following statement. Ask each person to write it down as you read:

The sadness I feel is a badge of honor. I wear the brokenness of my life at this moment with pride.

These expressions of my grief testify to the importance of _____ [each person will fill in the name of person, place, or condition that has been lost] to me.

I am willing to feel the full impact of my grief as a final act of tribute and love. I will make my way through this experience and will not run from it.

Signed, [your name]

Before anyone signs the statement, take time to talk about how each one feels about it. In what way does each one see his or her grief as a badge of honor? What feelings do people have about signing this statement?

Some members of the group may want to make a change in the statement before signing it. Allow whoever wishes to make whatever changes are necessary to make the statement true for them.

Have each person sign his or her statement. Then, using tape, post it on a wall where all can see it. Do this one person at a time. As the group members individually post their statement, have them read it aloud, including any changes they have made.

After all statements are posted, take time to talk about the experience.

The homework assignment for the following week is to write letters to and from one's grief. You will find a full description of this exercise on pages 235 to 236.

Close the group by having everyone gather the statements from the wall, put them in a pile on a chair, and gather around it, holding hands. Join in a short prayer or some other affirmation of what the statements represent.

Session Ten: Letter to and from Grief

Begin the session with an opportunity for open sharing about significant events of the week. Ask people to report on their experience with writing to and from their grief. Those who have brought their letters with them may want to read them to the group. It is important to affirm anyone who was unable to carry out the assignment. It is not unusual to have several who can't face the task at the present time. If you are accepting of everyone's experience, a valuable discussion can follow, regardless of whether the letters were written.

Talk about how people felt as they wrote each letter or found they could not write one or both of them.

When all have shared, have the group lay aside everything they are holding. Tell them the next exercise is one of relaxation as reward for all their hard work.

Everyone should get in a comfortable position with feet flat on the floor, arms and hands in lap, and eyes closed. Begin with a few repetitions of the 8–8–8 Breather exercise (page 290).

Read aloud the exercise beginning on page 259 titled "Making Peace with Grief." Your vocal tone should be peaceful and soft, but easy to hear. If you are uncomfortable reading the monologue, have someone else record it on a cassette and play it for the group.

When the exercise is completed, take time to talk about individual experiences with it. Remember, no particular response is "right." Whatever reaction people have is valid for them and will reflect their own personality and stage of grief.

As a homework assignment, ask the group to keep a daily log of their food intake. These logs should be brought to Session Eleven. Close the session in whatever manner has become most appropriate for your group.

Session Eleven: Grief Work and Good Nutrition

As you open this session, remind the group that you have only one more session to go. Ask people to talk about the issues of grief and loss that are most important to them at this time. What is there that each person wants the group to hear before it is disbanded? Remember, as leader, you should be ready to deal with issues of loss during this next-to-last group session. These issues, too, should be talked about freely. Call the group's attention to the material found in Chapter 20 about the role of nutrition in grief recovery. Ask each person to discuss his or her daily log of food intake for the past week. Did everyone keep the log? If not, why not? If it was kept, what was learned from it about each one's nutritional strengths and weaknesses?

If it is possible to get a nutritionist to come to the meeting for this portion of it, that is a real plus.

Next, talk about what each person is doing in the area of physical fitness. Just forty-five minutes of brisk walking can do wonders for lifting spirits and easing depression. Urge everyone to have a physical examination if he or she hasn't had one since the loss. This is especially important for those who are four to six months past a major loss experience.

Any program of exercise and fitness should be done with the involvement and direction of each person's doctor.

Close the session in the manner that is most appropriate for your group.

Session Twelve: Best Friend—Worst Enemy; The Secret Box

Plan to have some special refreshments at the close of this final session. Allow time for casual interaction and fellowship before people leave.

Open the session by reminding everyone that it is the last session. Ask for sharing about what people have gained from the sessions and how they feel about its ending.

In most cases, some of the group members will want to go on meeting. You should decide before this session whether you wish to continue in the group or as its leader. In any event, it is best to take a break of at least one week before going on.

Another decision that often must be made at this time is whether to take in new members to the group. Keep in mind that newcomers will not have gone through the exercises and experiences of the "veteran" group members. In most cases, unless a trained leader is in charge, I think it is best either to disband and start over again or to create a second group for newcomers and go on with those of the original group who wish to continue meeting.

It is very important that no one in the current group is pressured into continuing. After everyone has shared on the opening subject, ask the group to do the exercise on page 266 titled "Best Friend–Worst Enemy." Share the results of the exercise with one another.

Close the session and the series by doing the exercise beginning on page 281 titled "The Secret Box." Narrate it rather than having the group read it individually.

When the exercise is completed, gather the group in a circle and express thanks to one another for everyone's support and caring. Close with a short prayer or other affirmative statement.

Notes

Introduction

1. Alan Wolfelt, *When Your Soulmate Dies* (Fort Collins, CO: Companion Press, 2016), 27.

Chapter 4

1. J. R. Martinez in "Fighting the Battle of a Lifetime" by Nicole Smith Dahmen, *Phoenix Society Burn Support News*, no. 3, 2008.

Chapter 8

1. Glen W. Davidson, *Understanding Mourning* (Minneapolis, MN: Augsburg, 1984).

Chapter 12

1. Ann Kaiser Stearns, *Living through Personal Crisis* (Notre Dame, IN.: Thomas More Publishing, 1983).

2. Steve Lobel, *Recognition Beyond Burned: Portraits of Survival, Rebirth & Hope* (self-published, 2006).

3. Ibid.

Chapter 13

1. Richard Taylor, *Alzheimer's from the Inside Out* (Baltimore: Health Professions Press, 2007).

Chapter 19

1. Earl Grollman, *Time Remembered* (Boston: Beacon Press, 1987).

Chapter 20

1. Betty Jane Wylie, *Beginnings: A Book for Widows* (Toronto: McClelland and Stewart, 1997).

Acknowledgments

Because this book reflects not only the experiences of others, but my own grief as a result of June's death, the list of people to whom I am indebted has multiplied many times over.

I do not have words to express my gratitude to those who have shared the deepest experiences of their lives with me in grief support groups, seminars, and conferences. Every time I think I have seen it all, I encounter someone's tragedy that makes me realize I haven't seen the half of it. In the past few years I have met wounded military personnel, survivors of horrible burns, and some who are surviving the loss of loved ones in catastrophic events. These incredibly brave and determined people have opened a new and deeper understanding of the depth of grief and strength of the human spirit. The one thing I learned new following June's death is the depth of sorrow and feelings of being overwhelmed are so much greater than I imagined. When I told people in the past that I would listen to them but never tell them I knew how they felt because my wife was still with me, I was so right on!

I continue receiving letters, telephone calls, and e-mails from people who have found guidance and comfort from the book through all the editions—and give it their best endorsement by recommending it to their friends and family. Some credit it for saving their life. They are the reason I will keep working and writing in the field of loss and grief as long as I am able.

My mentors are among the great pioneers: the late Dr. Howard Clinebell Jr., Dr. Earl Grollman, and Dr. Glen Davidson. Their work provided the foundation upon which I could formulate the guidelines that have helped so many. There is a special place in my heart for Maryann Makekau, founder of Because Hope Matters and author of amazing children's books that help adults help children with life's deep challenges. Dr. Alan Wolfelt is a respected author and educator whose works are a healing balm to those dealing with grief. My editor, Claire Ivett, deserves the gratitude of readers and this author for not only helping create a sharp, easy-to-read book, but providing insights and guidance to the content as well.

I am grateful to the people of Gold Canyon United Methodist Church and Velda Rose United Methodist Church who have allowed me into their lives and losses and demonstrated how churches can be powerful places of healing after a major loss.

Most of all I am grateful to my beloved June whose depth of spirit, incredible courage in the face of death, and love for her family was amazing to the second she died.

—*Bob Deits*

Index